THE FOUNDATIONS
OF FREEDOM

THE
FOUNDATIONS
OF
FREEDOM

WITH SPECIAL REFERENCE TO
SOUTHERN AFRICA

D. V. COWEN

PROFESSOR OF COMPARATIVE LAW
UNIVERSITY OF CAPE TOWN

CAPE TOWN
OXFORD UNIVERSITY PRESS
LONDON   NEW YORK
1961

Oxford University Press, Amen House, London E.C.4
GLASGOW   NEW YORK   TORONTO   MELBOURNE   WELLINGTON
BOMBAY   CALCUTTA   MADRAS   KARACHI
CAPE TOWN   IBADAN   NAIROBI   ACCRA   KUALA LUMPUR

SET AND PRINTED IN
10 ON 11 TIMES
❀ BY RUSTICA PRESS, PTY., LTD., WYNBERG, CAPE

The King ought not to be under any man, but he ought to be under God and the law, since the law makes the King. Therefore let the King render unto the law what the law has rendered unto the King, namely dominion and power; for there is no King where will prevails and not the law.

Bracton

Preface

This book is much concerned with the travail of the land in which I was born and have lived. But though it has grown out of the contemporary African—and more particularly Southern African—situation, the themes with which it is concerned are of enduring and universal significance; they are the themes from which men throughout history have drawn courage and strength in their efforts to achieve a society in which they can flourish.

In attempting a restatement of the ideal of government under law, and of what is needed to implement it in an African context, I am very conscious that I have undertaken a most formidable task; one that would tax the capacity of men far wiser and more learned than I am. I can only hope that the urgent need at the present time for this work to be done will make it easier for readers to forgive my shortcomings.

To Deborah, my wife, I owe more than I can say. She has read and re-read, worked at and improved every page, every line, of this book; whatever merit it may have could not have been achieved without her constant sacrifice, forbearance, encouragement and guidance.

To my colleague and friend of long standing, Dr. Marthinus Versfeld of the Department of Philosophy in the University of Cape Town, I should like to make the special acknowledgement of a grateful student. Many years have passed since I first attended his lectures on ethical and political theory, and we have never really left off debating and discussing 'The Perennial Order' with, to me, abiding pleasure and profit.

I am very grateful to Miss Winifred Greenshields, Miss Elsa Oudschans Dentz and Mrs. Jean Bowes-Taylor for typing the manuscript quickly and efficiently, and for their unflagging generosity in working cheerfully far beyond normal hours. Miss Greenshields also gave invaluable assistance in making the index, as did Mr. W. J. Luker. I would record my thanks, too, to Miss Ellen Roberts, of the Jagger Library, for checking statistical information in Chapter 1.

Finally I must say how very much I have appreciated the

co-operation of Mr. Leo Marquard and Mr. James Currey of the Oxford University Press. Their advice and technical skill were a great comfort to me. I have learned much, too, from Mr. Marquard's sane and balanced book on *The Peoples and Policies of South Africa*.

D. V. C.

University of Cape Town
March 1961

Contents

PART ONE

Race and Community

1 Community or Schism

The history of every community reveals a struggle between the forces which cause men to live together, and those which disrupt communal life and keep men apart. Trade and economy, geography, defence, language, religion, race, education, law and custom, indeed the whole fabric of cultural heritage and its emotional content—these are the pervading forces of attraction and repulsion in human affairs. These are the hard facts with which every constitution has to deal; and, in devising a framework of government for a country, it is essential to have them constantly in sight. Their action will either preserve or destroy a constitution—preserve it if it has given them due recognition and scope; destroy it if its provisions turn out to be opposed to the sweep of irresistible currents. Indeed, the forces which tend to unite or dissever society are to the constructive statesman what the forces of nature are to man. They can be overcome, in Bacon's phrase, only by obeying them. If he defies or misunderstands them, they overthrow his work. If he knows how to use them, they preserve it.

The operation of these two groups of forces presents a particularly difficult and perplexing problem where races of different colour and culture are juxtaposed on the same soil—a problem which Lord Bryce once observed was the despair of the statesman, and, if not insoluble, was probably beyond the skill of the constitution-maker; though after a subsequent visit to Brazil he was less despondent.[1]

Putting on one side, for the moment, the obvious importance of the power of arms and money in maintaining an already existing structure of government, and in resisting change, the problem with which we are here concerned has two aspects.

In the first place where whites and non-whites are present together in the same country, and the average non-white differs from the

---

[1] I have attempted in these opening paragraphs to summarize the theme of Bryce's well-known essay on *The Action of Centripetal and Centrifugal Forces on Political Constitutions*. See, generally, *Studies in History and Jurisprudence*, vol. 1, pp. 255 sqq., published in 1901. Bryce's South American Impressions were first published in 1912.

average white in background and culture, is it possible to achieve the sense of security, the tolerance, and especially the community of interest and aspiration, which are necessary to provide the basis for a healthy and stable society? Is it possible, in short, to fuse the racial groups into one coherent nation? Or are the disruptive forces, particularly those of fear and prejudice, likely to prove so strong that the only expedient is to acknowledge their supremacy, and arrange for the races to live apart in separate territories and separately organized communities?

The second aspect of the problem is no less challenging. Assuming that it is possible to disarm fear and prejudice, and to find a way for races of different colour and culture to live together in one community having a single economy, is it practicable to organize that community on a democratic basis? Do individuals or minority groups require special protection against the power of a majority, and especially against racial discrimination? If so, should such protection be sought in constitutional machinery; how may such a constitution best be devised; and can it be effective?

In parts of South America—notably Brazil—and in the West Indies, it would seem that a solution of these problems has been found along the lines of integration and non-discrimination in a single politically organized community.[2] Writing in 1912 Lord Bryce observed that white Brazilians (who are outnumbered by negroes and persons of mixed blood) do not feel towards the negro race 'that repression which marks the attitude of the whites to the negroes in North America and South Africa'. Brazil, he noted with satisfaction, was one country at least where solidarity existed between European and African races, and where fusion was allowed to proceed unchecked by law or custom, with good results.[3] Today 'it might almost be said that "race relations" do not exist in Brazil: a society has developed in which, in the relationships between people, race is subordinate to human and social values'.[4] The distinctions which exist are primarily those of economic class, not race. Thus there is a common saying in Brazil that 'a rich negro is a white man, and a poor white man is a negro'.[5]

It is true that even in Brazil some racial prejudice is still occasion-

[2] See generally J. A. Comacho, *Brazil*, R.I.I.A., 1954, p. 3; Charles Wagley, *Race and Class in Rural Brazil*, 1952, pp. 7–15; 142–5; Bryce, *South America: Observations and Impressions*, Revised ed., 1914, pp. 479–83.
    Also the following works on Brazil by Afrikaans-speaking authors: B. J. Marais, *Colour—unsolved problem of the West*, 1952, pp. 254–84; P. Serton, *Suid-Afrika en Brasilië*, 1960, pp. 193–206.
[3] Bryce, op. cit., pp. 479–83.
[4] Wagley, op. cit., p. 14.
[5] Quoted by Liston Pope, *The Kingdom Beyond Caste*, New York, 1957, p. 39.

ally found, but it is neither serious nor disruptive.[6] Very recently a well-known Afrikaans-speaking scholar, Professor Serton, made a comparative survey of Brazil and South Africa; and in a valuable book on the subject, he reached the conclusion that 'Brazil has avoided much of the misery for which we in South Africa have no remedy. . . . It has achieved a national unity which we can only envy.'[7]

In the United States the course is now set deliberately, if not very speedily, in the same direction. But the picture is quite different in those parts of Africa where the white man has put down roots, and desires to settle permanently; there the dominant traits are still uncertainty, indecision—and in some places, potential disaster. There the issue of symbiosis or schism between the races, of living together harmoniously in a common society, or of acknowledging failure in this respect, is still dangerously unresolved.

The test case both in difficulty and importance is probably that of the Union of South Africa. If, as it seems, the problem of the relationship between whites and non-whites is only manageable with relative ease where one of the groups forms an insignificant minority (as for example, the Maoris in New Zealand, and the whites in the West Indies and Tanganyika),[8] or if it be true, as some have suggested, that colour prejudice and race feeling are primarily Teutonic phenomena,[9] or as Toynbee would have it, an Old Testament aberration of Protestantism,[10] then, indeed, the elements of the problem are compounded in South Africa in a most harassing way.

To begin with, the over-all numerical ratio between whites and non-whites in South Africa (1 to 4 in favour of non-whites) appears to be more disquieting to whites than the over-all ratio in the United States (10 to 1 in favour of whites). I do not say that the South African ratio should be more disquieting, but in fact it is so to many.[11] Though there are some authorities who contend that the importance of numerical ratios has been exaggerated,[12] there can be little doubt that it is easier to play upon fears of racial swamping or submersion in South Africa than it is in, say, the northern areas of the United States.

[6] Comacho, op. cit., pp. 18–19; Wagley, op. cit., p. 149.

[7] Serton, op. cit. Passage in text translated from the Afrikaans original.

[8] See, generally, Gunnar Myrdal, *An American Dilemma*, 1944, pp. 167 sqq.; cf. Gordon W. Alport, *The Nature of Prejudice*, Anchor Edition, New York, 1958.

[9] See Bryce, *South America: Observations and Impressions*, 1914, p. 482.

[10] *A Study of History*, vol. 1, 2nd ed., pp. 211 sqq.; cf. Marais, op. cit., pp. 115, 229.

[11] Marais, op. cit., p. 300. See also p. 31 below.

[12] Liston Pope, op. cit., p. 43.

Again, the problem in South Africa is complicated by significant differences within both the white and the non-white groups themselves. And here it may be helpful to summarize briefly the most important differences. While support for the policy of apartheid is by no means confined to Afrikaans-speaking white South Africans, and though colour prejudice and fear of racial submersion are very widespread among the English-speaking group, there can be no doubt that there are certain incentives for supporting apartheid which operate with special strength among Afrikaans-speaking South Africans. To begin with, the 1948 General Election marked the winning of decisive political power among the whites by the Afrikaans-speaking section of the community. After a long struggle their political supremacy among the whites became assured.[13] And many of them fear, rightly or wrongly, that the extension of political rights to the non-whites might enable the English-speaking section to jeopardize the political balance by soliciting the non-white vote[14] —a fear similar to that which is responsible for the Government's very cautious attitude towards the encouragement of immigration. Indeed, in this regard, it is important to note the conclusion reached by two of the most articulate apologists of apartheid, N. J. Rhoodie and H. J. Venter,[15] that 'apartheid is one of the prominent symbols of Afrikaner nationalism'.

There is admittedly a growing tendency among white South Africans to view continued strife between the English and Afrikaans groups as short-sighted, and increasing stress is being laid on the alleged need for all white South Africans to combine, or close their ranks so to speak, in an effort to find a solution of the country's overriding racial problems. But notwithstanding these developments (which are themselves both short-sighted and dangerous, for no real solution is possible without African co-operation), there still exists, and for some time there is likely to remain, an attitude of marked reserve to any policy which might impair Afrikaner political supremacy.

At a deeper level, there are strongly rooted cultural differences within the white group which are even more relevant to race relations. Thus there is a language question which can and does influence the attitude of the two main sections of the white people towards the non-whites; for although there is fairly widespread bilingualism in English and Afrikaans among both the whites and the coloured

[13] This is the theme of an important book by the Hon. H. A. Fagan, *Our Responsibility*, Stellenbosch, 1959.

[14] See the much-quoted passage on the alleged abuse of the coloured vote in B. K. Long, *In Smuts' Camp*, 1945, pp. 129–30. Also the speech by Dr. D. F. Malan, *House of Assembly Debates*, vol. 67, cols. 2821–2, March 1949.

[15] N. J. Rhoodie and H. J. Venter, *Apartheid*, Cape Town, 1959, p. 244.

people of mixed blood, among Africans English has far the stronger appeal. And so the fear is often expressed that it is Afrikaans rather than English which stands to lose in an integrated society. It is not without significance that under the system of Bantu education, which since 1953 has been one of the features of apartheid, literacy in English among young Africans has declined; the course is now firmly set against anything that might encourage the emergence of what are sometimes called 'black Englishmen'.

Even more powerful than language, is the influence on the Afrikaans-speaking section of Calvinistic religious and political thought, with their uncompromisingly anti-egalitarian character. This was exemplified in the Cape Colony early in the nineteenth century when the rigid Calvinistic outlook of many Afrikaners came into conflict with the more tolerant and liberal attitude to colour which was developing, mainly under English influence.[16] It was precisely this conflict of outlook which contributed in large measure to the Great Trek, and the subsequent establishment by Afrikaners of new states beyond the borders of the Cape. Indeed, in the words of Prof. E. A. Walker, if any one factor can be named as the cause *par excellence* of the Great Trek, it is fear of what Anna Steenkamp called 'ungodly equality' between black and white.[17]

Accordingly, in the constitutions of the new Afrikaner Republics it was categorically stated that 'the people will not permit equality between white and non-white inhabitants either in Church or State'.[18] And today, more than a century after these events, we may still read in a leading text-book on apartheid, the statement that each successive development of racial discrimination in the Afrikaner's history, up to the present time, should properly be regarded as 'a defeat of the Cape liberal tradition' (or, to speak more accurately, of what is left of it).[19]

Then, too, one constantly finds evidence of an almost Teutonic taste among Afrikaans-speaking South Africans for symmetrical theories and logical principles. On the whole they dislike loose ends in argument and planning, and are impatient with the Englishman's belief in *solvitur ambulando*, or 'doing the thing you want and saying

[16] See generally H. A. Reyburn, 'Studies in Cape Frontier History' in *The Critic*, vol. 3, No. 1, 1934, pp. 52–6; No. 2, pp. 101–9; No. 3, pp. 148–63.

[17] *A History of South Africa*, 1928, p. 207. Also de Kiewiet, *A History of South Africa*, 1941, p. 54.

[18] See art. 9 of the Grondwet of the old South African Republic (Transvaal), 1858; similarly, art. 1 of the Constitution of the Orange Free State, 1854; Eybers, *Select Constitutional Documents Illustrating South African History*, pp. 361, 286.

[19] Rhoodie and Venter, op. cit., pp. 116, 140.

as little as possible about it even to yourself'.[20] As we shall see, some of the details of apartheid legislation in recent years may be traced to this hankering after symmetry and logical tidiness.[21]

Among the non-whites differences are equally marked. Africans in the urban areas, who in 1951 numbered about $2\frac{1}{4}$ million,[22] have in large measure acquired values and western ways of living which contrast sharply with the customs obtaining in the Reserves, where attempts are being made to hold together the tattered and disintegrating fabric of tribal life; and the same is true, though to a lesser extent, among the $2\frac{1}{2}$ million Africans who (again 1951 figures) are living in rural areas outside the Reserves. And, of course, among tribal Africans themselves customs differ from tribe to tribe.[23] It would, admittedly, be unrealistic to give too much emphasis to the degree to which Africans in South Africa have become detribalized and acculturated to modern ways of living, but the degree is very considerable and growing, despite all attempts to arrest the process. Certainly those who sometimes attempt to deny or minimize this fact,[24] or who equate the relative cultural position of the African to that of American Indians living in the Reservations, are very wide of the mark.[25]

The Cape Coloured people of mixed blood (and the comparatively few Malays), who are predominantly Afrikaans-speaking, live for the most part in the Cape Province and number about $1\frac{1}{2}$ million.[26] Though legally segregated from the whites, the Cape Coloured people have no separate culture which is clearly distinct from that of the whites.[27] At the present time they occupy a fluid position; and there is currently a movement among some whites, especially among Afrikaners, to draw the Cape Coloureds (to the exclusion

---

[20] See the passage from 'The Etchingham Letters' quoted by a Scottish Law Lord, the late Lord Macmillan, in his essay on 'Two Ways of Thinking' in *Law and Other Things*, 1937, pp. 76 sqq. The preference for system is shared by the Scots.

[21] See below, p. 47.

[22] The most recent decennial census figures are not available at the time of writing, but all indications suggest that the number of Africans in urban areas has increased considerably.

[23] For a general survey, see I. Shapera, *The Bantu-speaking Tribes of South Africa*, 1937.

[24] As, for example, does Dr. W. W. M. Eiselen in his article on 'Harmonious Multi-community Development', *Optima*, March 1959, p. 2.

[25] This is a point of view which I have not infrequently heard expressed in some quarters in the United States.

[26] In 1957, the estimated figure was 1,319,000. Official Yearbook of South Africa, 1956–7, p. 712.

[27] See J. S. Marais, *The Cape Coloured People*, 1939; W. M. Macmillan, *The Cape Coloured Question*, 1937; D. P. Botha, *Die Opkoms van Ons Derde Stand*, 1960.

of the Africans) into the white camp. And finally, there are approximately half a million Asians,[28] living mainly in Natal, who are regarded as culturally distinct by the other groups, and who 'by exclusion, have been forced into self-consciousness'.[29]

These considerations may suffice to illustrate the complexity of South Africa; but despite its complexity, the country still presents a test case. For it is essential to recognize that the problem of race relations in South Africa is emphatically not a unique problem, in the sense that South Africans may claim exemption from fundamental standards of right and wrong. Nor would it be true to say that comparable problems are not being experienced in other countries. Much as South Africans, especially apologists of apartheid, may seek comfort in the alleged uniqueness of their situation — which is admittedly difficult—there is no health in this kind of self-deception.

Moreover, despite the fact that many persons abroad are beginning to wilt at the very mention of South Africa's interminably argued and troublesome affairs, there is no escape from the truth that what happens in South Africa matters in the context of international relations, and in the yet wider perspectives of world history. Nothing indeed could be further from the truth than the contention that South Africa's racial problems, or for that matter the racial problems of America, are exclusively the domestic concern of those countries. In an interdependent world, race relations everywhere have become the concern—the legitimate concern—of people everywhere.

The significance of these points was brought out in the clash of beliefs and policies expressed in two remarkable speeches which were made in Cape Town early in 1960; one by the Prime Minister of the United Kingdom, the Rt. Hon. Harold Macmillan, the other by the Prime Minister of the Union of South Africa, Dr. the Hon. H. F. Verwoerd. And it is well worth reminding ourselves briefly of what they said; for these two speeches give expression, in memorable and concise language, to sharply conflicting points of view on an issue whose importance both Mr. Macmillan and Dr. Verwoerd recognized as being neither ephemeral nor confined to Africa.

Mr. Macmillan said:

> What is now on trial is our way of life. Our judgment of right and wrong and of justice is rooted in the same soil as yours—in Christianity and in the rule of law as the basis of a free society. It has been our aim to create a society which respects the rights of individuals—a society in which men are given an opportunity

[28] In 1957 the estimated figure was 431,000. Official Yearbook, 1956–7, p. 712.
[29] Hilda Kuper, *Indian People in Natal*, 1960, p. 270.

to grow to their full stature, and that must in our view include the opportunity of an increasing share in political power and responsibility; a society finally in which individual merit, and individual merit alone, is the criterion for a man's advancement, whether political or economic.

Then in a very significant passage, he added:

In countries inhabited by several different races, it has been our aim *to find means by which the community can become more of a community* and fellowship can be fostered between its various parts. This problem is by no means confined to Africa. Nor is it always a problem of a European minority. In Malaya, for instance, though there are Indian and European minorities, Malays and Chinese make up the great bulk of the population, and the Chinese are not much fewer in number than the Malays. Yet the two peoples must learn to live together in harmony and unity, and the strength and future of Malaya as a nation will depend on the different contributions which the two races can make.

And he concluded this theme by endorsing a declaration made at the United Nations General Assembly in 1959:

We [that is the British] reject the idea of any inherent superiority of one race over another. Our policy is therefore non-racial; it offers a future in which Africans, Europeans, Asians, the peoples of the Pacific and others with whom we are concerned, will all play their full part as citizens in the countries where they live, and in which feelings of race will be submerged in loyalty to new nations.[30]

In his reply, Dr. Verwoerd made it quite plain that he was no less conscious than Mr. Macmillan of the magnitude of what was at stake:

I wish to assure you that in the Christian philosophy which you endorse, we find a philosophy which we wish to follow. If our methods should be different, let us try to understand one another, and may we at least find in the world at large that trust in our sincerity which must be the basis of all good will.

Elaborating this, Dr. Verwoerd said that the policies deemed advisable by the Union Government 'should, if rightly understood, make an impact upon Africa and upon the world' to the advantage of the very ideals in which both Mr. Macmillan and he believed. And he rounded this off by saying:

We never presume to criticize the application of other policies in the areas for which you are responsible, but when on an occasion such as this, on which we are perfectly frank, we look

---

[30] *Souvenir of a Visit*. Printed on the authority of Mr. Speaker, Cape Town, pp. 8–11. My italics.

at them critically, then we see, different to you, that there may be great dangers inherent in those policies. The very object at which you are striving may be defeated by them.

And in further explanation of government policy, Dr. Verwoerd said:

We have nowhere else to go. We settled a country which was bare. The Bantu too came to this country and settled certain portions. It is in line with the thinking of Africa to grant those fullest rights to them there which we also, with you, admit all people should have. But we also believe in balance. We believe in allowing exactly those same full opportunities to remain within the grasp of the white man in the areas he settled.[31]

Whether Dr. Verwoerd is correct in seeing the issue between Mr. Macmillan and himself as merely one of difference in the application of the same basic philosophy, is a question which must be deferred to the next two chapters. At this stage I have quoted fairly extensively from their speeches in order to put the issues raised by apartheid into true perspective; and that perspective manifestly transcends all national boundaries.

No one will deny that South Africa's racial problems, as indeed all human problems, should be approached with compassion, and charity, and humility. No one will dispute that angry and biting criticism, if it lacks charity, will often do more harm than good. But let there be an end to the dangerous fallacy that South Africa's problems, and how she manages them, are exclusively her business— uniquely domestic in character and significance. Indeed, the very complexity of South Africa's racial problems, so far from isolating or insulating the country, makes her a microcosm, or epitome of the world itself. Problems of race and colour, which are essentially world problems, are merely experienced in their quintessence in South Africa. Nor, in this connexion, is it without significance to note that the ratio between whites and non-whites in South Africa is roughly the same as the over-all world ratio—a fact which perhaps gives added point to Mr. Macmillan's statement that it is impossible today for nations to live unto themselves alone; for we are all members one of another. 'What Dr. John Donne said of individual men three hundred years ago is true today of every country in the world:

"Any man's death diminishes me,
because I am involved in mankind.
And therefore never send to know
For whom the bell tolls:
It tolls for thee." '[32]

[31] Ibid., pp. 15–16.
[32] Ibid., p. 12.

And finally the South African scene compels attention because, after twelve years of implementation, the Government's policy of apartheid is now showing unmistakable signs of failure and disintegration. When it grinds to a standstill, or is brought to a halt, the question will still remain: can it, will it, be replaced by any better alternative? Apart altogether from the absorbing interest—almost fascination—of this question to every serious student of government and society, the question has immediate and potentially tragic significance not only for millions of human beings living in Southern Africa, but also for the future of world peace; for the threat of international repercussions of the very gravest kind can no longer be disregarded. These considerations might not apply with such force were South Africa a small and insignificant state to which the world was indifferent. But South Africa is not insignificant; quite apart from her strategic importance, she is and, if she survives, may continue to be the most highly industrialized, minerally rich, and desirable state on the continent.

THE BASIC PROBLEM OF COMMUNITY

There are those who pin their faith for a better future in Southern Africa upon constitutional reform, a liberalization of the franchise, and the guarantee and safeguarding of Human Rights. That there is room for hope along these lines I firmly believe. But as I have written elsewhere[33]—and it would seem that the point requires emphasis and elaboration—it is manifestly foolish, and I would add politically illiterate, to place too much confidence in the efficacy of constitutions. No constitution can artificially fuse racial groups into one healthy community, one nation or shared society, if in fact the operative currents are flowing too strongly in a different direction.

No plans for constitutional reform in South Africa are likely to be of much more than academic significance unless they first grapple with two far more basic problems.

In the first place there are the plain facts of existing power. The governing party in South Africa is sternly resolved to maintain the existing constitutional structure and the policies which are now being implemented. Not only is the existing constitution felt to be satisfactory by the present Government, but it is also acceptable to the overwhelming majority of the white electorate. Moreover the forces of opposition, both white and non-white, are at present deeply divided. For this reason there are those who contend that all plans for radical constitutional revision, calculated to bring about a more integrated community, are either unrealistic or hopelessly premature.

[33] See 'Constitution-Making for a Democracy', *Optima*, Supplement, March 1960, especially at pp. 2, 12, 40, 41.

Nevertheless, for reasons which will be stated in a later chapter, I am convinced that such plans are by no means premature. On the contrary, if anything, they may be too late. But despite the lateness of the hour, I shall try to show why it is still realistic not to give up hope; and why it is important and urgent that alternatives should be very seriously thought about, and widely discussed.

Secondly, and even more daunting to the constitution-maker than the determination of power groups to maintain the existing structure, is the problem of community and nationhood. Even if the present Nationalist Government were entirely replaced by, say, a liberal but predominantly white government, there would still remain a harrowing problem of community, namely, is it possible to fuse the relevant groups of different colour and culture into one stable society. This is basic. And when, in addition, one asks the further question: assuming that it is possible for the various groups to live together peacefully in one community, can that community be organized on a democratic basis?—prospective constitution-makers should, to say the least, feel a due sense of humility.

Recently a new political party in South Africa (the Progressive Party) put forward certain proposals for constitutional revision, and for a qualified franchise which would not exclude any racial group. The plan was criticized by one of the country's most thoughtful and influential newspapers, *Die Burger*,[34] on the score that it failed to take account of the underlying sociological realities. *Die Burger* emphasized its point with graphic force by describing the plan as an attempt to create unity between a cat and a dog by tying their tails together in a constitutional knot. And much the same kind of criticism was put forward in more academic terms by another thoughtful South African, at one time a professor of constitutional law and now a Nationalist member of Parliament, Dr. L. I. Coertze. Speaking in the House of Assembly in February 1960, Dr. Coertze, in the course of a penetrating and lucid speech, made the point that cultural values and principles matter far more in binding people together into one society, than any system of government that can be established, so to speak, from the outside.[35] Reminding the House of views which had been expressed by Lord Balfour, and earlier by J. S. Mill, he maintained that there must be an inherent unity among a people, a sharing of values, and a like-mindedness on fundamentals, before a democratic system of parliamentary government could have any hope of success. And precisely because there was, in his view, no such unity of ideals and aspirations

---

[34] Leading article, 16 November 1960. This paper supports the Nationalist Party and apartheid, and circulates mainly in the Cape Province.
[35] *House of Assembly Debates*, vol. 103, col. 1022.

between white and non-white in South Africa, and no hope of such unity, he felt that all plans for constitution-making which presupposed a common society, were simply ignoring the crucial facts of the situation.[36]

For reasons which will be stated later, I do not accept the validity of the objection that black and white in South Africa are irreconcilable elements which cannot fuse into a single society. Nevertheless I believe that critics like *Die Burger* and Dr. Coertze are entirely correct in giving emphasis to what is, after all, the really basic problem; namely, the problem of community.

Considering the importance and urgency of the South African situation it is alarming how little fundamental thinking has been devoted, especially by critics of the Government, to the real problems that are here involved. It should never be forgotten that the late Dr. D. F. Malan once gave it as his considered view that the difference between white and non-white in South Africa was 'the physical manifestation of a contrast between two irreconcilable ways of life'.[37] And this is still, as we shall see, the deeply held conviction of the supporters of apartheid, and probably, if they search their hearts, of the overwhelming majority of white South Africans, including many who sincerely believe in fairness and justice for all. Leaving entirely aside the rightness or wrongness of this conviction, it would plainly be monstrous to ignore the only too real fact of its existence, and proceed with plans for constitution-making on the *unexamined* assumption that the colour and culture groups of Southern Africa can achieve together a symbiosis, an organic and viable community, and that they have the will to do so.

No amount of loud declamation will make South Africa one society if in fact it is not such. Nor will any amount of strong assertion get away from the fact that to the extent to which it is correct to describe the South African people as one community or nation, they are as yet a very deeply fissured, indeed schizophrenic, community. Every day in thought, conduct, and emotion, white South Africans behave for some purposes as if the non-whites belonged to the same community as themselves, and for other purposes, as if they did not. For generations the whites have both desired the benefits and feared the consequences of integration. And today, so far from acting on the principle enunciated by Mr. Macmillan of 'finding means by which the community can become more of a community', the majority of white South Africans both think and act in the firm belief that the forces which favour a common society for whites and non-whites should be actively discouraged.

[36] Ibid., col. 1024.
[37] Quoted by Rhoodie and Venter, op. cit., p. 30.

Merely to assert confidently that South Africa is a society, albeit a 'plural' or 'multi-racial' society, gets one absolutely no further; and indeed merely avoids the real problem and obscures thought. Some years ago a liberal-minded and very distinguished South African scholar, the late Professor R. F. A. Hoernlé, made a vigorous and now famous attack on the so-called 'multi-racial society' which we have hitherto known in South Africa. It was, he said, a caste-society, an instrument of domination in which whites dominated non-whites politically, economically and socially. And he reached the conclusion (in theory at any rate) that the evils of a multi-racial society in South Africa could only be mended by ending it. Either, he felt, one should encourage the operation of forces which would lead to the establishment of one entirely assimilated non-racial society, or one should work for a separation or 'dissociation so complete as to destroy the very possibility of effective domination'.[38] And of these two courses he preferred, again in theory, complete separation, because 'so long as whites and non-whites are united in the same socio-political structure, the former will not consent to surrender their dominance;[39] and also because he felt that when faced with the possibility of total assimilation, white South Africa would say 'rather withdrawal from South Africa, rather death and racial extinction, than this'.[40] Accordingly, in his view, a clear-thinking and liberal-minded man should, in principle, favour a solution which 'envisages an organization of the two warring sections into genuinely separate self-contained self-governing societies, each in principle homogeneous within itself, which can then co-operate on a footing of mutual recognition of one another's independence'.[41]

Hoernlé's thinking, as is well known, has been used to supply a theoretical foundation for apartheid[42] which, on the face of it, could be defended;[43] though as we shall see later, what Hoernlé actually envisaged has in practice been emasculated and caricatured, for the very good reason that he did not himself believe that his idea of complete separation or partition was practicable. On the contrary, he felt that the will to realize it did not exist; nor 'was there

[38] *South African Native Policy and the Liberal Spirit*, Phelps-Stokes Lecture, 1939, p. 168; *Race and Reason*, 1945, p. 158. And for a good summary of Hoernlé's views, see Roskam, *Apartheid and Discrimination*, Leyden, 1960, pp. 95–9.

[39] *South African Native Policy and the Liberal Spirit*, pp. 182–3.

[40] Op. cit., p. 168.

[41] Op. cit., p. 169.

[42] See, for example, Rhoodie and Venter, op. cit., pp. 147–8; and for critical discussion, Roskam, *Apartheid and Discrimination*, pp. 96, 97, 99. Also W. W. M. Eiselen, 'The Meaning of Apartheid', *Race Relations*, vol. 15, pp. 69 sqq.

[43] But see Prof. E. E. Harris, 'Heartbreak House', in *Race Relations Journal*, vol. XXII, no. 4, 1955, pp. 33 sqq.

any power on earth', he said, 'which could bring it into being'.[44]
Indeed, despite its professions, apartheid has in practice turned out
to be domination masquerading in the guise of Hoernlé's idea of
separation.

It is nevertheless important to keep in mind the realism of
Hoernlé's approach. Liberal humanitarian that he was, he reluctantly
came to the conclusion that there was in South Africa *no hope* for
fair and sound race adjustment, no hope for the liberal spirit, in a
shared multi-racial society.[45] Again, it was Hoernlé who said, as
far back as 1939, that in South Africa complete separation 'may
yet turn out to be the path of political wisdom'.[46] And it was Hoernlé
who in reply to the question 'Watchman, what of the night', reported
not the breaking of dawn, but an intensification of darkness.[47]

Hoernlé was criticized by well-meaning but less perceptive people
for lacking confidence in the future, for being a pessimist. The
criticism left him entirely unmoved. 'I have no use', he said, 'for
confidence based on illusion or on ignorance; I have no use for a
faith which is unthinking, or which can flourish only in the atmosphere of an intellectual holiday.'[48] And let me add, he had no use
for sloppy platitudes about 'good will' as the solvent of racial
problems. He recognized that the South African situation demanded
courageous and clear thinking of a truly fundamental kind, not
wishful thinking or blurred thinking.

It is precisely because I believe that it may yet prove practicable
for whites and non-whites to live together harmoniously in one
community; because I believe that such a symbiosis is necessary,
and, what is more, practicable on a democratic basis, that I propose
in this book to give particular attention to the difficulties in the way
of such a goal. I do not say, nor do I believe, that this goal will be
reached soon or without much suffering. But I do think that its
difficulties have been exaggerated. And I believe, further, that
compared with the difficulties, evils and almost certain disaster of
any other alternative, the goal of one integrated society organized
on a democratic basis is not only within the bounds of practical
politics, but is in fact the only solution which contains any hope of
future peaceful development; and that it is, in addition, spiritually
uplifting in its challenge.

However, to achieve this goal, it will be necessary to do very
much *in addition* to constitution-making. It will be necessary, as
we shall see, to explode the myths and disarm the fears upon which

[44] *South African Native Policy and the Liberal Spirit*, p. 183.
[45] Op. cit., pp. 164, 168.
[46] Op. cit., p. 101.
[47] Op. cit., p. 185.
[48] *Race and Reason*, p. 145.

apartheid and allied policies rest, and from which they draw their vital force. And still more important, it will be necessary to foster the idea of one inclusive community by daily conduct which is consonant with it. It will be necessary, in short, to devise and carefully plan a comprehensive *strategy for integration*.

At the rather more pedestrian level of constitution-making, such a strategy for integration would involve the devising of adequate constitutional safeguards of basic human rights. And it should be a sobering reflection that much serious thought will have to be given to the very real difficulties involved in the establishment of such guarantees. It is, however, because I believe in the usefulness of properly devised constitutional guarantees that I propose in this book to give as much emphasis to their defects and limitations as to their good qualities; for I hold that, like truth, they will not be put to the worse in a free and open encounter. But I would repeat that before we can usefully begin to discuss these problems of government, we must first give attention to the underlying social and economic forces, the dynamic cultural forces, upon which the whole structure of organized government ultimately rests.

SOME ESSENTIAL CLARIFICATION OF TERMS

As will already have become apparent, it is not possible to discuss the subject with which we are concerned without continually using such terms as society, community, nation, state and government. All of these words are, however, either ambiguous or lacking in precision, and the looseness with which they are used in everyday life, even among professed authorities, is remarkable. If confusion is to be avoided, therefore, it is desirable that I should specify at the outset the exact sense in which I intend to use them.

The term society is sometimes used in a wide sense to include every collection, large or small, of human beings who live together in an enduring relationship of any kind.[49] In this wide sense the term embraces such diverse groups as a single family or the members of a church. In a more specific sense of the word, society is often used as a synonym for community, and unless otherwise stated, I shall so use it in this book.

The term community, as currently used by sociologists and political scientists, connotes two sets of characteristics concerning human groups. Both are implicit in the meaning of the term, though in some contexts an author might give more emphasis to one aspect than to the other. In the first place, a collection of human beings is said to constitute a community when it occupies a defined

[49] Cf. L. T. Hobhouse, *Social Development*, 1924, p. 39; R. M. MacIver, *Community*, 1920, p. 22.

geographical area, engages in interrelated social and economic activities, and acknowledges some form of common rule, which may, in underdeveloped communities, be wholly customary law unaccompanied by specialized organs of government.[50] This is sometimes called the structural aspect of community to distinguish it from the functional aspect.[51] In the second place, from the functional point of view, when one describes a collection of human beings as constituting a community, the emphasis is on the fact that they share common interests and sentiments. As Professor MacIver puts it, 'wherever men live together they develop in some kind and degree distinctive common characteristics—manners, traditions, modes of speech, and so on. These are the signs and consequences of an effective common life.'[52] When, however, the emphasis is on the functional aspect of community, i.e. the sharing of common interests and sentiments, the question of geographical boundaries is not necessarily of the essence; and one may appropriately speak of a community whose members are scattered all over the world, as for example the members of a church.[53]

The extracts which I quoted earlier from Dr. Coertze's speech are perhaps sufficient to indicate that it is the functional aspect of community which is particularly relevant to this book. However, there is a passage in the writings of the sociologist, Professor L. T. Hobhouse, which should, I think, place beyond doubt the significance for us of this aspect of the idea of community. Hobhouse stressed the fact that the word community suggests something much more than rule in common. He said:

> It would suggest a common sentiment and a common interest, and it must be asked whether it is applicable to a population in which the majority are the unwilling subjects of a powerful oligarchy. The question how far this is possible, how far the writ of government runs if it is opposed to sentiment, has been and remains a live issue of politics, and the only general answer to be given is that it is certainly possible—to a limit. But the position of the limit varies very greatly in proportion to the strength of political factors of resistance, which can only be determined by dismal and often disastrous experiment.[54]

The relevance of this passage in the context of Southern Africa needs no emphasis.

[50] See generally, MacIver, op. cit., London, 1920, pp. 22–3; *The Web of Government*, New York, 1947, pp. 192 sqq.; *The Encyclopaedia of the Social Sciences*, vol. 4, s.v. Community.

[51] *The Encyclopaedia of the Social Sciences*, loc. cit.

[52] *Community*, p. 23.

[53] *The Encyclopaedia of the Social Sciences*, loc. cit.

[54] *Social Development*, London, 1924, p. 41.

The word nation is notoriously ambiguous; but with a little care it should cause no difficulty. Three meanings may be distinguished. In one sense of the term, nation signifies a cultural phenomenon. It implies a sense of special unity which marks off those who share it from the rest of mankind. It is not easy to trace this sentiment of unity to any single factor; for nationhood, in the cultural sense, is invariably the resultant of many forces: community of language and art and religion, the outcome of common history and traditions, and the sharing of moral, economic, and political aspirations.[55] In another sense of the word, nation signifies a political and legal concept, that is to say, a people who adhere or owe allegiance to a particular state.[56] And finally, the term is sometimes used in a racial sense to designate a people who share an ethnic unity or blood-bond.[57]

It will be noted that, in its cultural sense, the word nation signifies an idea which is almost identical with that of community. As MacIver points out, 'the nation is community'.[58] And it is in its cultural sense that I shall use the word nation unless a contrary indication is given. It is, moreover, in the cultural sense that the idea of nationhood is particularly significant for the purposes of this book. Thus it is relevant to ask whether, and in what sense, the peoples of South Africa constitute one nation or several? Ethnically, of course, there are in South Africa several nations within the political boundaries of a single state. Culturally, however, the idea of an overriding or all-embracive South African nationhood is still in the making; and whether it will ever be allowed to develop as between white and black is the really critical question. Here, again, there is a passage in MacIver's book on community which is very relevant. He points out that as culture advances, the like-mindedness which holds a community or nation together 'supports itself less and less on the idea of consanguinity'. 'A community', he says, 'must transcend the idea of race or remain limited, thwarted and irrational.' And he adds these significant words:

> A community that finds its unity and its inspiration in the blood-bond alone, and not on any intrinsic interests this may be held to involve, can scarcely have any definite object beyond mere aggrandisement and the reduction of rivals.[59]

Today in South Africa race is the main factor which is being exploited (not by any means only by the Government) to prevent

[55] Laski, *Grammar of Politics*, 1937, pp. 219–20.
[56] *Encyclopaedia of the Social Sciences*, vol. 11, s.v. Nationality, p. 231.
[57] For references, see Appadorai, 1952, *The Substance of Politics*, p. 16.
[58] *Community*, p. 277.
[59] Op. cit., p. 278.

the growth of a common South African community or nationhood; indeed, it is being used to foster the idea of smaller and *mutually exclusive* communities. Whether this process can be arrested, and whether the ethnic groups can live together harmoniously within the framework of a wider South African nationhood, are the fundamental questions upon which the future of the country depends.

Turning now briefly to the idea of the state, perhaps the most helpful approach to a clear understanding of the idea, is to begin with what MacIver calls an 'association'. If, as we have seen, the sharing of common interests and sentiments is one of the marks of a community, we must have recourse to the idea of organization for a purpose, to understand what is meant by an association. An association is any group of persons considered from the point of view of how they are organized for the achievement of a particular purpose.[60] Associations may, however, correspond to every possible interest of human beings. As MacIver puts it:

> no student of social life can help being struck by the enormous number of associations of every kind, political, economic, religious, educational, scientific, artistic, literary, recreative, philanthropic, professional, which today enrich communal life.[61]

In short, within one and the same community many different associations may co-exist.

Associations vary, of course, in degree of permanence and significance, ranging from comparatively minor and temporary associations, like a committee to organize the centenary of an historical event, to the most comprehensive of all organizations, namely the state. The state, then, is a particular kind of association or organization, namely an association for the purposes of maintaining law and order in a given society. While, however, it is entirely appropriate to speak of the state as one among other associations, it obviously has a peculiar and distinctive place. Other associations are limited to the pursuit of one or at most a few interests, but the state's range of jurisdiction is marked by its comprehensiveness. Thus, in the process of maintaining law and order, the state is concerned with most human interests. Again, other associations do not have the right, on their own initiative, to use force to compel obedience to their decisions, but the state does.

The state has been defined as society, or the community, organized for the purposes of maintaining law and order;[62] and subject to an

[60] Op. cit., pp. 23–4. Readers of Tönnies, *Community and Association*, will recognize that MacIver's use of the term association differs from that of Tönnies. See *Community*, p. 24, note 1.

[61] Op. cit., p. 24.

[62] Appadorai, op. cit., p. 14.

important reservation, this is not an inapt definition. But it should not be allowed to obscure the fact that state and community are nevertheless two different ideas. Because the state, like the community considered from the structural point of view, has territorial boundaries; and because it exercises control over all or nearly all other associations, writers on politics sometimes fail or refuse to distinguish between the state and the community; and also fail to analyse the relationship between the state and other associations within the community.[63] This, however, is a grave mistake which has far-reaching consequences, some of which will be noted in a subsequent chapter.[64]

At this stage it is relevant and sufficient to call attention to one point only concerning the relationship between the idea of community and the concept of the state. A people may belong to a state without having any common feeling of community or nationhood, as in the case of Austria-Hungary before the war of 1914-18. In such a case, as J. S. Mill pointed out, it is not easy to work democratic institutions. It is indeed precisely the sense of community, the sense of belonging together, which creates a readiness to subordinate differences to the common good. A political society is in an unsatisfactory condition when its members have no consciousness of unity except obedience to a common government.[65] On the other hand, the existence of a strong state is by no means incompatible with the existence of several communities within its borders, provided always that a larger, more inclusive and overriding sense of community is capable of developing. Indeed there may be great advantages in having several communities within one and the same state; for as Lord Acton showed, the presence of different communities within a state helps to tame power; and acts as a barrier against the intrusion of law-making power into fields which are beyond its reasonably legitimate jurisdiction.[66]

As regards the word Government, little if any difficulty should be experienced. Dr. Appadorai defines Government as the organ or organs through which the will of the state is formulated, and expressed organized; and so defined it includes the sum total of the legislative, executive and judicial organs which are engaged in making, administering and interpreting the law.[67] In a narrower sense,

[63] Probably the clearest and most convincing criticism of this failure is to be found in the works of MacIver, on which this passage in the text is largely based. See particularly, *Community*, pp. 28 sqq.; *The Web of Government*, pp. 129 sqq.; and *The Modern State*, 1926, *passim*.
[64] See below, pp. 89 sqq.
[65] Appadorai, op. cit., p. 17.
[66] *The History of Freedom and other Essays*, pp. 289–90.
[67] Appadorai, op. cit., pp. 12–13.

however, the phrase 'the Government' is used, especially in countries where the British parliamentary system operates, to designate the body of men who are responsible for Executive policy and administration. The context in which the word government is used in this book should suffice to indicate which of these meanings is intended.

Thus far we have dealt with terms of wide general use. There remains, however, one more group of terms, of somewhat greater domestic significance, which require preliminary definition. Dealing with the possible patterns of socio-political life in South Africa, the late Professor Hoernlé usefully distinguished between four different concepts. Firstly, a policy of repression in the interests of white domination. This policy, long practised in South Africa and familiarly known as *segregation*, seeks to maintain a caste-like multi-racial society.[68] And by a caste society, in this context, he meant one in which membership of the various groups is acquired by the accident of birth and cannot be modified either by the effort or volition of the person concerned.[69] Segregation in a caste society is a policy which Hoernlé felt could not be acceptable to any fair-minded man.

Secondly—and more defensibly he felt—one might adopt a policy of *parallelism*, which would seek the co-ordination of different racial groups within a single multi-racial society; the emphasis here being on co-ordination as distinct from domination.[70] Parallelism, he said:

accepts the fact of race difference, elevated by articulate consciousness and mutual appreciation into a principle of mainly voluntary organization—'birds of a feather flock together'. Subjecting no racial group to legal or other discriminations it credits each with the desire to preserve its own integrity, and hence to maintain by mutual consent all necessary distances between itself and other groups. Given such desire and consent, intergroup differences may be re-enforced by legislation.[71]

Thirdly, one might aim at *total assimilation*. This too, in a sense, seeks to maintain a multi-racial society.[72] But according to Hoernlé, it cannot do so indefinitely; for it attempts 'to abolish race conflicts by abolishing race differences', treating people as equal in all matters, regardless of race, colour or creed. And the reason why, according to Professor Hoernlé, such a policy cannot indefinitely maintain a multi-racial society is that such equality or treatment would lead

[68] *South African Native Policy and the Liberal Spirit*, p. 158 note 1.
[69] See also Liston Pope, *The Kingdom Beyond Caste*, pp. 52 sqq.
[70] Hoernlé, op. cit., p. 160.
[71] Op. cit., p. 160.
[72] Op. cit., p. 158.

first to cultural assimilation; then to economic assimilation; this in turn would lead to social and political assimilation, and 'lastly there could not fail to be racial assimilation, i.e. inter-marriage and the actual formation of one new race by the fusion of two races originally distinct'.[73]

It was because Hoernlé considered the first course, namely repressive segregation, to be unjust; because he felt that the second, namely parallelism, would in practice be indistinguishable from the first; and because he regarded the third, total assimilation, as likely to be utterly unacceptable to white South Africans, that he turned somewhat despairingly to the fourth possibility—*separation* and the total dissevering of the 'multi-racial' society. And as this too, in his view, was impracticable, he reached the gloomy conclusion that South Africa was indeed 'Heartbreak House'.[74]

I do not propose at this stage to go into the question whether Hoernlé was right in assuming that miscegenation and racial fusion are inevitable if one embarks upon a policy of non-discrimination and equality of treatment in all fields. Nor, at this stage, will I attempt to analyse the nature of the particular fear which is here involved, and the various methods of dealing with it. I have called attention to the distinctions drawn by Professor Hoernlé primarily because I believe that we are in need of a more precise vocabulary in the field of race relations; and because Hoernlé's definitions may help to give greater clarity to thought.

It is of course easy to understand why people, especially white people, tend to telescope these various distinctions and speak simply of 'the problems of a multi-racial society', or of a 'colour problem'; for in the mind of the average white person, race and colour have become convenient tokens of present differences in traditions, background and cultural attainments. But colour differences should not be mistaken for cultural differences; for the obvious reason that whereas one cannot change one's colour, cultural attributes can most certainly be acquired. Indeed, without in any way attempting to minimize the existence and significance of cultural differences among the racial groups in Southern Africa, I would say that it is precisely the failure to recognize the difference between colour and culture that is responsible for so much dangerous thinking about race relations.

While, however, it is important to acknowledge the fact of cultural differences among the people of Southern Africa, I know of no good reason why these differences should not in large measure be cherished and preserved within a larger unity—the Afrikaans

[73] Op. cit., pp. 165-7.
[74] Op. cit., p. 178 sqq.

language being a case in point. It by no means follows that the existence of cultural differences gives any real support to the policy of apartheid which is now being practised by the Union Government; or to the case for territorial partition or separation which Hoernlé envisaged; nor does it follow that within a single community they warrant group political representation, or constitutional guarantees of group rights, involving legal definition of the various groups. These, however, are matters which, together with the influence and relevance of aggressive nationalism, will be discussed more fully later.

Some years ago, Mr. G. H. Galpin wrote a book with the arresting title *There are no South Africans*,[75] a sentiment which has recently been repeated by an eminent Afrikaner, Professor P. V. Pistorius.[76] Though these writers were concerned primarily to call attention to the lack of basic unity and inner coherence among the white groups, their thesis was *a fortiori* valid in the wider setting of the population as a whole. Yet despite the prevailing gloom and despondency; and despite the very determined, but I believe mis-guided, efforts now being made to encourage the forces of division and arrest the forces which bring men together, there is still hope that the races in South Africa, and in countries with similar problems, will develop together a healthy communal life. It may well be that before this hope is realized there will be much deep travail. It may even be that the hope is a slender one. But the hope remains; and it is to help forward its realization that this book has, in humility, been written.

[75] London, 1941.
[76] *No Further Trek*, Johannesburg, 1957.

The Politics of Division—I

FROM SEGREGATION TO APARTHEID

It is usual for writers on apartheid, especially those who oppose it, to emphasize the difficulty of defining the concept with particularity and accuracy; for there are gaps and hesitations at several points both in theory and practice. Moreover, leading upholders of the policy have been at pains to emphasize that within the broad framework there is room for experiment, flexibility, and gradualness in implementation. But it would not be fair to conclude from this, as some critics still do, that the policy is a mere election slogan with no definite content. On the contrary, not only have the essential outlines and rationale of apartheid been often and clearly stated at the highest level of authority, but what is perhaps more important, the doctrine has been systematically enforced by its apostles for more than twelve years; and as each year has passed, an accumulation of legislative Acts and regulations has made the unfolding pattern ever clearer.

Probably the best way to gain a clear understanding of the nature of apartheid is to begin with the earlier policy of segregation, out of which it evolved. As we have seen, the late Professor R. F. A. Hoernlé defined segregation, in its precise sense, as meaning domination by the whites in a multi-racial caste society living within the boundaries of a single state.[1] And he distinguished this idea sharply from separation, which aims at establishing distinct racial societies politically organized in separate territories.[2] He said:

> Both segregation and separation have a common feature in being techniques used by whites for establishing distances (territorial, social, economic, etc.) between themselves and non-whites. But they differ none the less in principle, in that segregation establishes such distances in the form of a multi-racial caste society, whereas separation aims at establishing distinct racial societies.[3]

[1] *South African Native Policy and the Liberal Spirit*, p. 158 note 1; *Race and Reason*, pp. 95 sqq.
[2] *South African Native Policy and the Liberal Spirit*, pp. ix, 158.
[3] *Race and Reason*, p. 159.

In short, as envisaged by Hoernlé, separation (unlike segregation) seeks not to mend but to end the multi-racial society.[4] This is an important distinction; because in the eyes of the theoreticians of apartheid, it is claimed to be the justification for their policy, and one of the essential points of difference between it and the old policy of segregation.[5] Whether or not the claim is a fair one, is a question we shall examine presently.

In addition to the fundamental distinction between a segregated multi-racial society and separate racial societies, the theoreticians of apartheid draw attention to another distinction which they consider to be essential for an understanding of apartheid; namely the distinction between differentiation and discrimination. These two words are sometimes used synonymously; and according to the dictionary, they may legitimately be so used. But the more usual meaning of discrimination, especially in racially mixed societies, is to 'differentiate to the prejudice of', or to 'draw an adverse or detrimental distinction'. And the word was so defined by the United Nations Sub-Commission on the Prevention of Discrimination and the Protection of Minorities.[6] As practised in South Africa, segregation has for generations involved white supremacy and a subordinate status for the non-white groups: in short, it has involved discrimination.[7] But the supporters of apartheid claim that their policy aims not at adverse discrimination, but rather at differentiation between the groups for the mutual benefit of each.[8] Here, again, the question whether the claim is a fair one will answer itself as we proceed with our examination of the evidence.

Much light would undoubtedly be cast on almost every aspect of South African life by a comprehensive historical survey of the practice of segregation and the way in which apartheid has evolved out of it. Such a survey, however, has yet to be written,[9] and this is

[4] Ibid., p. 158.

[5] See especially Rhoodie and Venter, *Apartheid*, p. 148. And see, generally, Dr. W. W. M. Eiselen's *The Meaning of Apartheid*, Race Relations, vol. 15, pp. 69 sqq.; and 'Harmonious Multi-Community Development', *Optima*, March 1959, pp. 3 sqq. Dr. Eiselen is, of course, one of the main architects of apartheid.

[6] *The Main Types and Causes of Discrimination*, 1949, p. 26.

[7] Hoernlé, *South African Native Policy and the Liberal Spirit*, pp. 1, 48–9, 158–9.

[8] Rhoodie and Venter, op. cit., pp. 159, 216.

[9] The relevant literature is extensive. But three recent books—the first by supporters of apartheid, the other two by critics—are particularly revealing: N. J. Rhoodie and H. J. Venter, op. cit.; K. L. Roskam, *Apartheid and Discrimination*, Leyden, 1960; Gwendolen M. Carter, *The Politics of Inequality*, 2nd ed., 1959.

The earlier pioneer studies by Professor Macmillan are still indispensable. See also E. H. Brookes, *History of Native Policy in South Africa*, 1926; *The Colour Problems of South Africa*, 1934.

not the occasion to undertake it. But one or two brief conclusions must nevertheless be stated. There are critics of the Government who regard apartheid as an entirely new phenomenon in South African affairs, and who are disposed to attribute all the tensions and frustrations and bitterness of the contemporary situation to the activities of the Nationalist Party Government since its advent to power in 1948. On the other hand, there are supporters of apartheid who are at pains to give this policy the respectability of old lineage by emphasizing its wholly 'traditional character' in South Africa. Both attitudes are historically inaccurate, though the Government point of view is nearer the truth than that of their critics.

Professor Hoernlé, whose analysis of the South African racial situation includes some of the most penetrating observations of an historical nature that have yet been written on the subject, expressed the conclusion that:

> subject to the over-arching fact of white domination, South African Native Policy is an odd patchwork, exhibiting traces of Parallelism, Assimilation, Separation. Historic accident and deliberate policy—even conflicting policies—have contributed to this result.[10]

This, I think, is a very fair and balanced conclusion. Indeed it would not be difficult to quote chapter and verse in support of each aspect of it; and more particularly to show that the technique of white domination has historical roots which may be traced back to the early days of the settlement, and especially to the eighteenth century.

Much of the evidence has been brought together by Professors Hoernlé, Brookes, Macmillan, de Kiewiet and Frankel, and more recently by Rhoodie and Venter; and there would be no point in summarizing it here. The evidence goes a long way, however, towards supporting the view that the policies of the present Government are nearer to the main stream of South African tradition and thought than their opponents are generally prepared to concede. Nor would I deny Hoernlé's conclusion that rather too much importance is sometimes attached to the alleged strength of a contrary tradition of 'Cape liberalism'. Cape liberalism, as he observes, was in large measure an exotic, stimulated by officials from outside; it was not primarily an indigenous growth. Moreover it was never as completely colour-blind in practice as it was in theory—in fact it was sometimes transparently hypocritical—and, by the time of Union, on the decline.[11]

[10] Hoernlé, op. cit., p. 159. And see pp. 46, 55, 60, 63, 67.
[11] Op. cit., pp. 60–1, 103 sqq. And see E. E. Harris, 'Heartbreak House', vol. 22, *Race Relations Journal*, 1955, pp. 33 sqq.

The South Africa Act itself, which established the Union's framework of government, is often and very rightly quoted as discriminatory legislation openly adverse to non-whites, who were barred from being elected as members of an all-white Parliament; and save in the Cape, and to a minute extent in Natal, were excluded from the franchise.[12] Though it was a former Prime Minister of the Cape Colony, the liberal W. P. Schreiner, who courageously led a delegation to Westminster to remove 'the blot' of colour discrimination from the draft South Africa Act, the tide was flowing too strongly against him. Calmly and truthfully he described the Act as being not one of Union 'but rather an Act of Separation between the minority and the majority of the people of South Africa'. But his mission failed;[13] and Rhoodie and Venter are probably correct when, after hailing 'the statutory entrenchment of racial differentiation' in the constitution, they comment: 'Thus the Cape liberal tradition suffered a blow from which it has not yet recovered.'[14]

Year after year, subsequent to Union, discriminatory legislation has been added to the statute book by successive governments, both United Party and Nationalist: the Mines and Works Act of 1911; the Native Labour Regulation Act of the same year; the Natives Land Act of 1913; the Railways and Harbours Act of 1916; the Stock Theft Act of 1923; the Native Urban Areas Act of the same year; the Native Taxation and Development Act of 1925; the Master and Servants Amendment Act of 1926; the Native Administration Act of 1927; the Liquor Act of 1928; the Old Age Pension Act of the same year; the Women's Enfranchisement Act of 1930; the Natives Act of the same year; the Arms and Ammunition Act of 1937; the Industrial Conciliation Act of 1937; The Apprenticeship Act of 1944; the Pension Law Amendment Act of the same year; the Native Urban Areas Consolidation Act of 1945; the Asiatic Land Tenure and Indian Representation Act of 1946, and the Disability Grants Act of 1946. These have now been catalogued and usefully summarized by Roskam.[15]

The record of discrimination is equally plain in the pages of the South African Law Reports. In 1911, a year after Union, the Chief Justice, Lord de Villiers, declared that:

As a matter of public history we know that the first civilized legislators in South Africa came from Holland and regarded the aboriginal natives of the country as belonging to an inferior race,

[12] Roskam, *Apartheid and Discrimination*, p. 55. And see per Gardiner A.J.A. in *Minister of Posts and Telegraphs* v. *Rasool*, 1934 A.D. at 188.
[13] L. M. Thompson, *The Unification of South Africa*, 1960, pp. 402 sqq.
[14] Op. cit., p. 116.
[15] Op cit., pp. 55–8.

whom the Dutch, as Europeans, were entitled to rule over, and whom they refused to admit to social or political equality. . . . these prepossessions, or as many might term them, these prejudices have never died out, and are not less deeply rooted at the present day among the Europeans in South Africa, whether of Dutch or English or French descent. . . . We cannot as judges, when called upon to construe an act of Parliament, ignore the reasons which must have induced the legislature to adopt the policy of separate education for European and non-European children.[16]

In 1934 an Asian challenged the provision of separate post office facilities, but the Appellate Division, by a majority, gave countenance to the now widely discredited 'separate but equal' doctrine, which we shall have occasion to examine more fully in a subsequent chapter. In that case the regulations providing separate facilities were held to be valid and reasonable because in fact substantially equal facilities were provided.[17] One of the judges who formed the majority of the Court went so far as to hold that it was not relevant to go into the question whether the separate facilities were equal, in view of the fact that 'in important respects Europeans and non-Europeans had never been treated as equal in the eye of the law'. Only Mr. Justice Gardiner, strongly dissenting, held that under Roman-Dutch and modern South African law a classification on the basis of colour was *per se* invalid.

So deeply have notions of inequality permeated South African life that in 1948 a trial judge actually took into consideration the fact that an injured person was an African in awarding lesser damages for pain and suffering than he would otherwise have done. Not surprisingly, the Appellate Division overruled this decision with the remark: 'the fact that the appellant is a native earning only £2 a week, is not evidence that he is insensitive to pain.'[18]

These considerations are perhaps sufficient to reveal the hollowness of the contention that racial discrimination is a new phenomenon in South Africa; or in any way the exclusive characteristic of any one section of the white population, or of the Nationalist Government.

On the other hand it would equally be a mistake to assume that the policy inaugurated by the Nationalist Government in 1948, under the name of apartheid, was merely a continuation of the old segregation policy. In the first place, Rhoodie and Venter correctly emphasize the fragmentary character of the old policy of

---

[16] 1911 A.D. at 643–4.
[17] *Minister of Posts and Telegraphs* v. *Rasool*, 1934 A.D. 167.
[18] *Radebe* v. *Hough*, 1949 (1) S.A. (A.D.) at 386.

segregation, and of the measures designed to implement it; and they contrast this feature with the far more systematic and comprehensive policy of apartheid.[19]

Not only was the earlier segregation policy empirical and sporadic, but—what is much more important—it allowed the forces of integration to operate in many important fields free from legislative barriers. Before 1948 the operative social, economic and political forces in South Africa—those that tend to unite as well as those that tend to divide—had been allowed to exert their influence without much deliberate planning; and, broadly speaking, the trend was increasingly towards integration. The strongest forces working to bind whites and non-whites into one South African society with a single economy have, of course, been trade and industry; the white man needs and desires the benefits of non-white labour and the non-white market; and the non-whites need and desire employment and the benefits of white capital and skills. By 1948, these incentives had already operated for many generations and had produced a considerable degree of economic integration. Indeed, as a distinguished authority once observed, 'the economic entanglement of whites and non-whites is one of the oldest and most solid facts of South African history'.[20] And in addition to the obvious economic incentives, a careful and sensitive observer might have discerned feelings of interdependence between the races in other less tangible spheres of life.

Today, after twelve years of apartheid, economic and other incentives towards integration remain powerful, and have indeed been strengthened by the needs of rapidly expanding industry. But no longer can it be said, as in the old segregation days, that attempts to differentiate and discriminate between the races are fragmentary and unplanned. On the contrary, ruthlessly calculated efforts are being made to discourage the operation of unifying tendencies, and to foster the growth of forces that dissever the races.

Education, for example, which can be a most potent unifying factor when used to give a society ideals and aspirations in common, is being used to divide and set up racial barriers. As Dr. Verwoerd once explained in the House of Assembly: 'It is necessary that Native Education should be controlled in such a way that it should be in accord with the policy of the state.'[21] By providing for

[19] Op. cit., pp. 147–8.

[20] The late Professor R. F. A. Hoernlé: *South African Native Policy and the Liberal Spirit*, p. 173. And see, generally, *Report of the Native Laws Commission* (Fagan Report), U.G. 28/1948.

[21] *House of Assembly Debates*, 17 September 1953, col. 3776.

separate housing areas,[22] separate transport facilities and other
public amenities,[23] separate education with a tribal curriculum for
Africans at the school level,[24] and separate higher education;[25]
by differential laws in industry denying the Africans the right to
strike,[26] and reserving skilled jobs for whites;[27] by restrictive legislation concerning land,[28] marriage,[29] and other relationships;[30] by
the rigours of a population register;[31] by pass laws restricting freedom
of movement;[32] and a whole series of complementary measures
radically curtailing the basic human rights and freedoms;[33] in
short, by differentiating in the eye of the law between whites
and non-whites wherever their paths cross, the exponents of apartheid seek to arrest and devitalize the power of the forces of
unity.

Another fundamental respect in which apartheid differs from the old
segregation policy is the subtle emphasis now being placed on the
alleged relevance of race; and especially its relation to culture.
Naïve statements about racial inferiority are seldom openly expressed
by leading exponents of apartheid. On the contrary, the late Dr.
D. F. Malan's view that black and white are merely the physical
manifestation of two fundamentally *different* ways of life; and the
conclusion which he draws from this, namely that these two ways of
life cannot both flourish within a common society, are now being
more openly and clearly articulated in South Africa than ever before.
Indeed, this view is being put forward with an intelligence which it
would be folly to underestimate; and the emotional force which it
derives from an appeal to the 'law of self-preservation' has hitherto
proved to be devastating. This, however, is an aspect to which we

[22] The Group Areas Act, No. 41 of 1950, as amended and consolidated by
the Group Areas Act, 1957; Natives (Urban Areas Consolidation) Act, No. 25
of 1945, as amended.

[23] The Reservation of Separate Amenities Act, No. 49 of 1953.

[24] The Bantu Education Act, No. 47 of 1953.

[25] The Extension (*sic*) of University Education Act, 1959.

[26] Native Labour (Settlement of Disputes) Act, No. 48 of 1953, sec. 18.

[27] Native Building Workers Act, No. 27 of 1951, sec. 15; Industrial Conciliation
Act, No. 28 of 1956, sec. 77.

[28] Natives Land Act, No. 27 of 1913; Natives (Urban Areas Consolidation)
Act, No. 25 of 1945, as amended.

[29] The Prohibition of Mixed Marriages Act, No. 55 of 1949.

[30] The Immorality Act, No. 23 of 1957, sec. 16.

[31] The Population Registration Act, No. 30 of 1950.

[32] Natives (Abolition of passes (*sic*) and Co-ordination of Documents) Act,
No. 67 of 1952.

[33] Several of these measures have conveniently been brought together by
Leslie Rubin in *This is Apartheid*, Gollancz, 1959. See also *Civil Liberty in
South Africa*, by E. H. Brookes and J. B. Macaulay, Oxford, 1958; and K. L.
Roskam, *Apartheid and Discrimination*, Leyden, 1960.

shall return presently when we deal more fully with the rationale of apartheid.

Finally, there is one other important respect in which the policy of apartheid differs from the old segregation policy. Unlike segregation, apartheid has been underpinned with an extensive academic literature, fostered mainly by the South African Bureau of Racial Affairs (SABRA), which was founded in 1949. Building largely on ideas contained in Professor Hoernlé's Phelps-Stokes Lectures for 1939, the academic apologists of apartheid have constructed a theoretical foundation for their policy, supported by elaborate statistics, especially in regard to population movements, urbanization, and the economic implications of apartheid.

THE RATIONALE OF APARTHEID

It is relevant at the outset to call to mind a few facts obtaining in South Africa on the eve of that eventful election which brought the Nationalist Party into power in 1948. World War II, and its immediate aftermath, had given the country a tremendous industrial spurt—indeed its own industrial revolution. Whites in large numbers, and blacks in yet larger numbers, came from the rural areas to the towns for employment. It has been estimated that the population of the Witwatersrand gold reef, in and near Johannesburg, rose rapidly by more than a million. A housing shortage led to great overcrowding. Slums and 'shanty towns' grew. Nevertheless a shortage of skilled workers advanced the black man considerably; and as he developed his aptitudes, he came more noticeably than ever before into competition with white labour. Tribal ties increasingly disappeared as the non-whites fitted themselves into the framework of a modern economy. The Nationalist Party looked to the future and feared that the results of this integration, if unchecked, would be the 'swamping' of the whites. They noted that over the years the rate of increase of Africans in the urban areas had far outstripped the white rate. And they also feared that in the short run inexpensive black labour would prove more attractive to industry than white labour.

The stage was set for an election platform whose central plank was to be 'the colour problem'—seen in basic and simple terms, namely the self-preservation of the white man. To quote Senator J. Grobler: 'Racial discrimination does not imply a sense of superiority. It is actuated in circumstances such as apply in South Africa by the law of self-preservation.'[34] And in the result, as is well known, apartheid swept the polls.

[34] *Africa's Destiny*, 1958, p. 45. Also Rhoodie and Venter, op. cit., pp. 37, 131, 186.

This is how the policy appeared, and still appears, to thousands of voters. Nor is the appeal to 'the law of self-preservation' in any way confined to the hustings. In a slightly elaborated form it wins assent among intellectuals as well. In its elaborated form the argument runs broadly as follows. The non-whites outnumber the whites by roughly four to one. Were they allowed the same rights as the whites in the same socio-political structure, this would lead either to the domination of the whites by blacks, or—as suggested by Professor Hoernlé—to the gradual disappearance of the white race, as such, in a society of mixed blood. And in either event, so the argument runs, civilization as the whites know it today would disappear. (One might add, in parenthesis, that at this point the upholders of apartheid conveniently ignore the teaching of Hoernlé, who never equated race with culture.) Continuing the argument, however, it is contended that the whites are, in the remarkably candid language of the Government-appointed Tomlinson Commission, 'unshakeably resolved to maintain their civilization undiluted', and 'to preserve their existence as a separate entity'. Therefore, if peace is to be kept, the races should be kept apart, and encouraged to go forward along their own lines of development on the basis of separate cultures and traditions. The Tomlinson Commission said:

> In the absence of discrimination what would happen is that the foundations on which European civilization rests would vanish before the European disappeared. It is for this reason that the European population will not tolerate any conduct which may endanger the foundations on which its continued existence depends.[35]

And again:

> That the European people will not be prepared willingly to sacrifice their right of existence as a separate national and racial entity, must be accepted as the dominant fact in the South African situation.[36]

The argument outlined in the previous paragraph is, of course, capable of elaboration and change of emphasis at several points; and, in fairness, it is necessary to give the gist of this elaboration. For example, when defending the policy of apartheid, the Union's representative at the United Nations has frequently referred to the tensions, frustrations and racial animosity to which integration and an ever-increasing African urban population lead; and among the attendant evils he has stressed overcrowding and unemployment.[37]

[35] Summary of Report, U.G. 61/1955, ch. 4, para. 9.
[36] Summary of Report, ch. 25, para. 20.
[37] See also *Highway to Harmony*, 1958, by Wentzel C. du Plessis, at the time the Ambassador of the Union to the United States.

Nor is the Nationalist Government always on the defensive. There is, for example, a great deal of force in their argument that much of the allegedly liberal multi-racialism in South Africa is deeply inconsistent and humiliating to non-whites. Time and again, in recent years, during debates on the provision of separate university facilities for whites and non-whites, Government supporters have struck home with the legitimate argument that the notion of 'academic equality coupled with social segregation' in the so-called 'open' universities, is not only inconsistent with full university life, but also very frustrating to both whites and non-whites. This, of course, was not a sufficient reason for the Government's decision to deprive non-white students of their right to choose 'half a loaf' if they so wished, by compelling them to attend tribal universities. But when this has been said, the very solid point remains that all the non-whites get at present in the open universities *is* half a loaf.

Moreover, in any attempt to give a fair review of apartheid, it would be quite wrong and malicious to suggest that the policy is, in abstract theory, an entirely negative and selfish policy designed only to prevent the white man from being submerged, and to avoid racial tension. The Government has declared its resolve to build up homelands which Africans may call their own, areas where they may develop to the utmost of their potential and ultimately, perhaps, after a period of 'creative trusteeship', achieve independence. Nor can it be denied that a good deal of money and selfless hard work has been contributed to the rehabilitation of the African Reserves. Whether, in the nature of things, the Government's conduct can ever be equal to its professions is, however, another matter—on which judgment must inevitably be harsh.

Again, I have no doubt that many of the upholders of apartheid are men of high integrity, no less honourable than their opponents; and that, honestly believing their policy to be in the best interests of all, a few of them are prepared to make personal sacrifices to achieve the goal of providing separate territories for the autonomous development of each racial group. They recognize, too, that their self-appointed task is gigantic, even if they could obtain the full co-operation of all sections of the population. In the words of the Tomlinson Commission, its undertaking is, indeed, an act of faith.

However, after five years of intensive and dedicated work, the experts on the Commission reported that the only alternative to apartheid would be the eventual creation of a completely integrated society if social and economic factors were allowed free play in an evolutionary process. And this, as we have seen, they rejected mainly on the grounds that the whites are unshakeably resolved to maintain their existence as a separate entity with all the force at their command; and that if peace is to be kept, there is only one way out for South Africa, namely separate development of the racial groups in their own areas. Accordingly, to this end, the Tomlinson Commission recommended the massive expenditure of £104,000,000 towards the rehabilitation and development of the African Reserves, for a first period of ten years in a not over-ambitious programme.

This, then, is the theoretical framework of apartheid. Let us now examine the various aspects of this policy in the light of its prospects of success, and particularly in the light of what we have hitherto seen of its actual working and implementation during twelve long years. Let us ask whether, in practice, it is improving race relations, and whether in fact it exemplifies the western Christian way of life to which Dr. Verwoerd referred in his reply to Mr. Macmillan. Such an appeal to fact is not an unfair criterion for, as the Gospel says, by their fruit shall ye know them.

THE BANTUSTAN POLICY

I shall start with the Union Government's policy of developing the African Reserves, generally known as its Bantustan policy; because this is sometimes thought to be the better and positive side of apartheid.

The Government proposes to reserve about 14 per cent of the territory of the Union (that is to say, the existing Reserves, augmented by $7\frac{1}{4}$ million morgen of land contemplated under legislation passed in 1936) as separate areas for the development of African homelands. It is accepted that the Reserves must be rehabilitated, and that South Africa must shoulder the financial and technical responsibility of increasing the carrying power and prosperity of these areas.

There have been, understandably enough, conflicting statements by members of the Government as to whether it is envisaged that the African areas will eventually become independent states—free, for example, to make alliances with any foreign power of their choice. The more academically and idealistically inclined supporters of apartheid tend to give a mildly affirmative answer. The more politically conscious, aware of the use that would be made of such a concession by political opponents, tend to be more cautious. However, the official policy on this point, made quite clear by the Prime Minister, is to use the analogy of the British Commonwealth. Dr. Verwoerd has stated that for a considerable period while the Africans are learning to govern themselves, the South African Government will have to act as supervising trustee. At the same time, unlike Dr. Eiselen and others,[38] the Prime Minister, with his usual candour, does not exclude the possibility of eventual independence; everything, he says, must depend upon the actual capacity shown by the Africans themselves and upon the prevailing circumstances.[39]

That, in general terms, is the outline of the Bantustan plan. Now let us examine it in rather more detail. At the outset, it is desirable to dispose of two matters of controversy which are, in fact, peripheral and subsidiary, but which tend to divert attention from essentials; namely the question of incorporating the High Commission Territories into the Union, and the question: who settled in South Africa first, the white man or the African?

If the territories which are at present under the jurisdiction of Her Majesty the Queen of England (the High Commission territories of Basutoland, Bechuanaland and Swaziland) are included in the area reserved for Africans—as apologists of apartheid tend to include them—then the Union would be considerably increased in size, and about 45 per cent of the whole would become part of Bantustan. While one appreciates that 45 per cent of the land area looks more equitable and generous than 14 per cent, it is relevant to make two observations about the suggested accretion. First, it is entirely in the realm of speculation and very improbable speculation at that. The inhabitants of the territories do not wish to lose their present status in order to become part of the Union's Bantustan plan, for reasons which are not difficult to appreciate when one looks more closely at that plan. Moreover, as long as opposition by the inhabitants remains firm, the British Government is likely to turn a deaf ear to the Union's requests for incorporation or closer association.[40]

Secondly, even if the High Commission territories were available, any plan to settle additional millions of Africans from the Union in those territories would meet with difficulty. Quite apart from the fact that the High Commission territories cannot carry a much larger population than they do at present, the new-comers would have to be acceptable to the local organs of government: there could be no question of South Africa unilaterally foisting populations upon the territories. And certainly there would be no room for the removal of whole tribes from place to place by a white

[38] See 'Harmonious Multi-Community Development', *Optima*, March 1959, pp. 1 sqq.
[39] *House of Assembly Debates*, vol. 101, col. 6221, 20 May 1959.
[40] See, on the whole question of incorporation, *History of Discussions with the Union of South Africa*, Cmd. 8707, 1952; *Negotiations Regarding Transfer*, G.P-S. 4846, 1952/3, Government Printer, Pretoria.

government—along the lines envisaged under the Native Laws Amendment Act of 1952.[41]

In regard to the suggestion that Africans really have no better moral claim to the land of South Africa than the whites because, as Mr. Eric Louw once informed the United Nations, 'when more than 300 years ago the Cape of Good Hope was settled from Europe, the first Bantu immigrants from Central Africa had come down the East Coast and were crossing the Limpopo River',[42] Professor Monica Wilson has shown that this statement rests on a serious misconception, and is, in fact, a piece of myth-making conjured up to support apartheid. In a careful historical study she has demonstrated that in much of the territory which, according to the Government's plans, is to be under white control, it was the Africans who arrived and settled first.[43]

But all this argumentation about the past, and speculation about the future, is not of the essence. What is more to the point is to examine the Bantustan policy on its merits or demerits in those areas where it actually does obtain. And when this is done, it shows up in a poor light. It has been claimed that the main object of the Bantu Authorities Act, 1951, 'is to put the traditional Bantu form of government into practice by degrees'.[44] And it is sought to justify this policy on the ground that 'there is much in the old Bantu tribal system worth preserving'.[45] More particularly, it is claimed that the form of government embodied in the Bantu Authorities Act 'is the traditional Bantu democracy, and the Tribal Chief, together with his Tribal Council, provides the protective shelter under which the highest and the lowest can feel at home and find self-expression and fulfilment'.[46]

It may be conceded immediately that the old Bantu tribal system was indeed imbued with the democratic spirit; but there are at least two conclusive reasons why the Bantustan system will not be at all like 'the traditional Bantu democracy', save in the most superficial appearance. On the contrary, the Bantustan system will be distinctly undemocratic.

In the first place, even with the best will in the world, it would be very difficult—if not impossible—to restore the conditions which enabled the traditional tribal system to function democratically. In the old days the main sanction against a tyrannical chief was for his men to leave him, and offer their loyalty to another chief in

[41] See below, p. 52.
[42] *Cape Times*, 29 September 1959.
[43] See *African Studies*, vol. 18, no. 4, 1959.
[44] See the official Report of the Department of Native Affairs, 1954–7, p. 49.
[45] See article by Dr. Eiselen in vol. 29, *South African Year Book*, p. 368.
[46] Official Report of the Department of Native Affairs, 1954–7, p. 49.

return for the allocation of some of his land. In those days, moreover, men and followers were more important to a chief than land, which was plentiful. And the sanction that his followers might leave a tyrannical chief, and join a rival, operated as a powerful incentive to moderate and responsible government. But today land in the Bantu areas is far from plentiful, and freedom of movement is restricted. In short, the essential conditions which enabled the earlier sanctions to operate no longer exist.[47]

But, secondly, even if it were possible for the Government to put the clock back and restore the conditions of a century ago (conditions which obtained before the conversion of Africans to Christianity), the actual pattern of government which is being imposed is both undemocratic and radically different from the traditional system. Thus, for one thing, under the old tribal system if the people were dissatisfied with a chief, and the way in which he performed his functions, he could be impeached.[48] But under the Bantu Authorities Act, the chief and his council are carefully insulated against the popular will; and, what is more, they are expressly made subject to the control of the responsible Minister and the Government.

The insulation of the chief and his council from the popular will is most clearly exemplified in the decision of the Government to sweep away the idea of the popular vote, which had been in force for many years in the Bantu areas prior to the passing of the Bantu Authorities Act. And the reasons given for this decision are so remarkable that they are worth recording. Explaining the Bantu Authorities Act, the authors of the Tomlinson Report say:

> Councillors will be appointed by the chief or headman himself and not, as under the old Local Council System, by popular vote. The idea is to foster strong progressive action by tribal authorities whose councillors should be able to act independently of a less progressive and probably dissatisfied electorate.[49]

An even more ironic justification is given by the Department of Bantu Administration itself. In the 1956 handbook explaining the Bantu Authorities Act, it is said: 'The Councillors will perform their task without fear or prejudice *because* they are not elected by the majority votes.'[50] One has to read a passage like this several times to realize that it was actually written and seriously meant in the mid-twentieth century.

[47] Ashton, *The Basuto*, p. 217.
[48] See generally I. Schapera, *Government and Politics in Tribal Societies*, 1956, pp. 135 sqq.
[49] Full Report, chapter 17, para. 223.
[50] At p. 18. My italics. Quoted, what is more, with approval by Dr. Eiselen in *Optima*, March 1959, p. 6!

5

Again, the Minister of Bantu Administration may, at any time, depose any chief or headman, and cancel the appointment of any councillor; a commissioner may veto the appointment of any person appointed as a councillor by a chief or headman; and the police are authorized to attend the deliberations of a council. It is, of course, true that under the traditional Bantu system councillors were not democratically elected; but, as we have seen, there existed restraints upon tyranny and caprice which are conspicuously absent from the new dispensation.

When one reflects upon this governmental pattern, it is not altogether surprising that its introduction has been accompanied by widespread disaffection and rioting in such areas as Sekukuniland, Zeerust, Tembuland and Pondoland; and that even where rioting has not broken out, sullen acquiescence by the people, and not willing acceptance, is the dominant note.[51]

There are indeed at least four very solid reasons why Africans resent Bantustan. First, it is the creation of a white government; it springs from white initiative, even though the *ex post facto* appearance of local African acceptance may sometimes be obtained. Secondly, it is a regressive return to ideas of indirect rule, i.e. direction and control from above, which in the experience of other countries were outworn decades ago. Thirdly, it is difficult to see how Africans could accept with enthusiasm an attempt to perpetuate a tribal system which can only qualify them for the role of an unsteady museum piece, in no way fitted to take their place in the modern world. And fourthly, the many thousands of Africans whose tribal ties have been broken, and who for years have lived and worked in the urban areas, do not wish to be relegated to the more primitive tribal structure which is being prepared for them. Not only do tribal ways belong to their past, but in most cases, relegation to the Reserves would mean a sentence of dire poverty and deprivation; for it should never be forgotten that to the African from the Reserves migration to the big towns has hitherto been the road to progress and prosperity, and the escape from grinding poverty.[52]

It just will not do for Government spokesmen to attribute all the unrest in the Reserves to Communist agitators. It may be that some agitators are indeed active; but the central fact remains that the material for discontent is very much at hand for them to work on.

If the political structure of Bantustan is not calculated to inspire confidence, the economic outlook is equally forbidding. There is a growing volume of expert opinion that the implementation of the

[51] For the main facts, see Muriel Horrell, *Survey of Race Relations in South Africa*, 1957–8, pp. 62 sqq.; 1959–60, pp. 39 sqq.
[52] De Kiewiet, *The Anatomy of South African Misery*, 1956, p. 38.

Bantustan policy (if economically possible) would gravely injure
the Union's economy; but this is an oft-repeated criticism and,
however cogent, it looks at the matter primarily from the point of
view of the white taxpayer. Let us look at the economic outlook from
the point of view of the inhabitants of the Bantustans.

Making due allowance for some very good farming land in the
Reserves, the areas as a whole are very poor and stricken with
erosion. Again, after making every allowance for progress that has
been made towards rehabilitation, the process is still pathetically
slow. Ironically enough, this is not wholly the fault of the Government. The Tomlinson recommendation of an initial expenditure of
£104,000,000 was rejected as excessive by the Government, partly,
it would seem, because the Opposition proposed to remind the
electorate that the Government were being expensive 'kafferboeties'
(friends of the Africans). No doubt the charge should have been
scorned; but then politicians are, as they say, concerned with the
art of the possible. Meanwhile many supporters of apartheid have
come to appreciate ruefully that the 'act of faith' envisaged in the
Tomlinson Report has lost its dynamic.

More serious still, the Government rejected the recommendations
of the Tomlinson Commission in regard to white privately owned
industries inside the African areas; and decided instead to establish
white-financed and white-controlled industries outside the Reserves,
but on their borders. It is difficult to resist the conclusion that what
is envisaged is the establishment, on the old segregation pattern,
of vast labour reservoirs which will be close at hand to the new
industrial towns but as far removed as possible from the older
established cities. In fact this decision is very damaging to the claim
that the Bantustan policy aims at making the African areas self-
sufficient and self-supporting. It has long been the policy of white
South Africa to bring indirect pressure to bear (mainly by taxation)
upon the Africans in the Reserves, and to induce them to seek
employment in white industry and on the farms. This was part of
the pattern of the old segregation policy; and it must be galling to
those who had hoped for a less immoral dispensation under apartheid, to see merely a perpetuation of the old order under a new
name.[53]

BANTUSTAN AND BASUTOLAND

It is sometimes claimed by supporters of the Bantustan policy that
in essence it does not differ from developments now being promoted
by the British Government in Basutoland. This claim is wide of the

---

[53] See, for example, P. V. Pistorius, *No Further Trek*, pp. 32 sqq.

mark. Here, for example, are five points of difference between the position in Basutoland and Bantustan; and they are radical.

In the first place, the new Basutoland Constitution was established upon the initiative of the Basuto themselves, after they had been given an opportunity to put forward their own proposals in consultation with a professional adviser of their own choice, namely the present writer. Moreover, after long and comprehensive discussion in Whitehall, the final constitutional documents closely followed the recommendations made by the Basuto.[54] I am giving prominence to these facts for this reason: unless and until the lesson is learned — and this is perhaps the real significance of the Basutoland example — that it is both insulting and futile to work out a framework of government *for*, and not *with* Africans, as if they were very young children, no progress in race relations will be made.

Secondly, the organs of government set up in Basutoland are not based on the authoritarian principle that those who rule should be strong enough to 'act independently of a less progressive and probably dissatisfied electorate'. On the contrary, 50 per cent of the national legislature, called the Basutoland Council, are indirectly elected by district councils which are in turn almost wholly elected on a very wide franchise. Moreover, the principle of parity between elected and non-elected members, as well as indirect elections, were envisaged as merely an interim stage in the advance towards an elected majority and direct elections for the national legislature. Again, in Basutoland there is an Executive Council of eight members, three of whom are freely elected by the legislature from among their own members. Considerable publicity was given at the time to the grant by the British Government of a legislative council; but no less significant was the establishment of the Executive Council on the standard pattern to be found in other parts of the Commonwealth. The Executive Council of Basutoland is an emergent Cabinet; and it was designed to develop into a fully fledged Cabinet responsible to the legislature.

Thirdly, the actual powers of self-government entrusted to the Basuto are at present very considerably wider than those to be given to the Bantu Authorities in South Africa. Under the Basutoland Constitution legislation on all subjects save a few reserved ones (chief among which are external affairs and defence, internal security, postal services and the public service) requires the consent of the Basutoland Council, which has thus passed beyond the stage of merely advisory body. And even in the reserved field, where the High Commissioner may still legislate without requiring the consent of the Council, all proposed laws must nevertheless be placed in

[54] *Report on Constitutional Discussions*, 1959, Cmd. 637.

draft before the Council for their advice. Under the Bantu Authorities Act the powers entrusted to African assemblies are not only merely advisory, but they are also markedly narrower in scope than is the case in Basutoland.

Fourthly, although the emergency and 'reserve powers' of the British Government under the Basutoland Constitution are still very substantial, the provisions of the Constitution reflect a readiness not only to transfer real power to the Basuto, but also to surrender prerogative powers and control in a way which is wholly absent from the Bantustan plan. To give two examples. If the High Commissioner vetoes legislation, he is required to give reasons for the veto. Again, the appointment and deposition of chiefs and headmen are no longer in Basutoland the prerogative of the High Commissioner as they were under the previously existing law. A decision on these matters by a Basuto body—the College of Chiefs—is now an essential element. In Bantustan, however, any chief or headman may be deposed entirely at Government discretion. Of course the British Government may, in theory, withdraw the whole constitution, but powers once given are not in fact easily revocable.

And fifthly, colour discrimination between whites and non-whites in Basutoland is increasingly being obliterated. Admittedly there are only some 2,000 whites in that territory out of a population of over 600,000 residents, but most of them are concentrated in the capital township of Maseru; and this juxtaposition of the races may lead to a pattern of racial adjustment very different from the pattern obtaining in the Union—albeit on a small scale. Already whites and non-whites vote together on a common roll. Already one may find whites and non-whites enjoying hotel amenities together without incident or friction. Admittedly whites in Basutoland do not enjoy ownership or freehold tenure of land; but then neither do the Basuto, for all land is held in trust by the Paramount Chief for the Basuto nation. However, the Basutoland Council has legislative competence to modernize land-tenure, and probably will do so in the near future. Admittedly, too, non-Basuto may not immigrate freely into Basutoland; but here again the Basutoland Council has power to legislate on the subject—in a word it will increasingly be for the Basuto themselves to determine their own destiny.

All this, it is submitted, makes the claim that Bantustan is a South African counterpart of Basutoland very thin. No one pretends that Basutoland has not its own share of very real difficulties and deficiencies; indeed it is not unlikely that severe strain and tension will be experienced as increasingly the traditional Basuto chiefs are required to become more democratic and accountable to the people in a modern framework of government. Again, no one believes that the Basutoland Constitution will not require amendment and improvement from time to time as experience is gained; but that is precisely what was envisaged. The system of government was meant to grow and evolve in accordance with the wishes of the Basuto. It is obvious, therefore, that what has taken place in Basutoland was conceived in a very different spirit from that which permeates the Bantustan experiment.

Finally, before leaving the subject of Basutoland and Bantustan, it is relevant to refer briefly to the subject of independence. Writing in March 1959, Dr. Eiselen stated that 'the utmost degree of autonomy in administrative matters which the Union Parliament is likely to be prepared to concede to [Bantustan] will stop short of actual surrender of sovereignty by the European trustee'.[55] Shortly before then the retiring High Commissioner for the United Kingdom in South Africa, Sir Percivale Liesching, was reported as having said that 'it is not to be foreseen that they [the High Commission Territories] would ever advance to the status of independence comparable with Ghana, that is complete independence within the Commonwealth'.[56] Dr. Eiselen used this statement to support the contention that it 'exactly reflects the way in which the question of the position of our own Bantu areas is envisaged under the present administration'.[57]

Three brief comments on this may here be made. In the first place, Dr. Verwoerd has indicated that Dr. Eiselen's article was written before the Union Government's latest policy statement in regard to Bantustan.[58] The Prime Minister showed, with respect, greater realism than either Dr. Eiselen or Sir Percivale Liesching when he refused to say or suggest that the white guardian would never grant independence to its ward. Secondly, while it is plain that Basutoland cannot stand on her own feet at present for very obvious reasons, which are mainly economic, and while no one can foresee how long it may take before the realities of the situation change,[59] it would be a bold—and I would venture to say rash—government that would deny the possibility for all time of a surrender of sovereignty to the Basuto people. As the French proverb puts it: *cent ans n'est guère, mais jamais c'est beaucoup*. And thirdly, remarks on the subject of independence along the lines of Dr. Eiselen's

---

[55] *Optima*, March 1959, p. 8.
[56] *Cape Argus*, 12 September 1958.
[57] *Optima*, loc. cit.
[58] *House of Assembly Debates*, 20 May 1959, vol. 101, col. 6221.
[59] Cf. *Report on Constitutional Reform and Chieftainship Affairs*, Maseru, 1958, para. 84.

article, invariably raise unnecessary blood-pressure. Unnecessary because the subject is academic; during the immediately foreseeable future practical politicians in Basutoland have more than enough to think about in building up the country's economy, getting used to a modern political structure, and preparing the way for the next steps in constitutional advance. And practical politicians in the Union will have to think and work even harder—and may one suggest, on rather different lines—if they are to have any hope of persuading the Basuto that closer political association with South Africa is the answer to a maiden's prayer.

3

The Politics of Division—II

Thus far I have examined the positive and, ostensibly, more favourable side of apartheid. Now we must deal with its impact in the so-called white but, in fact, very mixed areas outside the Reserves. It is not always realized how great an impact apartheid legislation has made upon the law and government of South Africa; how very gravely it has whittled away the basic human rights and freedoms, primarily, no doubt for non-whites, but ever increasingly for whites as well; what deep inroads it has made upon a whole way of life; and how tragically it is undermining the fibre of the whole population.

It is convenient to start with the constitutional crisis that harassed South African life for some six years during the period 1951–6. To understand this crisis in its true perspective it is necessary to look back briefly into South African history. In 1908 there were four colonies in South Africa—the Cape of Good Hope, Natal, the Transvaal and the Orange River Colony. Each was self-governing, but subject to the overriding authority of Great Britain; and in each Colony the constitution had as its pattern the constitution of Great Britain. The legislatures of these four colonies agreed to send delegates to a National Convention to consider whether some form of closer union should be brought about. During some seven months of intensive work, under the skilful chairmanship of Sir Henry de Villiers, who had been Chief Justice of the Cape Colony since 1873, the delegates hammered out a draft constitution. The agreed provisions were cast in the form of a draft bill, which was ratified by the legislatures of three of the colonies and by a referendum in the fourth. Delegates were then selected to take the draft bill to England for the purpose of obtaining its enactment by the British Parliament. The Bill received the Royal Assent in September 1909 under the title of the South Africa Act (9 Edward VII, c. 9), and came into force in the Union on 31 May 1910. In law it is an Act of the British Parliament; in fact it is the product of white South African deliberation solemnly agreed to by the constituent colonies. There were, however, no non-whites at the National Convention.

One of the first issues to be decided was whether the Union should be federal or unitary in character. The Convention rejected a federal Union and decided that the existing colonies should become provinces, enjoying such legislative powers only as were specifically mentioned in the Constitution, or as might from time to time be specified by the Parliament of the Union. The powers originally conferred upon the Provincial Councils included powers over hospitals, education, roads, local government and local taxation; but the Union Parliament was left free to modify those powers and even abolish them by ordinary legislation if it chose to do so.

There was another issue far more delicate than the choice between a unitary or a federal system of government. This was the question of the franchise for non-whites. Before Union each of the colonies had its own electoral system. In the Transvaal and the Orange River Colony the right to vote was denied to non-whites, and the Natal law was in effect very discriminatory. Only in the Cape of Good Hope were the qualifications for voters the same for all. Moreover, in theory, a non-white person might be elected to Parliament in the Cape Colony, though in practice this never occurred. Nevertheless, at the National Convention, the representatives of the Cape of Good Hope were resolutely opposed to any whittling away of their non-discriminatory franchise, and in fact they urged that it should be extended throughout South Africa. On the other hand, the Transvaal and Orange Free State delegates were equally resolute in their opposition to the granting of voting rights to non-whites.

The solution finally adopted was a compromise whereby, substantially, the *status quo* would be maintained and the pre-Union electoral laws would, for the time being, remain in force in each province. The Union Parliament was, however, to be given power to deal comprehensively with the franchise at a later date if it so wished, but a means was to be devised whereby the Cape franchise would be specially 'entrenched' or safeguarded. I have said that the compromise was based, substantially, on maintaining the *status quo*. But this was not entirely maintained, because the Cape Delegation was prevailed upon to concede that non-whites should not have the right of becoming members of the new Union Parliament. As we have seen there were those who deplored this compromise as a blot on the constitution; but their voices were drowned.

It now remained to devise constitutional machinery to make the compromise an effective safeguard of what was left of the Cape franchise. The crux of the problem lay, of course, in the manner in which the constitution could validly be altered. Was it to be completely flexible, with all its provisions alterable by Parliament in the same way as other laws? Or was it to be 'controlled', so that its provisions could only be amended by a special procedure?

Here again an unusual compromise was arrived at. The constitution laid down the general rule that its provisions could be amended by Parliament itself legislating in the same manner as it legislates for other matters; that is to say, by a simple majority in each of the two Houses. Moreover, after the lapse of ten years, Parliament— legislating in the ordinary way—was to be entirely free to modify its own composition and powers, as well as the composition and powers of the Executive and Judicial departments of Government. However, in respect of three important sections, and only three, a special procedure was laid down for their amendment. These were the so-called 'entrenched sections'; namely section 35, which prevented discrimination in voting rights in the province of the Cape of Good Hope by reason of a voter's race or colour only; section 137, which guaranteed equality for the two official languages —a subject on which there was also deep feeling; and section 152, which set forth the agreed provisions for amending the constitution. The special procedure agreed upon for the constitutional amendment of these sections was that amendments should be passed by both Houses of Parliament sitting together; and, moreover, they had to be agreed to at the third reading by not less than two-thirds of the total members of both Houses.

In the result, therefore, the constitution was to be what constitutional lawyers would call a 'partly controlled' constitution; most of its provisions were alterable by Parliament in the ordinary way, but certain of its provisions (those contained in the three so-called 'entrenched sections') could be amended only by a special procedure. It was for the future to show whether this device was an effective safeguard or entrenchment.

The first serious attack on the Constitution came in 1936 when the Hertzog-Smuts Coalition ensured the passage of an Act which provided for the removal of African voters in the Cape of Good Hope from the common electoral roll. In return these Africans were to be placed on a separate roll, and were given the right to elect three representatives to the House of Assembly—all of whom were to be white. The Act was denounced by the thinning ranks of old Cape liberals—and particularly by one of South Africa's really great men, former Chief Justice Sir James Rose Innes—but in vain. It was duly passed in accordance with the special procedure prescribed in the Constitution. Nevertheless the validity of the legislation was challenged in the courts in the case of *Ndlwana* v. *Hofmeyr*, 1937, and—not unexpectedly—the challenge failed. Unfortunately, the judgment of the Appellate Division of the Supreme Court in favour

of the Government was expressed in wide terms which were later
to prove pregnant with difficulty.

Stated very briefly the Court held, in effect, that the Union
Parliament had been created in the image of the British Parliament;
that at the time of Union there were certain limitations upon the
full sovereign power of the Union Parliament; among them, the
requirement of a special procedure to amend the three entrenched
sections. The Statute of Westminster, 1931, had, however, removed
all limitations upon sovereignty, and in the result it was held that
Parliament's will, as declared in an Act of Parliament, could no
more be challenged in South Africa than in England.

Fortified by this decision, by the opinion of its law advisers, by a
Speaker's ruling, and by a consensus of legal opinion,[1] the Government in 1951 decided to pass legislation altering the franchise
rights of coloured voters in the Cape Province by the ordinary
procedure—the two-thirds majority specified in the Constitution
being beyond their strength at the time. Legislation was drafted
along the same lines as the 1936 Act dealing with Africans; the
idea being to remove the coloured voters in the Cape Province from
the common roll, and give them in return the right to vote for four
special white representatives in the House of Assembly. The requisite
legislation—called the Separate Representation of Voters Act, 1951—
was in due course passed by a simple majority of each House sitting
separately. Its validity was immediately challenged; and in a great
legal battle which has become known as the *Vote Case*, the Appellate
Division of the Supreme Court held the legislation to be invalid.[2]

Overnight the Court was precipitated into the heat of bitter
controversy; and there began a long sustained series of manoeuvres
to circumvent the constitutional requirement. An attempt was made
by an ordinary majority of members of Parliament to convert
themselves into a High Court, which thereupon purported to overrule
the *Vote Case*. This was struck down by the Appellate Division.[3]
Rebuffed a second time, the Government now proceeded more
astutely. One piece of legislation increased the size of the Appellate
Division of the Supreme Court by the addition of six Government-
appointed judges to bring it to a total of eleven. Another measure—
the Senate Act—inflated the membership of the Senate with Government supporters in sufficient numbers to ensure that if the Coloured
Voters Act were again submitted to a joint session of both Houses,

---

[1] The fullest review of the authorities is probably still that given by Speaker
Conradie. See House of Assembly Debates, 11 April 1951, cols. 4201–4219.
See also D. V. Cowen, *Parliamentary Sovereignty and the Entrenched Sections
of the South Africa Act*, Juta and Co., Feb. 1951.
[2] 1952 (2) S.A. (A.D.).
[3] 1952 (4) S.A. (A.D.)

the necessary two-thirds majority would be obtained. The next step was to pass the Coloured Voters Act with the requisite majority, and this was done. Once more the validity of the legislation was attacked; but the relentless process of attrition had now done its work. With one dissentient voice, that of Mr. Justice Schreiner, the Court held that the coloured voters had been lawfully removed from the common roll.

It would be tempting, were it appropriate in a book of this scope, to elaborate upon the many legal questions raised by the long-sustained constitutional struggle whose main features I have outlined. The legal issues are important, but their technical nature has led me to the conclusion that elaboration would not be appropriate here.[4] It is relevant, however, and probably sufficient to make a few observations.

The process of constitutional gerrymandering that was used to strip the Cape Coloured people of their slender franchise rights has done incalculable harm by destroying the faith of the overwhelming majority of the people of South Africa in *any* form of constitutional guarantee; though, as we shall see later, it is nevertheless possible to devise far stronger guarantees than those fashioned in 1910. Again, the defeat of the Constitution has done much to undermine faith in the moral worth of the white man's pledged word; for apart from the guarantees in the Constitution, the Cape Coloured franchise was most solemnly assured in the 1930's by leading members of the very Government which took them away.

Today there are many white supporters of the Government, who, I believe, are ashamed of the whole performance. Why then was this great damage done, especially when it is recalled that the Cape Coloured people formed less than 3 per cent of the electorate spread over twelve constituencies, most of which the Nationalist Party won in the 1953 General Election, even with the coloureds on the roll? Several answers may be proffered. In part it was done to establish the right, or rather ultimate power, of Parliament to legislate on *any* matter (including a projected Republican Constitution) in the ordinary way; in part there was pique and resentment that the judges had presumed to test the validity of Acts of Parliament; and in part too—and this is by no means the least significant explanation—we may see here evidence of a Teutonic desire for logical symmetry and tidiness. The coloureds were an illogical blot on an all-white electoral roll; their colour excluded them from sharing the citizenship of the whites.

[4] I have dealt with some of the more strictly legal issues elsewhere: See note 1 above; also 15 *Modern Law Review* 282 sqq.; 16 *Modern Law Review* 18 sqq.; and 70 *South African Law Journal* 258 sqq.

In 1959 the remorseless pattern, initiated in 1936, was taken one step further. The Promotion of Bantu Self-government Act, 1959, took away from the Africans even the representation which had been conceded in 1936. In the result, the Africans outside the Reserves are now entirely voteless and unrepresented, and cannot influence the legislation of the Union Parliament. In no fair and proper sense of the term can these people be regarded as migrant labourers with homes in some foreign country, yet they are to be denied effective political rights in the 'white' area. And in this connexion it is difficult to understand the suggestion, made, for example, by Dr. Verwoerd, that the Africans will be compensated by having 'an anchor' in the Bantustans.[5] Or the more recent notion that they will be compensated by the provision of 'local government councils' in the white areas outside the Reserves, coupled with 'diplomatic' exchanges and consultation with their representatives in the Reserves.[6] For the stark fact remains that huge numbers of Africans have completely lost their tribal ties and (unless genuine partition is resorted to) will remain permanently resident in the white area, where indeed many of them were born and grew up. It is not easy for any person to contemplate the fact of this vast, disenfranchised and disillusioned proletariat with any equanimity; or, indeed, with an untroubled conscience.

THE TWILIGHT OF CIVIL LIBERTY

Having seen what damage has been done to the constitution by the logic of apartheid, let us now see how the common law of the land has been mutilated in order to accommodate it.

There is nothing in South Africa comparable to the Bill of Rights and the constitutional guarantees which are familiar in American government. Fundamental human rights and freedoms are left in South Africa, as in England, to the ordinary or common law of the land, and to the courts. They may therefore be extended or reduced by the decision of Parliament in whose jurisdiction they lie; moreover, they are not placed beyond the reach of ordinary parliamentary majorities.

In Great Britain the real protections against legislative and executive abuse of power are ingrained habits of constitutional observance. Magna Carta and the Bill of Rights are such deep-rooted traditions that no British Parliament would have the temerity to abrogate them; for the values which they embody are the very essence of civilized life in a free world. The fathers of the South African Constitution believed that in their country—no less than in

[5] House of Assembly Debates, May 1958.
[6] Dr. the Hon. T. E. Dönges in the *Star*, 13 September 1960.

Britain—such basic values would be held equally sacred. They pointed out that in the Roman-Dutch common law of South Africa we had a system no less jealous of human rights and fundamental freedoms than the law of England. There was no need therefore, they thought, to follow the American example of entrenching a Bill of Rights in a rigid constitution.

There were others less sanguine. They called attention to the facts that the British system presupposes a remarkable degree of political adulthood and sophistication; that on the whole, it worked well; but it had been a slow and painful growth, aided by many favourable factors, not least of which is the homogeneity of the peoples of Great Britain and especially a fundamental unanimity among them on basic issues of government.[7] Having regard to conditions actually obtaining in South Africa, they doubted whether the British way of doing things could be successfully imitated. But those who would trust men with unqualified power over other men won the day. Let us see now what apartheid has done to that trust.

There are several ways in which the impact of apartheid legislation upon basic human rights and freedoms might be illustrated. One way would be to set out the familiar rights which are guaranteed in the constitutions of most modern states; and then proceed to show how each and every one of them has either been denied or seriously violated by apartheid legislation. Such an exercise, which has, in part, already been done,[8] would however tend to be jejune; and, what is more, not wholly in point, because the record of South African legislation long before the advent of apartheid in 1948 would make innumerable dents in any Bill of Rights. I have chosen, instead to analyse critically two official pronouncements on the protection of human rights in South Africa; one made in 1947, a year before the present Government came into power, the other made nearly ten years afterwards.

THE POSITION IN 1947

In 1947 the Law Advisers to the Union Government, in consultation with the Department of External Affairs, published a statement on the position in South African law concerning human rights and fundamental freedoms.[9] After pointing out that fundamental human rights and freedoms are left in South Africa, as in England, to the ordinary law of the land and the courts, the Law Advisers give an

---

[7] Cf. Lord Balfour's introduction to Bagehot's *The English Constitution*, World's Classics edition.

[8] See the two reports sponsored by the United Nations: Supplement No. 16, A/2505, of 1953 and Supplement No. 16, A/2719, of 1954.

[9] This appears in the *United Nations Year Book on Human Rights for* 1947, pp. 304 sqq.

encouraging quotation from a judgment of a former Chief Justice of the Union:

> Every subject high or low is amenable to law, and none can be punished save by a properly constituted legal tribunal. If a man's rights or personal liberty or property are threatened by the Government or by a private person, the courts are open for his protection. And behind the courts is ranged the full power of the State to ensure the enforcement of their decrees.

The statement goes on to say, in words which are particularly relevant to the subject of apartheid:

> The courts preserve the utmost impartiality when dealing with different racial groups; and the same treatment is enjoyed by all, whether they be alien, black or white.

The Law Advisers then proceed to elaborate upon what they consider to be basic freedoms, namely personal freedom; freedom of speech; freedom of the press; and freedom of assembly (including the right to free association). Under the heading of personal freedom they point out, *inter alia*, that:

(i) No person may be punished without having been tried before a properly constituted Court and any person arbitrarily detained may obtain a writ known as *de homine libero exhibendo* for his immediate release. The writ is similar to the English writ of *habeas corpus*.

(ii) It is a presumption of the South African common law that a person is presumed to be innocent until the contrary is proved. The onus is on the prosecution to prove the guilt of the accused person beyond a reasonable doubt.

(iii) Every person who has been unlawfully arrested or detained has the right to approach the Court and obtain damages for wrongful arrest and malicious imprisonment.

Freedom of speech, it is said, is a fundamental right of all members of the community; and there exists full freedom of the press. Under the heading of freedom of assembly, the official statement goes on to say that:

> In general there are no prohibitions against persons meeting for any lawful purpose. Certain restrictions have, however, been imposed by statute to prevent disorders, and in protection of life and property: e.g. the Riotous Assemblies Act of 1914.

And with particular reference to freedom of association, it is stated that: 'South Africa has been generous in recognizing the right of association.' They add, too, that full freedom of religious worship exists in South Africa.

In a final paragraph the Law Advisers summarize the position as follows:

In conclusion it may be stated that the freedoms described above are regarded as fundamental. They are there to be enjoyed by all members of the community, which include widely differing racial groups. They are not withheld from or limited in respect of any person on the ground of his class, colour or creed. They are jealously guarded by the courts of which it was said by one of South Africa's greatest judges that their 'first and most sacred duty is to administer justice to those who seek it, and not to preserve the peace of the country'.

Quite a healthy picture, it will be thought. And let me say immediately that, *so far as the common law is concerned*, this was a reasonably fair statement of the position as at 1947; though, of course, it will be remembered that there were in force, at the time when the statement was written, a considerable number of racially discriminatory statutes which made deep inroads on fundamental human rights. There were, for example, pass and other laws restraining freedom of movement among Africans and Asians; laws circumscribing the rights of both whites and non-whites to acquire land; laws reserving skilled labour in the mines to whites; and, indeed, all the other examples which I have scheduled on an earlier page.[10] But when all the statutory exceptions had been accounted for, the common law was still a powerful bastion of liberty without regard to race, colour or creed. And here perhaps a specific illustration of its strength—an example dealing with *habeas corpus*—may be useful.

Although the term *habeas corpus* was not in use in the Roman-Dutch law, the protection afforded by the writ *de homine libero exhibendo* was for all practical purposes the same as that enjoyed under the English writ of *habeas corpus*. A striking illustration of the way in which this protection once operated in South Africa is afforded by the case of *Sigcau* v. *The Queen*.[11] Sigcau, an African chief living in Pondoland towards the end of the last century, was a source of irritation to the Cape Government. Sigcau's country had been annexed to the Cape Colony, and the Annexation Act gave extensive authority to the Governor of the Cape Colony to make new laws for Pondoland. Professing to act under this authority the Governor issued a proclamation which set aside the established law of Pondoland with respect to arrest, trial, conviction and punishment; and he condemned Sigcau—untried and unheard—to imprisonment, the place and duration of his captivity being left to the uncontrolled will of the Governor. This proclamation was countersigned by Cecil John Rhodes, who was then Prime Minister and Minister of Native Affairs of the Cape Colony.

[10] Above, p. 26.
[11] 12 S.C. 283.

Sigcau applied for his release to the Supreme Court where the application was opposed by the Attorney-General. The Court held, however, that the Governor had no power to issue the proclamation under which Sigcau had been condemned, and ordered his immediate release. In a forceful judgment the Chief Justice, Sir Henry de Villiers, said:

> The civil courts have but one duty to perform and that is to administer the law without fear or favour or prejudice, independent of the consequences that may ensue. . . .

These are, of course, stirring words; and so long as the law itself remains favourable to liberty, an upright and independent judiciary and a fearless Bar may shield the citizens from tyranny. But what when the law itself is made adverse to freedom? Let us now look at a few of the more basic pieces of apartheid legislation to see what they have done to those provisions of our common law, which in 1947 were proclaimed by the Law Advisers as the foundation of human rights and fundamental freedoms in South Africa.

1. Personal freedom

Personal freedom was the first topic mentioned by the Law Advisers in 1947. What, so far as Africans are concerned, has become of this freedom?

As far back as 1927 in the Native Administration Act of that year, it had been enacted that if an African, ordered to leave an area, refused to comply with the order, the Governor-General might in his unfettered discretion order that, without trial in a court of law or further investigation of any kind, the African be summarily arrested, detained and removed from that area. After 1948, however, the position deteriorated seriously. Detention and banishment, without trial or judicial warrant, at the sole discretion of the Executive Government, has, for Africans, become a feature of the legal system. Indeed, under a law passed in 1952 whole tribes may be moved from one area or province in the Union to another; and no court interdict, or other legal process, may intervene to stop the removal.[12]

2. Presumption of innocence

What again has become of the presumption of innocence? One of the alarming features of apartheid legislation is the extent to which it reverses the common law by placing the onus of proof on the individual. Examples are legion; and it will suffice to mention three. In 1949 the Mixed Marriages Act was passed making it an offence for a marriage officer knowingly to celebrate a marriage between a

[12] Native Laws Amendment Act, No. 54 of 1952, sec. 20.

4

European and a non-European. Section 3 of that Act provides that 'any person who is in appearance obviously a European or a non-European, as the case may be, shall for the purposes of this Act, be deemed to be such unless and until the contrary is proved'. Secondly, under section 28 of the Native Laws Amendment Act, 1952, it is provided that in criminal proceedings against a Native (African) for remaining in a prohibited area for more than seventy-two hours, it shall be presumed, until the contrary is proved, that he did so remain.[13] Under the same Act, a Native may be arrested and brought before a magistrate. The Native may then be required to give a satisfactory account of himself. If he fails to do so, he may, according to the circumstances, be declared an idle or undesirable person and be sent to a work colony.[14]

3. *Freedom from search without a warrant*

What has become of the common law freedom from search without a warrant? A perusal of the Native Urban Areas Act of 1945 as amended, the Group Areas Act of 1950, and the Criminal Law Amendment Act of 1953, discloses drastic invasions of domestic privacy, as well as the privacy of correspondence, without judicial warrant of any kind.

4. *Freedom of speech and of the press*

Have freedom of speech and the press fared better? Serious inroads upon this particular freedom have been made under several Acts,[15] notably the Suppression of Communism Act of 1950, the Public Safety Act, and the Criminal Law Amendment Act of 1953. In the main, apart from putting down obscenity, the law has up till now been directed against serious and potentially effective opposition to apartheid. Thus, for example, the Criminal Amendment Act of 1953 provides, in effect, that if a person does or says anything which causes any other person by way of protest against the apartheid laws, to use, for example, a counter in a post office reserved for the exclusive use of white persons, such person commits a criminal offence and is liable to a fine not exceeding five hundred pounds, or to imprisonment for a period not exceeding five years or to a whipping not exceeding ten strokes or to both such fine and such imprisonment and such whipping; and in the case of a second or subsequent conviction the court may not impose only a fine but is obliged to impose a sentence of imprisonment or a whipping. This provision applies to both the written and the spoken word.

[13] Sec. 28, subsec. 5.
[14] Sec. 29.
[15] See generally, A. Hepple, *Censorship and Press Control in South Africa*, Johannesburg, 1960, pp. 11–23.

5. *Freedom of association*

And what about the fifth head of freedom mentioned by the
Law Advisers in 1947—freedom of association? The Native Urban
Areas Act (as amended) provides, in effect, that:

> The Minister of Native Affairs may, unless the local authority
> objects, by notice in the *Gazette*, prohibit a social gathering in a
> private home in a town at which an African is present, if, in his
> opinion, such gathering is undesirable having regard to the
> locality in which the house is situated. Any African attending
> such a gathering is guilty of an offence and liable to a fine not
> exceeding ten pounds or to imprisonment not exceeding two
> months or to both such fine and such imprisonment.

Similar inroads were made under the Suppression of Communism
Act, and the Public Safety Act, 1953. And, as we shall see presently,
in subsequent years the righ of effective political association has
been virtually destroyed for Africans.

1955 ONWARDS

The process of attrition outlined in the previous section is not
always realized in all its starkness, even by educated and profes-
sionally competent white persons in South Africa. As late for
example as 1955, in the official summary of the Tomlinson Report,
one finds the following very remarkable statement:

27.   (i) In terms of the South African Citizenship Act 1949, the
Bantu population, like members of other population
groups, are Union citizens. In terms of constitutional
law, therefore, no distinction is made, and this fact
naturally implies equality of persons, property and
rights;

  (ii) All individuals of all population groups are equal in
the eyes of the law and receive equal protection from
the law. This implies that nobody can be illegally
deprived of his liberty or held in slavery, or be exposed
to arbitrary arrest, detention or banishment; that any
person may apply to our courts for redress when he is
threatened in the possession of his goods or when his
person, honour or reputation is violated; and that the
South African courts are accessible to all persons on an
equal basis;

  (iii) Every person has the right to work;

  (iv) Every person (except a lunatic) has the right to marry
and procreate children. Marriages and extra-marital
relationships between Europeans and non-Europeans are
prohibited;

  (v) There is complete religious freedom in South Africa;

    (vi) The Bantu, like other population groups, have the full right to form either amongst themselves or together with members of other population groups:

        (*a*) organizations of a political nature (for example the African National Congress, the Liberal Party, etc.);

        (*b*) in the economic sphere, companies, etc. (subject to the general legislation concerned, to the provisions of the Group Areas Act and of other relevant legislation dealing with the acquisition of rights to land, etc. by such companies); also (unregistered) trade unions, mutual aid societies etc.; and

        (*c*) all kinds of associations and societies in the social sphere; and

    (vii) As regards the issue of passports, etc., there is no discrimination on the grounds of race or colour.

28. In a general sense, therefore, it can be said that, as regards these wider civil rights, there is no differentiation between the various population groups, and that in this respect the Bantu are substantially in no worse position than the other population groups.

This statement was euphemistic and very inaccurate when it was written. Nevertheless it is a useful peg on which to hang comment, because, among other reasons, the position has seriously deteriorated since it was written. Let us now review the main points:

1. *Equality of persons, property and rights*

It is difficult to believe that this statement was meant to be taken seriously; for it is contradicted by most laws in the Statute Book.

2. *Equality before the law, and access to the courts*

Here again, one can only assume that the authors of the Report were using the phrase 'all persons' as meaning only whites. Of course the South African common law, before it was corroded by legislation, maintained the alleged equality. But what was not mentioned by the Tomlinson Commission, and what should have been mentioned, was the fact of the corrosion. Moreover, subsequent to the Tomlinson Report, the adverse trend has continued. Thus section 9 of the Natives (Prohibition of Interdicts) Act, No. 64 of 1956, provides in effect that whenever the Governor-General (who acts on the advice of the Government), in his unfettered discretion, deems it fit to issue the necessary proclamation, an African who has been required by an order of court to leave a certain area must do so, and no court of law may grant an interdict preventing such removal, nor may appeal or review proceedings stay or suspend such removal, even where it can be established beyond all doubt that the order of court was intended for some other person and was served upon him in error. Any person who is not an African would, in precisely the same circumstances, be granted an interdict, or a stay or suspension of the removal order and would, therefore, not be obliged to leave the area.

3. *The right to work*

This right suffered diminution in the very first years of Union when it was laid down that no non-whites should be permitted to do skilled work in the mines. In 1956 the Union Parliament amended the Industrial Conciliation Act so as to give the Minister of Labour wide powers to reserve certain types of work for specified races. Determined attempts have since been made, in the face of the needs of industry and regardless of the personal considerations involved, to reserve certain skilled jobs for whites.

4. *Marriage and family life*

Quite apart from the merits or otherwise of the legal prohibition against mixed marriages—and I consider it to have no merits—the Natives Urban Areas Act, as amended,[16] deals with the case of an African male who was born and is registered as a worker in a particular town, but who has married somebody who is not registered as a worker in that town. Neither his wife nor his children (if 18 years old or more) are entitled *as of right* to live with him for more than seventy-two hours. Yet many of us have heard as part of the marriage service the words: 'Those whom God hath joined together let no man put asunder.'

Moreover, since the passing of the Bantu Education Act African parents have no choice whatsoever in regard to the kind of education which their children are to receive, nor has anyone the right to run schools for Africans which do not conform strictly to the terms of that Act.

5. *Religious freedom*

This too has been contaminated. The Natives Urban Areas Act, as amended in 1957, provides in effect that:

> The Minister of Native Affairs may, provided that the urban local authority concurs, by notice in the *Gazette*, prohibit the attendance of Africans at a Church service in any town, if in his opinion it is undesirable that Africans should be present in the Church in the numbers in which they ordinarily attend that service; and if he is satisfied that they are a nuisance.

There was strong opposition to this measure from the churches; the Act was therefore so phrased as to ensure that the burden of

[16] Act No. 54 of 1952.

punishment for infringement fell only on the African and not on the church authorities.

6. *Political association*

Comment here is almost superfluous. At the time of writing both the African National Congress and the Pan African Congress—the only two non-white organizations of any significant strength—have been banned.

7. *Economic association and trade unions*

It will have been noticed that the Tomlinson Commission said in 1955 that Africans were free to form trade unions, adding (in brackets) that these might not be registered—unlike white and Coloured unions. The difference between a registered and an unregistered trade union is, however, substantial. For example, Africans in an unregistered trade union cannot participate in collective bargaining. Again, under the Native Labour Act of 1953 it is unlawful for Africans to strike on pain of heavy penalties. And, of course, the Industrial Conciliation Act of 1956, by its policy of job reservation, has widened still further the difference between whites and non-whites in regard to the basic right to work and industrial organization.

8. *Passports*

On this subject the statement in the Tomlinson Report is, in an ironic sense, slightly more accurate. Both whites and non-whites have, on occasion, found it very difficult to obtain a passport! However, the statement is still not correct, because non-whites have experienced much more difficulty in leaving the country, even to the extent of having to obtain the privilege on condition that they never return.

9. *Civil liberties generally*

Year after year the process of attrition has gone on. In 1958 under the Criminal Law Amendment Act there was another glaring example of shifting the onus of proof on to the accused. If a document found on the premises of any association is produced by the prosecution at a trial, its mere production is prima facie proof of its authenticity; and if a name corresponding to that of the accused appears as its author, or as a member of the association, the accused is deemed to be the author, or a member as the case may be, unless the contrary is proved. In the same year another blatant example of invasion of freedom from search without a warrant was afforded by the Regulations governing the Evaton African Township. They provide that: 'any policeman may, whenever he wishes for any reason whatsoever to inspect the dwelling occupied by a resident of the township, enter that dwelling at any time of the day or night.'[17] And finally, for there must be an end to this dreary catalogue, there is at the time of writing a Bill before Parliament to impose pre-publication censorship; if passed, it will destroy freedom of the press and cripple the entire pursuit of learning and the discovery of truth in South Africa. Indeed in the Union's long history of legislative assaults upon freedom, it would be difficult to find a more sinister and dangerous threat than is contained in this Bill.[18]

EFFECT ON THE WHITES

Thus far, I have concentrated attention mainly upon the impact made by these laws upon freedom for non-whites. And I would submit that it is impossible for any fair-minded observer not to recognize that for them the fundamental common law freedoms and protections have been emasculated. This emphatically does not mean that all or most of the non-whites are physically ill-treated daily (as is sometimes represented) or anything like that (though one could wish that the record were better than it is): it does mean that they are, for the most part, denied the basic rights and freedoms deemed essential by white men for the fullness of their own lives.

At the same time it would be a grievous error to believe or hope that the programme of apartheid is not levying a vicious toll on freedom for the whites as well. In a very real sense freedom in a community is indivisible; measures aimed against one group invariably react on others; and it is in this context that the words of Dr. John Donne are particularly applicable: send not to know for whom the bell tolls; it tolls for thee. Here again, there are several ways in which one might illustrate the truth of this statement.

At an obvious—but perhaps the least significant—level it is plain that much of the legislation for apartheid has, either in specific terms or in effect, hit whites as well as non-whites. For example, the process of constitutional manipulation used to strip the coloured voters of their protection, in effect undermined at one stroke the protection for the equal status of the official languages—which were accorded the same so-called 'entrenchment'. Again, the Criminal Law Amendment Act, which makes it punishable to do or say anything that may cause some other person to commit an offence by way of protest against the law, has specifically struck at both whites and non-whites, and injured the freedom of all. Similarly the Suppression of Communism Act hits at all races alike, even

[17] G.N. No. 61 of 1958.
[18] See, generally D. V. Cowen, *Freedom of Thought and its Expression in South Africa*, Cape Town, 1960.

though it has been used primarily to prevent the organization of African political opinion.

But, when this has been said, it remains true that very few whites suffer in the same way as the non-whites. The few who are prepared to suffer in the same way are put on one side by kindly disposed fellow-whites as 'starry-eyed liberals' or 'hot-heads'; and are pilloried by those who are less kindly disposed, for being 'liberalist agitators', traitors, or worse.

The truth of the matter is that the encroachment upon civil liberties in South Africa affects the whole population, white and non-white, in a more subtle and pernicious way; but precisely because it is more subtle it too often escapes notice. In the first place it coarsens the moral fibre of individuals who belong to that section of the community which is responsible for making laws which are unjust and repressive. They must either acquiesce and stifle their conscience; or decide to become outcasts. As Socrates pointed out in Book I of the Republic injustice has a suicidal quality, and injures its perpetrator more grievously than the victim. Secondly, it causes deep fissures in the structure of society itself. And on this point there is indeed much wisdom in some editorial comment which appeared recently in the columns of the *Daily Telegraph* in London:[19]

> Apartheid is turning white against white. . . . The policy creates such tensions and doubts among the whites themselves that it can be made to work only in something like a police state. . . . This, then, is the fatal flaw in apartheid; it creates conditions which will poison the whites long before it goads the blacks into revolt—and all Africa will suffer.

Indeed, as Abraham Lincoln once pointed out, in a similar context, a house divided against itself cannot stand.

And there is yet more to it. I stated in Chapter 1 that white South Africa was not only deeply fissured because of its racial policies, but that it had also become schizophrenic. This is manifest in every aspect of national life. Let me give one or two examples. White South Africans sometimes like to proclaim that theirs is a Christian country. But they would do well to ponder the truth of what Professor Hoernlé once said on this subject. Christianity and the civilization which the whites value are by their very nature all-embracive; they draw people by their strength and rightness. Yet, while trying to hold to Christianity, too many whites by their actions repudiate the fact that its draw is universal, i.e. concerns all men equally.[20] This leads to an inner tension, a facing both ways, which can be morally devastating.

[19] 26 January 1959. [20] 'Race Mixture and Native Policy' in *Western Civilization and the Natives of South Africa*, ed. I. Schapera, London, 1934, p. 281.

Precisely the same phenomenon is to be found in social, and particularly in economic life. As Dr. de Kiewiet and others have observed, the economy of South Africa would surge forward if economic integration on a non-discriminatory basis were encouraged. Yet while many of the whites desire the ultimate economic benefits, they are held back by fear of racial equality. In de Kiewiet's words: 'If a nation cannot be half-slave and half-free, it cannot be half-poor and half-rich. The poverty of the natives is in the long run a subtraction from the wealth available to all.'[21]

IS ANYTHING ACHIEVED?

Is it possible to justify these heavy inroads upon human freedom, this load of suffering and indignity, in terms of any conceivable benefit that may be gained? Here again there are many factors which point inexorably to a negative answer. There are today some $5\frac{1}{2}$ million Africans, that is between 50 per cent and 60 per cent of the entire African population, living and working in the proposed (but vaguely defined) 'white' area. And, by the year 2000, according to the Tomlinson Commission, if the forces of integration and urbanization are allowed to go on operating, there will be upwards of 12 million Africans in the white area, the majority of whom will be in and near the towns. At the same time, on the commission's own estimate, even if apartheid policies are vigorously and uninterruptedly pursued on a more ambitious scale than the Government is, in fact, prepared to adopt, there will, by the year 2000, *still* be some 6 million Africans living and working there.[22] In other words, apartheid will have achieved parity in numbers between Africans and whites, as in some of the southern states of America where racial tensions are most acute; and if the Asians and the millions of mixed blood are taken into account, the whites will still be outnumbered!

THE DISINTEGRATION OF APARTHEID

However triumphant and dominant in South Africa the apartheid policy may appear to be on the surface, it is very plain to every reflective observer that it is at last beginning to disintegrate. This is the result of several powerful causes acting in combination.

First, it is being realized by many of its supporters that the promise which apartheid held out to arrest the flow of Africans to the urban areas, and their penetration into the economy, was largely vain. As Professor de Kiewiet writes:

[21] *The Anatomy of South African Misery*, pp. 71–2. See also Dr. Sheila van der Horst, *The Economic Implications of Political Democracy*, Optima Supplement, June 1960; and Prof. S. H. Frankel, *The Tyranny of Economic Paternalism in Africa*, Optima Supplement, December 1960.
[22] Summary of Report, U.G. 61/1955, ch. 7.

There are a number of frontiers across which natives are quietly drifting into more skilled and better paid occupations. The evidence is steadily mounting that behind a continuing barrage of speeches and gestures the Nationalist Government itself is yielding to economic pressure. Even in the rural areas, which are the stronghold of *apartheid*, the average wages in cash and kind of native workers rose by about 16 per cent between 1947 and 1952. Every step forward in mechanized and scientific farming also increases the demand for greater competence on the part of native farm labour. Even in government service it has been impossible to prevent natives from moving into positions where greater skill and responsibility are required. . . . South Africa is a land of contradictions. By the side of the rivalry of the races there is an even more fundamental struggle between the forces of separation, and the opposite forces of integration. The process of investment, industrialization and urbanization are processes of integration and amalgamation. In Great Britain what Disraeli once called the two nations were ultimately fused into one by the integrating power of technology, social conscience and economic understanding.[23]

Or, again, in the words of Professor P. V. Pistorius:

The position seems to have become worse. There are as many natives as ever. Integration, especially in the economic field, seems to be going on apace, and never in the history of South Africa has the number of natives employed by the South African Railways, to give but one example, been so great or the proportion of natives to Europeans been so much in favour of the natives as now.[24]

Secondly, it is being realized that the bitterness and tensions which apartheid arouses are leading to ruin. To quote Professor Pistorius:

The realization seems to have gained ground that the present trend is leading to ruin, and the doubts expressed in this respect no longer come only or mainly from the English-speaking side.[25]
     And perish we must, if group stands against group and sectional ideology against sectional ideology. By their [the Government's] very efforts to retain the identity and the predominance of the Afrikaans-speaking group, they are destroying that group. But the horror is that the inevitable cataclysm will strike all equally. That is hard and unemotional fact.[26]

Realization of national disaster, unless present trends change, is of course inescapable to all who are not blind to the facts. Internally,

[23] *The Anatomy of South African Misery*, Oxford, 1956, pp. 70–1.
[24] *No Further Trek*, 1957, p. 34.
[25] Op. cit., p. 37.
[26] Op. cit., p. 30.

we have been racked by the grim events at Sharpeville, Langa and Cato Manor, which of course have their counterpart in other racially tense societies, for example the recent riots in Southern Rhodesia. And as the months go by tension mounts, though it may not always be apparent on the surface.

Externally, throughout the civilized world, South Africa has aroused very deep anger; and among her friends or erstwhile friends, near-despair. Mounting opposition is annually becoming better organized and articulated in the United Nations. In the territory of South West Africa, which the Union has virtually annexed as a fifth province, apartheid policies are being carried out, and in consequence South Africa is being required to answer to the charge that this development conflicts with her international obligations. In the opinion of many competent observers, the South West African issue may yet prove to be the weak link in the chain of defence which the Government has attempted to raise against the pressure of external criticism.

At a level of awareness which is related to immediate financial interest, there is deep concern at the fact that capital is not easily attracted to the Union, and is in fact going out; and that during the period 1959–60 the number of emigrants from the Union exceeded the number of immigrants. Nor will it do to whistle up one's courage and seek to denigrate the emigrants as being 'rats deserting a sinking ship'. If the ship is in fact sinking, there is cold comfort indeed for those still on board; nor is it fair to call those who leave rats or 'just frightened'; on the contrary, they are often very courageous people forced to tear up roots because they see no future either for themselves, or more particularly for their children, in a country which seems bent on destroying itself. They are often among our finest citizens but are unable any longer to live a life of self-contradiction and muted conscience. South Africa cannot afford to lose them.

Again, who can be blind to the ever-mounting tide of African resentment which may (though God forbid) have to break before it recedes. No sane person can ignore the terrible warning of the African Msimangu, in Alan Paton's novel, 'I have one great fear in my heart, that one day, when they are turned to loving, they will find we are turned to hating'.[27]

And then there are the moral and philosophical objections to apartheid which, to many, seem to be overwhelming. Increasingly, moreover, they are being voiced by Afrikaans-speaking South Africans; and even avowed supporters of the Government are beginning to have misgivings.

[27] *Cry, the Beloved Country*, 1953, p. 42.

'A policy of segregation', says Professor Ben Marais, 'as long as there is economic integration, can never be applied consistently and with decency.'[28] 'Just apartheid', says Professor B. B. Keet, 'does not exist.'[29] Needless to say the Christian churches have denounced discrimination based on race as being contrary to the teachings of Christ.[30] In regard to the Government's decision to impose apartheid in places of worship, the denunciation of the Church has been particularly firm; and, more recently, there have been indications of an impending dispute between the State and the Dutch Reformed churches on the whole issue of apartheid.[31] Within the ranks of the Government, Senator de Klerk has reminded the electorate that if apartheid is to measure up to its ideals a change of attitude is needed; whites will have to learn to do semi-skilled work and not look down upon it, as in the past, as 'kaffir-work'.

CONCLUSION

All this makes it difficult to resist the conclusion that the values of civilized life, to which the Prime Minister of Great Britain referred in Cape Town,[32] are being corrupted and swept away in the determined pursuit of an impracticable ideal against the wishes of the majority of the people. Recently a group of prominent South Africans, including many leading figures in commerce and industry from both language groups, called for a reappraisal of beliefs in South Africa; and repeated the anguished cry: 'Where do we go from here.'[33]

The answers that have been suggested are analysed in the next chapter, together with what I believe to be the only possible, and ultimately—however difficult—the only morally defensible, and indeed uplifting, alternative.

[28] *Colour*, p. 323.
[29] *Cape Times*, June 1956. Also *Suid Afrika Waarheen*; and the *Ethics of Apartheid*, Hoernlé Memorial Lecture for 1957.
[30] See the recent condemnation of apartheid by the World Council of Churches reported in the *Cape Times*, 15 December 1960.
[31] See the statement of the World Council of Churches, reported in the *Cape Times*, 15 December 1960, and in the *Cape Argus* of the same date. And cf. the New Year Message for 1961 by Dr. H. F. Verwoerd.
[32] Above, pp. 7–8.
[33] *Cape Times*, 21 October 1960.

NOTE: On the eve of this book's going to press, the Government's attitude in regard to proceeding with the censorship Bill was equivocal.

4

Building a Common Society

In the last two chapters the main objections to apartheid, as I see them, were stated. But it must be stressed that it is by no means a sufficient answer to apartheid to reveal the suffering and unfairness, the inroads on liberty and human dignity, and the economic fatuity and wastefulness which the partial implementation of the policy has already entailed during twelve disquieting years of regulation and regimentation. Though apartheid now stands alone — barricading itself against world opinion, the forces of economics and all the truths revealed by reason — it must regretfully be admitted that the authors of the Tomlinson Report penetrated to the heart of the matter when they said that where the existence of a people is felt to be at stake, purely rational and economic considerations play a relatively unimportant role.[1]

Unfortunately, it does not win seats to remind the existing electorate of the Christian paradox that he who would save his life must lose it; and that white men who wish to remain in Africa will have to lose their racial pride and obsessions, and identify themselves fully with the ideal of an all-embracive community, which has put aside racial thinking. It is, unhappily, not enough to explain to a white electorate that what is needed is not so much absence of 'discrimination' but more discriminating discrimination. It is not enough to point out that a discriminating man is universally admired precisely because he discriminates wisely between the intelligent and the stupid, between the beautiful and the ugly, and bases his judgement of people and things on individual merit — and that merit knows no colour bar. One is not likely to get very far in the heat and dust of politics by stating — what is so true — that the fundamental objection to colour discrimination is that it is indiscriminate and blunt-edged working injustice to people who are as intelligent, good and worthy as any others, and coarsening the fibre of those who enforce the discrimination.

To criticize, to ridicule, even to demolish totally in rational argu-

[1] *Summary of the Report of the Commission for the Socio-Economic Development of the Bantu Areas*, 1955, Chapter 25, paras. 21 and 23.

ment, is not enough when once basic human fears and prejudices have been aroused; on the contrary, such a course may often merely confirm fear and harden prejudice. As we shall see, it will be necessary to strike at the very roots of fear and prejudice in order to destroy them.

THE FORCES OF UNITY

At present, in South Africa, one is regarded as starry-eyed, or a 'liberalist', or as something more heinous, if one seriously suggests that there could be health in exorcizing the race bogy and trying to build one undivided and democratic South African society. But there are in actual fact strong and persistent undercurrents flowing in that direction.

First, there is the fact that were South Africa's economy to be freed of the stultifying mass of apartheid legislation, and the waste of human effort and money which is involved in bolstering it up, the country would enjoy the fruits of unparalleled industrial expansion. Moreover, from an economic point of view, the situation is ripe for this; for here we have a newly and, as yet, far from fully industrialized country with a vast potential of labour and markets.

Then there is the fact that most of the whites claim to be Christian, although the whole theory and practice of apartheid, and indeed of any theory of racial discrimination, is deeply and completely unchristian. Those who wish to continue in the Christian camp must know in their minds and in their hearts—unless again they plead schizophrenia—that in Christianity there is no room for exclusiveness or for denying one's neighbour on racial grounds.

Again, there is the draw of a civilization which has come about through the fusion and spreading of ideas. As Professor Hoernlé wrote in a passage which upholders of apartheid conveniently ignore:

> to try to make Western civilization in South Africa the fenced-in prerogative of the white group, is to belie and betray the deepest drive of that civilization. For Western civilization just because it believes itself to be good, and its religion the highest, has in it the irresistible urge to self communication.[2]

A truly civilized, Christian and sane development in this country, would be for the whites to offer willingly the best of their civilization (from technology to Christian charity), secure in the knowledge that much will be added by the vitality and freshness which the newly initiated will bring. I say civilized development, because this has been the experience of the ages; I say Christian, because there is no warrant for the denial of universal brotherhood in the Bible, and

[2] 'Race Mixture and Native Policy' in *Western Civilization and the Natives of South Africa*, ed. I. Schapera, London, 1934, p. 281.

very little in twenty centuries of Christian experience. And I say sane, because present policies are bringing on that disintegration, called madness, which we are told precedes the end of those whom the gods wish to destroy.

And let it be emphasized that there is nothing exclusively 'Western' about our civilization. In religion, in art, in philosophy, in law, ideas from the East have mingled with those from the West, and have borne new fruit. Whatever is enduring in it will endure by becoming the possession of all civilized human beings. The great society of mankind which is slowly and painfully coming into being will have a great civilization to match it; in that society the Africans will have a place, and in that civilization they will share.[3] In this regard we do well to ponder, and ponder deeply, the fact that competing for the allegiance of men in the world today are two vital and antagonistic forces, government under law in a free society and communist authoritarianism—and in that struggle the way race issues are resolved will almost certainly be decisive.

And finally, among the unifying forces, is the fact that nearly all South Africans of all colours feel and want this extraordinarily beautiful country to be their only home; and they do not really want a ruptured country.

THE FORCES OF DIVISION

But the barrier in the way of these forces is very formidable. It has been built up by generations of racial thinking, prejudice, and fear; and buttressed by legislation and social taboo. Until recently whites have been able to get away with more or less naked domination and exploitation of non-whites, but as, in the modern world, this becomes increasingly less possible to maintain, fear of various kinds has more overtly gripped the white man.

This is demonstrated in South Africa by the attitudes of both the major white political parties. Fear has been the mainspring of apartheid. The official Opposition to the Government [the United Party] offers a policy of 'ordered progress' or 'white leadership with justice'. But stripped of verbal anodynes, this amounts to the old discredited policy of segregation, coupled with a humane relaxation of the asperities of apartheid. For some years it may continue to win white votes, partly because of old loyalties, partly because alternative leadership is not inspiring—and perhaps mainly because of the honourable character of the party leader, Sir de Villiers Graaff. But in the eyes of non-whites, especially Africans, the party just does not exist; and among whites it is dying.

Fear, too, or an over-sensitive consciousness of the potency of

[3] Hoernlé, op. cit., p. 281.

fear among the white electorate, is primarily responsible for a regrettable tendency in the more liberal Progressive Party to emphasize the significance of racial groups, and the need for group protection. Fear, too, it would seem, is responsible for the approval given by that Party in important fields to the 'separate but equal doctrine', and its categorical rejection of adult suffrage. Only the Liberal Party is at present committed to full non-racial democracy in an undivided country; and its influence, needless to say, is as yet negligible.

Fear too—the fear of a clash between mutually irreconcilable nationalisms—lies behind all plans for partition.

These various fears merit the closest analysis, for if they cannot be eradicated or disarmed there is no hope for a common society in South Africa. First, it is argued that equal social, political and economic rights would inevitably lead to miscegenation, and the loss of whiteness, in a society of mixed blood. And, as we have seen, the probability of this development was in fact conceded by Professor Hoernlé.[4] Fear of the consequences of such a development was articulated (though it was not shared) by Hoernlé in a lucid passage which bears quotation:

> Race-purity or blood-purity are valued not merely in themselves, but on the ground of the alleged 'superiority' of white over black blood. This superiority is held to justify the political and economic dominance of white over black, and to be itself attested by the 'higher' civilization which the whites have brought with them to South Africa, which they have established wherever they have settled, and the creation of which they claim for their own race. Granted these premises, it seems to follow that any mixing of superior white with inferior black blood must lower the culture-creating and culture-maintaining qualities in the offspring of such unions, and thus undermine the continuance of white civilization by deterioration of the human stock on which it depends. The oft-heard question: Would European civilization in South Africa survive if the whites were to leave the country or to be destroyed, is held to clinch the argument. For no one can deny that the Bantu, *as they are now*, could not take over the political system, the economic institutions, the railways, schools, universities, businesses, etc., of the country as going concerns and run them, as they are now being run by whites trained for their tasks and sustained by the necessary cultural tradition.[5]

Secondly, there is the hard fact that people who enjoy power and privileges do not willingly surrender them; and they both fear and oppose any policy that might weaken their position.

[4] Above, p. 21.
[5] Op. cit., p. 269. Written in 1934.

Thirdly, there is the fear of retribution or retaliation. What assurance, what security, it is asked, is there against the risk that, given political power and authority, the blacks will not retaliate in kind and victimize the whites. And if they have a taste for political theory, those who ask this question will pursue their fears by raising the more basic question whether the techniques of democracy are really suited to a mixed society where the majority are racially distinct from, and less experienced than, the minority. Was not the grant of the franchise to the negroes in the South after the American Civil War premature, they will ask. Did it not lead to the evil of 'carpet-bagging'; and in the result were the negroes not worse off than if wiser and more patient policies had prevailed in the era of reconstruction?[6]

And fourthly, there are those who say it is already too late to try to build a common society. Pointing to the undeniable fact of 'nationalism' among both the whites and the blacks, they argue, or rather assume, that each form of nationalism must inevitably seek to dominate the other. Fearing a conflict, they contend that if peace is to be kept, the two nationalisms should be separated by an immediate resort to partition.

Because it has suited the book of politicians, all these fears have been fostered and strengthened by the propagation of myths. And once again, if there is to be any hope of revising present trends of thought and policy among white people, these myths must be seen for what they are.

Pointing to the admitted fact that white men brought civilization to Southern Africa, the wholly false conclusion is drawn that the white man is the sole trustee and bearer of that civilization. The 'guardian', or 'bearer' of civilization myth has a deceptive and superficially scientific air about it; and it would be folly to underestimate its power.

Again, arguing from the fact that Africans did not independently evolve the wheel, or gunpowder, or the New York skyscraper; and have not produced a figure comparable to say, Shakespeare, it is sometimes contended that Africans are an 'inferior race'. Indeed there are those who have sought to give theological verisimilitude to this by the myth that Africans are the sons of Ham, 'cursed' by God to be hewers of wood and drawers of water.

A third myth, sometimes invoked to support either apartheid

[6] The traditional, and probably still 'orthodox' view of American historians is that the enfranchisement of the freed negroes led to corruption. See Dunning, *Reconstruction*, 1907; Donald, *The Negro Freedman*, 1952. For the contrary view, see Woodson, *The Negro in our History*, 1947; Franklin, *From Slavery to Freedom*, 1956.

or partition, is that the white man has an original claim to all the land which he seeks to set apart for himself—the myth of 'he got there first'.

In addition, the forces of division have long been fed by 'slanted' education; by encouraging ignorance; and by a calculated policy to discourage all individual contacts across the colour-line, except on a master and servant basis. This policy is enforced by the combined operation of law, convention and social taboo.

All this leads naturally to the growth of white nationalism, in the sense of consciousness by the group of its own identity and privileges, and a determination to maintain them: and in turn, it has inevitably begotten black nationalism. Rejected and dominated by the white man, black nationalists seek primarily an escape from their inferior position. But each passing year sees an ever-growing number of disillusioned Africans who (can one be surprised) have become frankly anti-white. 'Africa for the Africans' can no doubt be interpreted as a simple call for autonomy or self-determination; it no doubt includes in the eyes of many Africans a place for the white man who has fully identified himself with the ideal of a non-racial democracy in an integrated society; but to an increasing number it is coming to mean no truck with the white man.

Here then is the present South African situation:

1. Apartheid by its very logic is setting group against group, and leading to the disintegration of society.

2. At the same time there is no fair and just—or indeed any—alternative policy which has widespread support. All is confused, contradictory, tense.

3. Although there is still overwhelming white determination to stay on top, this is coupled with growing awareness among whites that their position cannot be maintained indefinitely.

4. Meanwhile world opinion is hardening against the country. And as indignation mounts, the independent black African states in the United Nations interest themselves increasingly in South African affairs, and address themselves increasingly to the means of making sanctions effective.

5. South West Africa, now within the Union's self-assumed jurisdiction, presents an obvious case for intervention; and may yet prove to be the Achilles heel of apartheid.

6. The yoke of apartheid falls with increasing weight upon a disenfranchised, underprivileged, and comparatively poor proletariat. Sporadic and spontaneous demonstrations of opposition are becoming more frequent, and as time goes on can be expected to become more serious.

In short, as Mr. Chester Bowles has observed, a truly classic revolutionary situation is developing in South Africa.

If these factors are carefully and honestly weighed, one cannot but recognize that the chances for South Africa's peaceful future are very slender. And it is probably for this reason that many have already given up hope. They accept that the white man has failed in his mission as a 'bearer of civilization', and that he is too self-seeking to live in peace with non-whites in the same society; they would therefore try to negotiate a partition as soon as possible.

A suggestion along these lines was recently put forward 'as a possible solution' by the economist, Dr. Jan Graaff, Sir de Villiers Graaff's brother. Dr. Graaff suggests what he calls demotomic partition. This is not, like apartheid, a plan to divide South Africa into separate racial communities, but to partition the country and its peoples into two sections, East and West. The East would be set aside mainly for Africans to live in, the West mainly for whites, although it would include a large number of Africans (who would however constitute less than half of the total population). Dr. Graaff envisages that the drawing of the frontiers would have to take place by negotiation either with or without an initial upheaval. However, while wishing to remain vague as to the outcome of such negotiations, he envisages as a possible boundary a line running from the mouth of the Great Fish River (between Port Elizabeth and East London), skirting Basutoland, following the Natal-Transvaal border, going round Swaziland, and ending along the edge of the escarpment in the eastern Transvaal.[7]

From the point of view of government, this scheme runs into precisely the same difficulties that vex South Africa at present in the so-called white but really mixed areas. Thus, for example, in the proposed western area, it must be asked what political, economic and social rights would be enjoyed by the large number of non-whites, and especially the Africans? These, however, are precisely the questions which have hitherto baffled politicians in South Africa; and it may be doubted whether they would become any more easily soluble (in the eyes of white politicians) by reducing the proportion of Africans in the population to 'something less than half'. If more than two million Africans remain in the western area (as Dr. Graaff apparently envisages; indeed to avoid this, the line would have to be drawn so as to exclude the gold- and diamond-mines from the western area), all the old problems would still be very much present. Moreover, when the Coloureds and Asians are taken into account, then unless there were substantial immigration, the whites would actually be outnumbered. What is more, they would

[7] *Cape Argus*, 15 October 1960.

have a predominantly black state on their borders—a state which, on Dr. Graaff's example, would be about 90 per cent non-white, and lacking the gold- and diamond-mines.

It might legitimately be asked whether it would be long before conflict broke out between the minerally rich western state and its less favoured eastern neighbour—a conflict in which the western state would be faced with, at least, an obvious 'Sudeten Problem', and in which the eastern state might not unreasonably expect support from other African states. Dr. Graaff's reply is that once the boundary had been agreed upon, and was internationally recognized, it might follow (from United Nations intervention in the Middle East and in the Congo) that it would be internationally enforced.

These are obstacles which Dr. Graaff's suggestion for demotomic partition does not really grapple with. Nevertheless I have given prominence to his suggestion because he has placed stress upon two important considerations. In the first place, his bold argument that such a partition need have no economic ill-effects, may—if sound—operate to weaken what has hitherto been regarded as a cohesive factor in the country's affairs, namely the economic advantages of an undivided South Africa. Dr. Graaff's conclusions were, however, immediately challenged by another economist, Professor W. H. Hutt, of the University of Cape Town.[8] And they would seem to be opposed to what the average man might reasonably feel to be the probabilities of the case.

Indeed, on this point, about a year before Dr. Graaff put forward his plan, I ventured to say:

> In South Africa a *fair* partition would present insuperable obstacles. Where exactly should the boundaries be drawn? Can South Africa's economy sustain the disruption involved in a fair partition? Would there be full and free consultation and consent on the part of all groups in its planning? Have white South Africans the will to face up to the material sacrifice and cost which would necessarily be involved? How, to be specific, would the gold, diamond and other mines and natural wealth of the country be divided? And, if a fair share of these is not to be given to the non-whites, will they not demand it when they grow in political organization and maturity? In short, unless the partition is genuinely fair, what real prospects are there for peaceful co-existence between the white and the non-white territories? And what prospects are there of getting the policy accepted by world opinion?[9]

I see no reason to change a word of this.

[8] *Cape Times*, 15 October 1960.
[9] *Optima*, Supplement, March 1960, p. 5.

Dr. Graaff's further contention, that we are already faced in South Africa with two antagonistic and mutually irreconcilable nationalisms, is more formidable. Basically this is very similar to the assumption upon which the whole policy of apartheid rests. Nor can it be doubted that fear of a destructive conflict between irreconcilable nationalisms is in the present situation a very real one. If Dr. Graaff's assumption is in fact correct, if the forces of division are intransigent, then indeed partition may be the only way out. But, and it is a very big but, it would, I think, be a partition far more favourable to the Africans than that which most white men could contemplate with equanimity. The whites might be lucky to keep the Western Province. And what is even more to the point, this could at best be regarded as a strategic withdrawal, a shortening of the lines of defence.

THE ALTERNATIVE

As I see it, the one and only hopeful alternative to the policy of apartheid, and its poor relations, is a policy whose goal is a democracy in which all men, irrespective of race, colour or creed, may enjoy the basic human freedoms and political and economic rights in one integrated society. In advocating this alternative, I do not exclude the possibility of an interim period of development during which non-racial democracy would be progressively fostered Indeed, I believe that Dr. Gikonyo Kiano of Kenya is right when he says that if white men would commit themselves genuinely and immediately to the ideals of non-racial democracy, then—subject to certain conditions to which I shall refer later—African nationalists would still accept a defined period of really genuine gradualism.[10] There are, however, certain subterfuges which sometimes masquerade under the title of gradualism, like the doctrine of 'separate but equal', which simply will not do. What should be put aside as both morally indefensible, and in any event opposed to the irresistible sweep of events, is any policy designed to buttress the white man as a permanently privileged minority group anywhere in Africa. Moreover, as the months go by, the prospects for even genuine 'gradualism' towards full non-racial democracy become more remote.

I shall not waste time weighing the relative merits and propriety of the adjectives 'non-racial', 'multi-racial' or 'inter-racial' as the appropriate label for the kind of society which may be offered as an alternative to apartheid. Many of the current terms are either inappropriate or have been debased by unhappy experience. Whatever label is chosen (and, if forced to choose, I prefer the phrase

[10] 'African Nationalism and the Problem of Minorities', *Colonial Times*, Nairobi, 21 August 1958.

non-racial democracy), if the alternative is a genuine one, it should, in declared principle, and as far as possible in daily practice, recognize no bar whatever to social, economic, cultural and political rights, merely on the ground of colour. It should, in short, be entirely colour-blind.

STRATEGY FOR INTEGRATION

I should not be writing this book if I did not believe that there was still a little time, and still some hope, for this latter alternative. It is the morally right and spiritually challenging solution. It is the only solution which offers to all the inhabitants of South Africa any hope of peaceful and fruitful co-existence, and indeed—to the whites—any hope of continued existence in this country. For it should be plain that the result of choosing any one of the alternatives based on fear will inevitably be the complete disappearance of the white race as such from Southern Africa, after a period of very ugly strife. However, the whites still have much to contribute; they have greater science, superior knowledge of technology, longer experience of modern government, and a great heritage in arts and the humanities. And they still have much to enjoy in this country, could they be persuaded in time to share willingly those things which at present they bind to their exclusive benefit.

Can this be done? It is plain that there can be no real progress along the road to true civilization in a shared and integrated South African society without a wholly fresh start in the national life of the country, without the excision from its entire constitutional and legal structure, and indeed in the course of time from men's hearts, of all traces of racial prejudice. Presently I shall give closer attention to the essential outlines of the strategy to be used for achieving this aim. Here it is necessary to observe that the aim itself must necessarily remain a dream, a vain phantasy, unless an immediate and powerful incentive can be provided for pursuing it.

Counter-fear

Perhaps the first step in bringing the whites to their senses will be the shock of national upheaval; though we may pray that it will not be so. However, there is, I believe, a less drastic solvent of the present impasse. It is to break fear with counter-fear; and to make the counter-fear felt. There is, I think, no other way. Indeed it might be accepted almost as an axiom that there is no prospect for the lasting success of any alternative to apartheid, and in particular no hope of bringing about a *peaceful* change in current trends of policy, unless it is possible to convince the white man that the dangers implicit in apartheid are very much greater than the risks involved in a common society organized on a democratic and non-racial basis.

The issues in South Africa are rapidly moving out of the sphere of rational argument and electoral appeals into the field of naked power. Tough and powerful as the white man unquestionably is—supported by guns, money, armoured cars and aircraft—he may soon have to reckon with mightier battalions, both internally and from abroad. Already organized boycotts have had an effect. The legally recognized instruments for a peaceful settlement—the voting and law-making power—are still in the white man's hands; he has not yet quite lost the opportunity for initiating a just and peaceful settlement. But the sands are running out for the white man all over Africa; whether he will come to his senses before it is too late remains to be seen.

It should be realized that the division of men into groups will work for the purposes of government provided that those excluded from a particular group, as well as those included within it, accept the division as sound; but a blunt-edged division into white and non-white is simply not acceptable to an overwhelming majority of non-whites in Africa—and cannot long be peacefully maintained. Each year of apartheid brings additional burdens and frustrations, and makes the risk of eventual retaliation greater. Each passing month will strengthen the case for economic boycotts in commodities and services that matter. In short, only the mentally blind can fail to see that the implementation of apartheid carries with it its own inherent and grave dangers of economic impoverishment and social turmoil; and fear of these may yet come to weigh as heavily with the whites as the fears which give life to apartheid itself.

These arguments, coupled with the spur of conscience, may still, I believe, tip the balance among white men in favour of a committal to non-racial democracy in an integrated society. At the same time it must be emphasized that such a committal would be sterile if, like the policy of apartheid, it rested only on the negative force of fear. What is needed is courage and a positive willingness—whether flowing from enlightened self-interest or moral conviction—to make the committal, and to work towards the realization of the goal.

What then can be done in this direction by those who still believe in the possibility of one society?

Exploding the myths

It is popular among the well-meaning to say that education and goodwill are the best methods for overcoming prejudice. Education can help in so far as prejudice is based on inaccurate information or deficient knowledge. But as Dr. Liston Pope, the Dean of the School of Divinity in Yale University, has pointed out, much prejudice is irrational in character and is little affected by educational approaches.[11] Again the cultivation of goodwill undoubtedly provides a more favourable climate in which to seek the solution of difficult problems than does indifference or hatred, but—again as Dr. Pope shows—'good feeling does not in itself provide formulas for desegregation and integration; and may actually be used to mask and render more bearable a pattern of segregation.'[12]

We should not, however, underrate the efficacy of education and goodwill. And so before turning to other techniques in the strategy for integration, I should like to say a little more about these, and especially about the role of education in eradicating disruptive fears and myths.

Take for example, the fear of miscegenation. This is a subject that is hardly discussed or even whispered about in South Africa. But like most fears, when courageously faced, it shrinks to insignificance. In part (though I believe this would be the least valid approach) the fear of miscegenation, and of its alleged consequences, may be met by challenging Hoernlé's assumption that equal social, political and economic rights for both white and non-white peoples will lead to racial mixture. Against this, it should be kept in mind that one cannot force people to marry people of different races if they do not wish to; and if the whites are so set upon the idea of racial purity, they should have no difficulty in remaining white. As Lincoln once observed in the course of his debates with Douglas, the number of mulattoes was proportionately greater in the slave than in the free states. Again, according to Dr. Liston Pope, 'in those American states that have not forbidden miscegenation by law, the ratio of interracial marriages has been extremely low', and he quotes interesting statistics on the point.[13]

In part, again, it may help a little to exorcize the miscegenation bogy to let it be known that there is no sufficient evidence that the mingling of the black and white ethnic groups leads to degeneration. Here again there is a very relevant passage in the writings of Professor Hoernlé which the apologists of apartheid are careful to suppress. 'There is no reason to think', he says, 'that the offspring of white and Bantu need be in any way intellectually or morally inferior, as measured by white standards. Bantu blood does not necessarily mean bad heredity, nor white blood good heredity.'[14]

Further, there is no evidence that blacks are inferior to whites in intelligence and innate endowment. To quote Dr. Liston Pope,

[11] *The Kingdom Beyond Caste*, p. 84.
[12] Op. cit., p. 86.
[13] See *The American Journal of Sociology*, vol. 57, 1952, pp. 587–9.
[14] Op. cit., p. 269. See also Liston Pope, op. cit., p. 34; and Bryce, *South America*, 1914 ed., p. 481.

'it has now become clear that no test of intelligence has yet been devised that can rule out such non-hereditary factors as education, social opportunities, and other environmental differences'.[15] And Professor Hoernlé is even more explicit. 'Perhaps the safest working principle', he concludes, 'is to assume that all human stocks are much alike in innate endowment.'[16]

In short, if with the passage of time a mixed society should come to be regarded as acceptable by our descendants, we today have neither right nor reason to interfere with their free choice. If people wish to remain white they will, and if they wish to mix there is no sufficient moral or genetic reason why they should not. All this propaganda about racial superiority—rationalized by the Comte de Gobineau, H. S. Chamberlain, and Lothrop Stoddard—was one of the evils which led to Hitler's War. It should have died with Hitler.

Dealing with the failure of Africans to initiate anything comparable to the Graeco-Roman civilization, Hoernlé demolishes the racialist argument with powerful strokes:

> Those whites of Teutonic or Anglo-Saxon descent who believe in the innate superiority of race and blood would do well to reflect that if their argument had been fashionable in the age of Tacitus, he would have looked down upon the Germans from the height of his Graeco-Roman civilization and declared the barbarians to be manifestly inferior in inborn capacity to himself and his own people.[17]

Then, too, the causes of the development of cultures in different parts of the earth, and at different eras in the history of the same people, are still, on the whole, utterly obscure.[18] We do know, however, that great civilizations flourished in China and India and around the eastern Mediterranean, among dark-skinned people, when Europe was still barbaric.

It should, moreover, never be forgotten that the richness and essential vitality of what we call 'western' civilization has come about through the fusion and spreading of ideas. Its secret has been its capacity to absorb what is best in many cultures and, on each occasion, to achieve a new synthesis; its mission must ever be to communicate itself. Again, it must be borne in mind that incapacity to *initiate* a culture is no obstacle to its acquisition.

Similar considerations apply to Christianity itself. Compounded of Judaic and Greek elements, which were given new depths of meaning

[15] Op. cit., p. 31.
[16] Op. cit., p. 273.
[17] Op. cit., p. 272.
[18] Op. cit., p. 272.

by the life of Christ, its mission, too, must be that of self-communication. And certain it is in the words of the Dean of the School of Divinity in Yale University, that 'where God truly reigns and his Kingdom prevails, men know no difference of colour or race. Forgiveness and oneness in Him are the way of life in the Kingdom beyond caste'.[19]

The old myth about the curse on the sons of Ham has been exploded, again by Dr. Liston Pope, in the following passage:

> Defenders of segregation derive comfort from the 'curse' (Genesis 9:25) placed on the son of Ham, Canaan, by his grandfather Noah (who had just risen from a drunken stupor)—'A slave of slaves shall he be to his brothers'. They associate this curse with the punishment meted out by Joshua to the Gibeonites (Joshua 9) when he placed some of them in slavery as 'hewers of wood and drawers of water'. Careful reading of the passages reveals that the curse was pronounced by Noah, not God, and that the old man was hardly in a fit condition to be God's spokesman at that moment. Besides, the Canaanites cannot be proved to be the ancestors of Africans. Why the Gibeonites should be dragged in is a mystery, except that perhaps any curse will do if cursing is intended.[20]

These are truths which will have to be kept constantly in mind if existing mental habits are to be changed. And on other less fundamental but still very important points too, existing misconceptions and distortions will have to be removed by a more wholesome and enlightened system of education. I have already shown how Professor Monica Wilson has exploded the 'he got there first' myth. There are many other misconceptions on race relations which should be excised from allegedly impartial school history books.

As regards the argument about retaliation, in part the answer is that such fears were often expressed in the West Indies before the non-whites took over; and that there they have proved groundless.[21] In part again, the answer is that the risk is inevitable, and that, in any case, in the world in which we live no assurance of complete security can be given:[22] therefore let the white man by means of education, and a steady and generous concession of rights, minimize the risk *now*.

The disinclination of a power group to surrender domination is another matter. People do not ordinarily give up power by rational

[19] *The Kingdom Beyond Caste*, p. 160.

[20] Op. cit., p. 146.

[21] See the letter by Mr. B. E. King in *Cape Times*, 6 December 1960.

[22] A famous English judge once suggested that 'certainty is the mother of repose and therefore the common law aims at certainty'—a proposition which evoked from Mr. Justice O. W. Holmes the remark that 'certainty is an illusion, and repose is not the destiny of man'.

argument; generally they do so only when confronted by greater power. But tough as white racialists may be, they cannot but realize that their days of domination are numbered. However they should also realize that to give up domination does not necessarily mean to be dominated. There is a third way; power may be shared. Indeed, the fear of mutually conflicting and irreconcilable black and white nationalisms is I believe, as yet, exaggerated.

In this regard, though the whites in Southern Africa must be prepared to make an act of faith in non-racial democracy, there is comfort for them here as well. First, they are very lucky in the general level of the non-white population. The non-whites, Africans as well as others, have had a very long experience of working with whites. Probably nowhere else in Africa is the average calibre of the non-white population higher, nowhere else in Africa are Africans more experienced in white techniques and ways of thinking—despite widespread poverty and lack of education. The serious pronouncements of African leaders have until now been on a high plane of restraint and dignity. Their demonstrations have been non-violent, and both the African National Congress and the Pan African Congress have stressed that they do not wish to reject the whites, but wish to build one nation, one South Africa, together with them. There is, moreover, still a strong sense of mutual interdependence between the races. The whites should try to have confidence in this fund of goodwill, before it is too late.

A word now on earning goodwill by conduct. Each individual who believes in an integrated society must by his conduct show that colour is irrelevant in all that matters. For this truly is a time when each individual must live according to his best lights, and be brave enough to act according to conscience. Political and business expediency have been with us too long: they have dulled conscience, sapped moral vitality, and wellnigh destroyed independence of mind.

And this leads me directly to a difficult field. Some years ago a group of social scientists at Cornell University, dissatisfied with evasive generalities about goodwill, investigated the concrete possibilities of breaking down racial prejudice and fear so as to encourage integration. They came to the conclusion that there was no simple magic formula. But there was much that could be done to help. This is not the occasion to give a full enumeration of their lengthy findings; still less, to discuss the importance of what might, superficially, seem one of their minor recommendations, namely the avoidance in social intercourse of such thoughtless and wounding phrases as 'free, white and twenty-one', 'boy' (for a grown man), 'Hey, John' (for any African), and so on.[23]

[23] See, generally, Liston Pope, op. cit., p. 87 sqq.

One essential point, however, does require emphasis. The experts came to the conclusion that the more contact a person has with other groups, the lower is his level of general prejudice against them. Certainly the psychological importance of this has not been overlooked by upholders of apartheid; for it is precisely their policy to maintain and perpetuate prejudice by erecting legal and conventional barriers against contact, especially *social* contact, across the colour line.

It follows, therefore, that an essential step towards any improvement in South Africa must be a radical revision of the entire body of the country's legislation, involving wholesale repeal of literally dozens of statutes. And no less important is the necessity to try to bring about changes in public opinion, and particularly in those unwritten laws or conventions, often called 'social mores'.

It is just here that a great responsibility for creative leadership rests with such institutions as the churches and the universities. And on this point certain conclusions reached by the Cornell study group are particularly relevant. There is a tendency among some university leaders, and even occasionally among the clergy, to emphasize the expediency of conforming in race relations to 'the accepted conventions of the community' and to 'public opinion'. But, as the Cornell scientists showed:

> Decisions about the practices of particular institutions in a community are seldom really made by 'public opinion', though appeal to that vague force may often be used to rationalize refusal to make decisions differently. Decisions are seldom made directly by 'the rank-and-file'. Most often they are made by those entrusted with policy making. In a democratic situation there is always an ultimate appeal to the total constituency. *But the constituency itself expects leadership.* And the leadership often has far more latitude, even in ticklish matters of race, than it supposes, as the variety of patterns to be found in almost any community will attest. Those who are actually in a position to make changes of policy within a certain organization or situation have, therefore, a great opportunity and grave responsibility to demonstrate leadership. A genuinely interracial, non-segregated situation seldom 'just grows'; it must be planned.[24]

It is, of course, not possible to blue-print a plan for policy changes in comprehensive detail, but the Cornell scientists have usefully called attention to particular points which may be kept in mind:[25]

1. It is better to have a positive policy than no policy, in order that the position may be perfectly clear to all.

[24] As summarized by Dr. Liston Pope in *The Kingdom Beyond Caste*, p. 92. My italics.
[25] Taken from Dr. Liston Pope's summary.

2. Examples of successful integration in kindred or neighbouring institutions can often be very helpful and reassuring.

3. No effort should be made to stifle potential opposition by facing it with an accomplished fact.

4. Even if no policy of desegregation is possible at the moment, a policy adopting desegregation as a goal to be achieved as rapidly as possible provides a direction for future movement.

5. Desegregation that proceeds by firm and decisive steps backed by the responsible authorities is more readily accepted and taken for granted than a halting desegregation that appears unsure of itself.

THE ROLE OF CONSTITUTION-MAKING

Thus far I have made little mention of the role which constitution-making has to play in building a common society. And I have adopted this course deliberately, so as to put constitutions and their efficacy into true perspective. As Lord Bryce pointed out, no constitution in the world can artificially create social unity and well-being, if, in fact, the operative currents are flowing too strongly in a different direction. The difficulties facing the constitution-maker for a real democracy in South Africa are so formidable as to be almost daunting. But, as we have seen, there are undercurrents which in fact give cause for hope. The forces of unity are still strong even though, for the time being, they are not as compelling as the forces of division. Given the necessary stimulus and encouragement, however, the situation could change dramatically.

It should be borne in mind, moreover, that the whole situation in South Africa is fluid. Opposition has already begun to move out of the parliamentary arena; already there are many persons in the country's gaols who have gone so far as to deny the legitimacy of national institutions of government (the attitude, for example, of the banned Pan African Congress), and there are others who have contended, significantly, that the apartheid laws are not binding in conscience on the score that they offend against the divine and the natural law.

In these circumstances it is more than ever urgent that the alternative to apartheid be worked at, and that its far-reaching implications should be widely discussed, so that as large as possible a body of informed public opinion on the subject may be ready to give effective support when the time comes. And it is for this reason that I still believe that proposals for a reformed constitution might have an important role to play in helping forward the idea of a common South African society.

At the same time it is of great importance not to be deluded into placing too much confidence in the value and efficacy of constitutions as such. I am not one of those who regard a constitution as a panacea for all a country's ills. Constitutions can never in themselves provide social stability and security. But having said this, there are, I believe, several major objectives which could be helped forward in South Africa by a properly drafted constitution, including among its provisions a genuine Bill of Human Rights.

In the first place, such a constitution should help to disarm fears about the risks of democracy and the abuse of power. Indeed it is with the problem of preventing the abuse of power that the rest of this book will be concerned; and as we shall see, constitutions can do much to tame governmental power and prevent its abuse. They can, of course, never provide complete security. But they can make the way of the tyrant difficult. They are what I like to regard as the outer bulwarks, the outer defences, of true freedom.

Secondly a Bill of Rights should become the basis of the political education of the community, with really profound effects upon the whole character of national life. The values embodied in a Bill of Rights provide a standard to which people can appeal when power is abused. Moreover, were these values properly taught in the schools in civics classes, they would become an important cohesive element in society. Indeed, from this point of view, it would be difficult to overestimate the importance of the role which the United States Constitution has played in establishing the fact of American nationhood. No one who has studied American society, even for a comparatively short period, can fail to be impressed by the central position of the Constitution in the affection, the thought, and the imagination of Americans. No enumeration of the characteristics and qualities which go to make up 'a good American' would be complete without a reference to the United States Constitution and its Bill of Rights.

Nor does the great educative effect of a constitutionally entrenched Bill of Rights end there. A Bill of Rights is likely to be a very shaky affair unless men are agreed about the philosophical basis upon which it rests. Jacques Maritain has observed that, from the point of view of philosophic doctrine, it may be said that in regard to human rights men are today divided into two groups; those who to a greater or lesser extent explicitly accept, and those who to a greater or lesser extent explicitly reject, natural law as the basis of those rights.[26] In the eye of the first, the requirements of his being endow man with certain fundamental and inalienable rights antecedent in nature and superior to society. These are *the source* of social life itself, and the duties and rights which it implies. For the second school, man's rights are constantly variable and in a state of flux, being

[26] Unesco Symposium, p. 13.

entirely *the product* of society as it advances with the forward march
of history.

For those who believe in natural law, as it stemmed from the best
thought of the ancient world and was developed by the medieval
Christian scholastics, there is a difference between right and wrong,
just and unjust. This difference is fixed in the order of nature, however,
being eternal and universal. It is the function of man's reason, and his
responsibility, to discover the right and the just. This *is* an act of
discovery; because the standards of right and wrong, just and unjust,
are not, on this view, the product of man's intellect or of his will.

Those who take the other view, also profess to have standards of
right and wrong, just and unjust; but they deny the existence of
eternal and universal verities. For them what is right and just is
what man establishes at the various stages of his development.

The consequences of accepting one of these points of view rather
than the other are great; for, as we shall see more fully later,
without the sense of direction given to a society by an understanding
of the natural law, and man's place within its framework, power
and expediency can become the highest arbiters of behaviour and
of the enactments of the state; and base emotions such as fear and
greed are given free rein.

It is because I believe that the natural law fulfils the essential
needs and yearning of men, and because I believe that contemporary
travail and confusion the world over are particularly favourable to a
great revival of natural law, that I consider proposals for Bills of
Rights in Africa to be particularly exciting. Indeed by opening the
way to an understanding of the natural law, they may help men to
understand what they really mean, or should mean, when they claim
to the bearers of 'western Christian civilization'.

PART TWO

The Taming of Power

5   The Challenge of Democracy

The fundamental problem of organized society is that of the use and abuse of power: how may men best prevent its abuse and direct its use to good ends. I take it as axiomatic that power, by which I mean the will and capacity of men to ensure the obedience of other men,[1] is neither good nor bad in itself, but only according to the ends which it serves[2]—a point worth stressing; for there are some who regard power as an unmitigated evil in the affairs of men, and set it in stark contrast to good government under the rule of law. But this, I think, is a sentimental and shallow view. Dante had clearer insight: after stating the great medieval doctrine that the authority of the ruler rests ultimately upon law, he added that a ruler must nevertheless be armed with power, 'for law does not extend beyond power'.[3] Law without power, in Ihering's phrase, 'is a lamp that does not burn'.[4]

As I do not believe in the unchristian doctrine of the perfectibility of human nature, I also take it for granted that as long as men remain men, there can be no complete assurance or guarantee against the abuse of power. It is possible, however, and also supremely important, to try to tame power so that its exercise shall not be capricious, but principled, and directed to the achievement of 'the good society' in an orderly way. What is meant by these ideals, and how to achieve them, are, of course, among the perennial problems of political theory and government.

In the modern world, however, the problem of power has become particularly urgent. Thus to quote a distinguished American historian, Professor C. H. McIlwain:

> The one great issue that overshadows all others in the distracted world of today is the issue between constitutionalism and arbitrary

---

[1] See, generally, B. de Jouvenel, *Power*, London, 1952, Ch. 1, 'The Metaphysics of Power'.

[2] Radcliffe, *The Problem of Power*, London, 1952, Ch. VI.

[3] *De Monarchia*, quoted by Sayers in her introduction to the Penguin edition of *The Divine Comedy*, Hell, p. 45.

[4] *Law as a Means to an End*, Husik's translation, p. 241.

government. The most fundamental difference is not between capitalism and socialism. . . . Deeper than the problem whether we shall have a capitalistic system or some other . . . lies the question whether we shall be ruled by law at all, or only by arbitrary will.

And again:

Never in its long history has the principle of constitutionalism been so questioned as it is being questioned today, never has the attack upon it been so determined or so threatening as it is now. The world is trembling in the balance between the ordinary procedure of law and the processes of force which seem so much more quick and effective. Never in recorded history, I believe, has the individual been in greater danger from government than now.

The first quotation is from an essay written three years before the outbreak of Hitler's War;[5] the second from a book written after Hitler's defeat.[6] Since then the urgency of the problem has increased rather than abated.

Power, as such, may be considered from several points of view: its origins and the various forms it assumes, its historical development, its purposes, and its credit or moral claim to obedience, as well as the possible methods of taming it. It is plain, moreover, that each of these various aspects of power are interrelated. Thus to know about what de Jouvenel calls the structure of power, that is to say how it operates, is essential for its effective control.

To illustrate: it is an historically observable fact that in most societies the power of rulers is maintained partly by the view which men take of the means and efficacy of physical compulsion at the rulers' disposal, that is to say, by fear; partly by habit and indolence, or the disposition of human beings to let someone else do what it would give them trouble to do for themselves; partly by the hope of benefit; but also, and perhaps primarily, by belief in the justness and legitimacy of the rulers' authority and conduct.[7] Government, being a human institution and not a mere physical phenomenon, is deeply influenced by the ideas men have of it. Indeed, to the extent that men expect their rulers to conform to certain standards of right and wrong, the power of a government which has become tyrannical— relying on brute force—is in actual fact enormously weakened. As we shall see more fully later, there are definite limits imposed by law

---

[5] 'Government by Law', Foreign Affairs, 1936, reprinted in *Constitutionalism and the Changing World*, 1939, p. 267. To the same effect, MacIver, *Leviathan and the People*, 1940, p. 39.

[6] *Constitutionalism, Ancient and Modern*, 1947, p. 1.

[7] In this enumeration I have supplemented de Jouvenel's analysis (*Power*, p. 33) with Bryce's earlier analysis contained in his essay on Obedience, *Studies in History and Jurisprudence*, vol. 2, pp. 6 sqq.

and morals to the claims which power may make upon men's obedience. And it is, of course, for this very reason that usurpers and tyrants have throughout history attempted to cloak their acts with the appearance of legality.

Again, a study of the origins of power may throw light upon the hopes which men have of its beneficence. This is an aspect of particular relevance in primitive societies. Frazer, for example, in his work on primitive societies, was of the opinion that all 'kingship' arose, and could only arise, on a basis of magical power; the royal road to political rule being an understanding of the occult powers and a capacity to control them. People, he considered, gave their obedience to particular rulers on the ground that they were best able to propitiate the gods or increase fertility, and so on. Though it would seem that Frazer's belief in the exclusively magical origin of authority is exaggerated,[8] to the extent that such beliefs are in fact held in a particular community, it is important to those who seek to tame power to be aware of the fact; for power resting on such foundations may be tamed in some measure (though perhaps not completely) by education, coupled wherever possible with a demonstration that the particular belief is false, and the substitution of a more compelling belief. Cortes, for example, threw down the idols on the Island of Columel to prove to the Indians that he could defy their gods with impunity.

But although these various aspects of power are all relevant to the problem of taming it, I mention them primarily in order to define my objectives in this book a little more closely. It is clear from what has been said that there are many techniques which help in the taming of power, ranging from the transfer of loyalty from one chief to another in a tribal society to the judicial enforcement of a Bill of Rights in a modern democracy. If, however, we are to deal with the subject in any detail, and at any depth, it is necessary to be selective.

I propose therefore to deal fully with two methods of taming power which I believe are particularly relevant to the problems now bedevilling Africa. I refer to: (i) the entrenchment and judicial enforcement of a Bill of Rights in a rigid constitution; and (ii) federalism. The former is a method which depends for its success on putting effective legal checks upon power. The latter technique also seeks to place legal restraints upon power, but it goes further by dividing it, and seeks to tame power by balancing one part against another.

The reason for my choice of subject-matter is not far to seek. We may, I think, accept it as almost axiomatic that if any new

[8] De Jouvenel, *Power*, p. 70.

dispensation in Southern Africa, for example, is to be workable, it will have to be acceptable to the bulk of the inhabitants of the country, both white and non-white. And, as I see it, to be so acceptable, it will have to conform to the criteria of a democratically organized society—for it is hardly necessary to emphasize the enormous prestige of democracy, not only among the nations of the free world, but especially among politically aware Africans throughout the continent.

Compliance with the criteria of a true democracy, however, presents everywhere and at all times a most formidable challenge. As Lord Acton once observed: 'The one pervading evil of democracy is the tyranny of the majority, or rather of that party, not always the majority, that succeeds by force or fraud in carrying elections.'[9] Nor can there be any doubt that to comply with the criteria of a true democracy will be the hardest test for those who would build a common society for whites and non-whites in Southern Africa. Indeed it is fair to say that fear of the risks of democracy, and especially fear of universal adult suffrage, are among the most powerful obstacles now standing in the way of any policy which could genuinely lead to the building of such a society.

If this challenge of democracy is accepted, then it is logical to focus attention upon constitutional guarantees of human rights and federalism. For if any one experiment in taming power, more than another, has been greatly justified by its works, it is the entrenchment in a written constitution of fundamental human rights, so that they may be placed beyond the reach of executive decisions and legislative majorities, and entrusted to the protection of the ordinary courts. In 1835 Alexis de Tocqueville described this experiment as 'one of the most powerful barriers that has ever been devised against the tyranny of political assemblies'.[10] And in the Reith lectures for 1952 we find Lord Radcliffe still praising the institution in almost the same words.[11]

And, in regard to federalism, a great modern student of the subject has said: 'One of the most urgent problems in the world today is to preserve diversities . . . and at the same time to introduce such a measure of uniformity as will prevent clashes and facilitate co-operation. Federalism is one way of reconciling these two ends.'[12] The relevance of this in contemporary Africa needs no emphasis.

However, before dealing with the various problems involved in establishing, entrenching and enforcing a Bill of Rights, and before

---

[9] *History of Freedom*, p. 87.
[10] *Democracy in America*, Reeve-Bradley text, Vintage Books, vol. 1, p. 107.
[11] Radcliffe, *The Problem of Power*, Secker and Warburg, London, 1952, p. 62.
[12] K. C. Wheare, *Federal Government*, 3rd ed., pp. 259–60.

discussing the idea of federalism, it is necessary first to have a clear view of the nature of democracy, and to be fully aware of the standards which it exacts.

DEMOCRACY AND GOOD GOVERNMENT

The term democracy is notoriously ambiguous. Both the United States and Soviet Russia claim to be democracies—and in South Africa frequent references are made, apparently with a straight face (though hardly ever by non-whites), to 'our existing democratic constitution'. Whether this is an illustration of the truth observed by Thucydides that words tend to lose their meaning in times of total conflict,[13] is an interesting speculation which need not detain us. Plainly what is needed is some preliminary definition. Indeed, as MacIver observes:

> in this age of ours, when the form of government has become the most momentous of the issues that divide men and nations, we have peculiar need for clear-thinking about democracy. If we defend it we should do so without misunderstanding what it is; if we attack it we should know what we attack.[14]

To begin with, it is necessary to distinguish between democracy in what might be termed the substantive sense of the word, and democracy in the procedural sense. From the substantive point of view, the word refers to certain essential principles and ideals of government; while procedurally it refers to the machinery whereby the basic principles may be implemented.

There is no fixed pattern for the procedural machinery of democracy: the question, for example, whether the legislature should be organized unicamerally or bicamerally; the relation between the executive and the legislature; the tenure and function of the judges; the use, if any, to be made of the federal principle; the organization of local government—all these are matters of machinery which can and do vary among democracies. There is, in fact, room for great flexibility, subject always to one overriding consideration: if a democracy is to be genuine, it must use procedural machinery which is compatible with its substantive and underlying principles.

Not all writers on democracy draw the line between substance and procedure in precisely the same way. But there is agreement on the validity and usefulness of the distinction; and there is substantial agreement, too, as to what subjects fall respectively within these two categories.

It is necessary, however, to define the substantive aspect of democracy a little more closely, because, even from the substantive

---

[13] *History of the Peloponnesian War*, Bk. III, ch. 10.
[14] *Leviathan and the People*, p. 86.

point of view, the word democracy is ambiguous. Thus, it is used to designate (*a*) a philosophy of government—a particular theory about the relationship between man and the state; and it is also used to describe (*b*) a particular method of government, more especially a method of reaching group decisions by a majority vote.[15] It is important for our purposes to examine each of these aspects in some detail.

A PHILOSOPHY OF GOVERNMENT

We hear a great deal nowadays of the battle of ideas going on in Africa. Are the principles of government which prevail in well-established democracies like Britain and the United States of America acceptable in African communities? Does Russia have more to offer? Do the African states wish to develop something different of their own in the theory and art of government?

Perhaps a first step towards answering these questions is to attempt a summary of what are generally understood to be the basic principles of democratic government in terms of 'western' culture. I would venture to say that at the heart of the matter there are two cardinal ideas, each of which has several facets. These are:

(1) a particular conception of man and his relationship to organized society, which is often expressed in the phrase 'the primacy of individual human worth';

(2) acceptance and recognition of the variety and complexity of social life.

As a philosophy of government democracy asserts, in the first place, the supreme worth, dignity and creative capacity of every individual human being. It presupposes that every normal man possesses a rational intelligence, a free will, and responsibility for his actions. And it insists that all organizations and, in particular, the state exist to enable men to fulfil their nature as men. This does not mean the isolation of individuals, nor does it mean anarchy; for, as Aristotle demonstrated long ago, a man can only be himself in society, and society cannot exist without rules and obligations. It does mean, however, that there is all the difference in the world between a state which lays down rules for the sake of encouraging the free life of its members, and a state which regiments its members for the sake of the state itself or its power.[16] We shall have occasion

---

[15] See, generally, A. D. Lindsay, *The Modern Democratic State*, 1943, pp. 230 sqq.; Carl Becker, *Modern Democracy*, Yale University Press, 1941; Sidgwick, *The Elements of Politics*, 1897, pp. 615 sqq.; Bassett, *Essentials of Parliamentary Democracy*, 1937, ch. 4; R.L. Calhoun, 'Democracy and the Natural Law' in (1960) *Natural Law Forum* 30 sqq.

[16] Maritain, *Man and the State*, Chicago, 1951; Lindsay, *I Believe in Democracy*, 1940, p. 13; Calhoun in (1960) *Natural Law Forum* 31 sqq.; Bassett, op. cit., p. 108.

to develop this more fully when, presently, we consider democracy as a method of government.

In the second place, it is an observable fact that man enters into relations with his fellow beings at many levels; families, churches, town councils, sports associations, clubs, universities, etc. It seems to be a law of his being to join many groups, none of which, however, not even the state, exhausts the social needs and possibilities of his nature. St. Thomas brings this out in a passage in which he emphasizes that *'homo non ordinatur ad communitatem politicam secundum se totum, et secundum omnia sua . . .'.*[17] And a modern Thomist has said equally clearly: 'The development of the human person normally requires a plurality of autonomous communities, having their own rights, their own freedoms and their own authorities.'[18] It is the business of government in a healthy democratic society to allow for this variety and complexity of social life. Totalitarian regimes, however, seem unable to endure such richness. They tend to suppress all forms of group life other than the state's or, alternatively, to absorb them as mere organs or agencies of the state, reflecting state policy. A true democracy, on the other hand, must embody an explicit and effective distinction between the state and the various aspects of community life.

The importance of recognizing the variety and diversity of social life may perhaps be illustrated in another way. Wherever groups of human beings are found, whether they be the family, a trade union, a club or a state, men are drawn into them because of the promise of some benefit. There exists some 'good' sought in common which unites men to remain in the association, and which determines the rights and obligations of both the members as a whole and the governing authority. Totalitarian states, however, adhere to a monolithic or monistic concept of the common good, and seek to realize it through the state's activity. The state then absorbs the common good of families, professional associations, municipal councils and so on, with the result that these groups lose their own individual character and become cogs in one vast machine. On the other hand, it is part of what I understand to be distinctively 'western' or, as I prefer to say, sane thought that no political association, no matter how grand it may be, in itself exhausts all the legitimate potentialities of human nature. In other words, there is not just one common good, but many; namely, the benefits which men seek within the state, within their church, within their universities and so on.

[17] Quoted by D'Entreves, *Medieval Political Thought*, New York, 1959, p. 29.
[18] Maritain, *The Rights of Man and the Natural Law*, New York, 1951, pp. 20–21.

Recognition of this fact involves the principle that all human associations should play what may be described as a supplementary role—a principle which may be explained as follows. With respect to both individuals and groups, every association should be satisfied to exercise a supplementary function, in the sense that it should abstain from doing in their stead what they are capable of doing for themselves.

This principle has far-reaching consequences concerning the relationship between man and the state. As regards individuals, it means that the state should not relieve men of responsibilities which are properly theirs. Though there are many services which the state should undertake for men, it fails as a democratic state if it does not create the conditions which permit its members to act freely within the law *for themselves*. Indeed a state which purports to be a universal provider actually wrongs men by treating them contrary to their nature; for a man's first duty is to fulfil his nature by assuming the responsibilities which are his.[19] 'If every action', said Milton, 'which is good or evil in men at ripe years were to be under pittance, prescription and compulsion, what were virtue but a name—what praise could be then due to well-being, what gramercy to be sober, just or continent.'[20]

Once the state's claim to be a universal provider is acknowledged or encouraged, it is difficult to resist a further claim to regiment men. But quite apart from the moral grounds to which we have already referred, there is a very practical reason why individual men should, as far as possible, be left to work out their own destiny free from state control and interference. It is this: men are fallible, and no man or group of men are good enough to be entrusted with absolute power over other men. Indeed the fallibility of man, is, if I have understood it aright, the essence of Socrates' refutation of Thrasymachus in Book 1 of the Republic; it was the core of Cromwell's appeal to the Scots on the eve of the Battle of Dunbar—'In the bowels of Christ I beseech thee, consider that ye may be wrong'; it is, according to many, the best justification for reversible democratic government;[21] it was the ground on which, basically, Milton rested his plea for freedom of the press; and it lies at the heart of Professor Hayek's recent defence of the philosophy of liberalism.[22]

[19] This is elaborated in a scholarly manner in the *Report of the Royal Commission of Enquiry on Constitutional Problems*, Quebec, 1956, vol. 2, p. 119. In writing this section I have derived great assistance from that Report.
[20] *Areopagitica*.
[21] See especially C. S. Lewis, *Transpositions and Other Addresses*, 1949, p. 39.
[22] *The Constitution of Liberty*, London, 1960.

The principle of the supplementary nature of associations also has important consequences in regard to the position of groups and associations within the state. In order to conserve the diversity and complexity of social life, the right of smaller groups to exist and to function must be recognized. Pope Pius XI stressed this in an encyclical letter when he said:

> Just as it is wrong to withdraw from the individual and commit to the community at large what private industry and enterprise can accomplish, so too it is an injustice, a grave evil and a disturbance of right order for larger and higher organizations to arrogate to themselves functions which can be performed efficiently by smaller and lower bodies. Of its very nature the true aim of all social activity should be to help individual members of the social body, but never to destroy or absorb them.[23]

In short, democracy involves a balance between pluralism and unity in regard to governmental initiative and control.[24]

And here we may pause to observe that in affirming these fundamental principles to be characteristics of democratic government, we are in fact giving our allegiance to principles of sane government and ideals in regard to the relationship between man and the state, which have been accepted by a succession of philosophers from Aristotle to St. Augustine, through the Middle Ages, to the present day. Judged by these standards totalitarian systems have no claim to the title of democracy.

It is perhaps the distinctive merit of the principles which I have outlined that they deny none of the works of man, and allow full scope for the flowering of small communities. There is 'more perfection in a whole whose parts are full of life and initiative, than in a whole whose parts merely reflect the initiative of a superior organisation'.[25] Bertrand de Jouvenel explained this in a memorable way when he said:

> The big state is a bad thing in itself. It becomes all the more blind to individual realities as its size increases. It becomes more inhuman, more geometric, more automatic. It cannot recognise individuals and their size, but only their classified files. If in a small state there may be injustice through favour consisting in the unequal treatment of similar cases, the big state presents another form of injustice—injustice through classification, and consisting in treating unequal cases in a uniform way. The Greeks believed that the dignity of the individual only finds assurance in a small state where each may make himself heard and where each is taken into consideration. 'The empire', said the Greeks,

[23] Quoted in the *Report of the Royal Commission*, Quebec, vol. 2, p. 119.
[24] R. L. Calhoun, op. cit.
[25] Yves Simon, quoted in the *Report of the Royal Commission*, Quebec, p. 119.

'is the work of barbarians, as the city is the work of civilized men.'

When governments use symbols for individuals or groups, as they must in big centralized societies and their planning, we have reached the stage where we are in danger of substituting political algebra for political humanism.

A METHOD OF GOVERNMENT

As a method of government, democracy rests on the assumption that the just powers and authority of those who govern derive from the active consent of those who are governed,[26] and, from this point of view, it is concerned with the technique for ascertaining that consent. The democratic method of government is, however, far more complex than might at first sight appear and it requires close analysis. Three major problems are involved.

First, there is general agreement that democracy presupposes that from time to time the people will be given the opportunity to control the government. Democratic government is, in short, reversible government. 'A form of majority rule which entrenches itself against the processes and tides of free opinion that could reduce it again to a minority; that silences all opposition and censors all contrary opinion is emphatically not to be named a democracy.'[27] In a true democracy the citizens learn to rule and be ruled by turns, they learn both to command and obey.[28]

But although it is agreed that democratic government must rest on the consent of, and may be controlled by, the governed, there is considerable difference of opinion as to how this objective may best be achieved. The essence of the matter is to determine *who* among the people shall have a say in controlling the government—the problem of the franchise; and further (in all states which are too big for regular and direct popular participation in government) to determine *the manner* in which those who have the vote shall choose their representatives (whether for example, by majority vote in single member constituencies, or by proportional representation, and so on)—the problem of electoral organization.

Secondly, it is necessary to determine how group decisions shall be reached; are they to be reached by an ordinary majority or in some other way—part of the problem of majority rule.

And thirdly, and most important of all, there must be clarity as to the conditions, if any, which must be observed in order that group decisions (whether reached by an ordinary majority or in

---

[26] Becker, op. cit.; Sidgwick, op. cit., p. 610.
[27] MacIver, *Leviathan and the People*, pp. 66–7.
[28] Calhoun, op. cit.

some other way) may claim validity; there must be clarity as to whether there are any limits to the authority of such decisions. This is the problem of constitutional government, or government under law.

These are topics which test statesmanship the world over. They are, moreover, precisely the topics which require most attention in working out a democratic alternative to apartheid.

THE FRANCHISE

Few problems of democracy have raised more controversy than those of determining (*a*) who among the people shall have a say in controlling the government; and (*b*) the manner in which those who have the vote shall choose their representatives (whether, for example, by majority vote in single-member constituencies, or by proportional representation, and so on). The former problem—the problem of the franchise—is logically the prior one, and will be dealt with in this chapter. The latter problem, that of electoral organization or system, will be considered in a subsequent chapter.[29]

On the question of the franchise, there are, on the one hand, the protagonists of universal adult franchise; and on the other, those who would qualify the right to vote and restrict it to certain classes of persons. It is not surprising that controversy on this subject should be intense; because, fundamentally, we are concerned here with an argument for or against the acceptance of democracy itself.

The franchise is, in fact, the very cornerstone of democracy. As stated by a former Attorney-General of the United States, 'it is the one right, perhaps more than any other, upon which all other constitutional rights depend for their effective protection'.[30] And again, 'it is a fundamental right of all people in a democracy. Every other constitutional right depends upon it. Without this, we have only an illusion of true democracy; history has shown us that when this basic right is abrogated democracy and freedom fail.'[31]

During the last century discerning writers on government, from de Tocqueville to Bryce, observed that the movement towards universal suffrage was in the natural order of development the world over.[32] Events have proved them right. In 1948 the principle of universal suffrage was firmly proclaimed in the Declaration of Human Rights adopted by the General Assembly of the United Nations. Article 21 of that Declaration lays down, *inter alia*, that:

[29] Chapter 8.

[30] Quoted in the *Report of the United States Commission on Civil Rights*, 1959, p. 19.

[31] Loc. cit.

[32] De Tocqueville, *Democracy in America*, Vintage Books, vol. 1, p. 59; Bryce, *Studies in Contemporary Biography*, p. 310.

(1) Everyone has the right to take part in the government of his country, directly or through freely chosen representatives.

(2) The will of the people shall be the basis of the authority of government; this will shall be expressed in periodic and genuine elections which shall be by universal and equal suffrage and shall be held by secret vote or by equivalent free voting procedures.

That these sentences reflect the considered opinion of almost the entire democratic world, there can be no doubt. Their applicability has, however, been questioned in communities comprising different races, and especially in South Africa. It is in such communities that the case for a restricted or qualified franchise finds its most determined supporters, especially among privileged groups. And if this conflict of opinion is to be resolved intelligently, it is plainly necessary that we should be clear about the grounds upon which the claims for universal adult suffrage, and for a restricted franchise, respectively rest.

THE CASE FOR UNIVERSAL ADULT SUFFRAGE

The case for universal adult suffrage has been argued on a wide variety of grounds which tend, on the whole, to emphasize the individual interest of each member of the community. And as the arguments for and against are not often brought together, it may be useful if I summarize.

The shoe-pinching argument

One of the strongest arguments in favour of universal adult suffrage is what Lord Lindsay called the 'shoe-pinching' argument. Thus: as it is the business of democratic government to promote the free life of *all* men, *all* men should, in principle, have their say as to how the work of government is promoting or hindering their interests. It is the individual affected by government who alone knows where the shoe pinches; and therefore—the argument runs—every individual affected ought to be free to ask for another shoe-maker when his feet have been pinched, even if he may not himself know how to make governmental shoes.[33]

It will be noted that on this basis educational and property qualifications are quite irrelevant. On this basis the qualification for the franchise is not wisdom or 'civilization', or 'responsibility', or 'sophistication' or 'skill', but simply and solely capacity to state grievances.[34] And on this basis the exponents of universal adult suffrage quite consistently exclude lunatics; and contend that the

[33] Lindsay, *The Modern Democratic State*, pp. 269–70.
[34] Lindsay, loc. cit.

age of majority is a convenient age to choose as a measure of ability to state grievances.

The requirements of justice
Another forceful line of argument rests the case for adult suffrage on the proposition that:

> it is a personal injustice to withhold from anyone, unless for the prevention of greater evils, the ordinary privilege of having his voice reckoned in the disposal of affairs in which he has the same interest as other people. If he is compelled to pay, if he may be compelled to fight, if he is required implicitly to obey, he should be legally entitled to have his consent asked, and his opinion counted at its worth, though not at more than its worth. There ought to be no pariahs in a full-grown and civilized nation; no persons disqualified, except through their own default.[35]

Jeremy Bentham, arguing on the same side, contended that if a man claimed the suffrage for any one human being but refused it to another, it lay upon him to justify the refusal.[36] He recognized the justice of disqualifying minors on the ground that 'a person who is not yet competent to manage his own affairs cannot have reason to complain of being debarred from interfering in the management of the affairs of others'. And he was also prepared to disqualify lunatics and convicted criminals.

In addition, there are two other aspects of the argument based on justice; and they are very compelling. In the first place it has been strongly urged that the suffrage is necessary for the development of individual character, a condition necessary for the recognition and realization of the worth of human personality. And it is urged that if this right is denied, the freedom of the individual to develop his nature is trammelled.[37]

Again, it is argued that the individual worth of a man, his title to be called 'civilized' or 'responsible', is not dependent upon either wealth or formal school education. This is a point to which we shall return presently.

There can be no doubt that these arguments have in the past had great influence, and that among Africans they have irresistible appeal all over the continent today. Every African who has studied the subject, and who favours universal suffrage, feels that to deny the vote to an adult person is an infringement of human dignity, or to use Mill's stronger language, a relegation to the status of a pariah.

---

[35] The quotation is from J. S. Mill, *Representative Government*, Everyman's ed., p. 279; though, as we shall see presently, he himself insisted on certain minimal educational and property qualifications.

[36] Bentham, *Constitutional Code*, Works, Bowring ed., vol. IX, p. 107.

[37] *Encyclopaedia of the Social Sciences*, vol. 14, s.v. Suffrage, p. 446.

Argument based on equality

Again, there are protagonists of universal adult suffrage who contend that it must necessarily be accepted as part of the democratic faith on the ground that equality is a fundamental principle of democracy.[38] Based as it is on the proposition that 'any honest citizen is, on the average, as well qualified as another to choose the government', this is probably the most controversial of the arguments in favour of universal suffrage.

However, there is more to this argument than meets the superficial eye. The illiterate peasant, poor and uneducated, is often far shrewder, far less prone to 'demagogery' than many a 'sophisticated' city dweller. Peasant bodies have resisted the blandishments of oratory, and the appeal to passion; just as highly educated bodies of university and professional men have made decisions on the most irrational grounds, or on no grounds at all—often swayed by a chance appeal to emotion or self-interest. Nor will it be forgotten that millions of educated Germans once voted for Hitler and his doctrines; and that, for the most part, those Germans were not intimidated; on the contrary, they acted with wild enthusiasm.

Natural right

And, finally, there are some who support universal adult suffrage on the ground that every person has a 'natural right' to vote, deriving from the very fact of adult humanity. This is, however, an ambiguous statement which requires clarification.

To the extent that it implies each or any of the three arguments in favour of adult suffrage which we have already considered, it has all the force which belongs to them.

To the extent, however, that it purports to carry the matter further, it suggests, in Mr. C. S. Lewis's words, that 'all men are so good that they deserve a share in the government and so wise that the commonwealth needs their advice'. But this, he submits, is a false and romantic view of democracy.[39] The claim to a 'natural right' to vote was, of course, the claim of the theorists of the French Revolution who believed in the inherent goodness of man, without Grace— the noble savage. Thus, Condorcet declared: 'We would have a constitution the principles of which are solely founded on the natural rights of man previous to social institutions. One of these rights we consider to be that of voting for common interests.'[40]

[38] See Appadorai, *The Substance of Politics*, Oxford, 1952, p. 466.
[39] *Transpositions and other Essays*, 1949, pp. 39–40. And to the same effect, Sir Lewis Namier, *Conflicts*, 1942, p. 195.
[40] Quoted by W. J. Shepard in *The Encyclopaedia of the Social Sciences*, vol. 14, p. 448, s.v. Suffrage.

THE CASE FOR A QUALIFIED FRANCHISE

The adversaries of universal adult suffrage start with the contention that the vote should not be regarded solely from the individual's point of view and as a right. On the contrary, they argue that the vote should be regarded also, and perhaps primarily, as a public trust. More fully, they argue that voting is merely one of the procedural problems of democracy, similar to the problem of organizing the legislature into one Chamber or two, or of selecting the Judiciary.[41]

The first point to note is that if this view is accepted, 'the problem of who shall vote' becomes in the words of Prof. W. J. Shepard, 'one of mere political expediency'.[42]

The second and more important point, however, is to determine the grounds upon which expediency should be judged. In broad terms, those who adopt the approach of expediency claim that the state is entitled to determine the qualifications for the franchise so as 'to ensure the general welfare', and avoid what Sidgwick called 'a dangerously bad use of the vote'.[43] They deny the equal fitness of adults to exercise the suffrage; and claim, moreover, that the doctrine of human equality, properly understood, does not conflict with their views, on the ground that the doctrine does not assert uniformity of human capacity, but rather the duty of the state to respect the common humanity of all its members.[44] Whether or not the state is in fact likely to respect 'the common humanity' of its unenfranchised members is, of course, another matter.

Moreover, when it comes to the fixing of qualifications which will prevent 'a dangerously bad use of the vote', doubt and confusion become rampant, as may be seen from the nature of the controversy on the subject in Southern Africa.

IS SOUTHERN AFRICA A SPECIAL CASE?

With those who regard 'whiteness' as the decisive qualification for the exercise of the franchise I have nothing in common.

There are, however, those who would like to move in the direction of creating a common society in which non-whites have their say in the government. But acting on the assumption that a peaceful change can be brought about only by an appeal to the existing electorate, they feel that one should not attempt to go too far too

---

[41] Cf. *Encyclopaedia of the Social Sciences*, loc. cit., p. 449.

[42] Loc. cit., p. 449.

[43] See generally, Sidgwick, *Elements of Politics*, p. 379; Maine, *Popular Government*, pp. 34 sqq.; Lecky, *Democracy and Liberty*, 1896, vol. 1, ch. 1.

[44] On the difficult concept of 'human equality', see Lindsay, *The Modern Democratic State*, 1943, ch. XI; and Maritain, *Redeeming the Time*, 1944, pp. 1 sqq.

soon, and thereby scare this electorate. This is a party political decision based primarily on an assessment of vote-catching possibilities and on a desire to ease non-whites into an existing political framework without dislocating it too much—without rocking the boat.

It is, however, very doubtful whether this 'don't scare the electorate' approach is likely to delude anybody. More than 100 years ago Alexis de Tocqueville concluded that 'the further electoral rights are extended, the greater is the need for extending them; for after each concession the strength of the democracy increases, and its demands increase with its strength . . . and no stop can be made short of universal suffrage'.[45] Needless to say, the upholders of apartheid argue on the same lines; nor, indeed, for the racialist is there much comfort in being told that if and when adult suffrage should ever come about, all the electorate will have achieved a junior school education; for with their own logic, or rather lack of it, upholders of apartheid, and other racialists, will contend that 'they have no more enthusiasm for their daughters to marry educated black men than they have for them to marry illiterate black men'. It does not help with this kind of voter to explain that there is no necessary connection between the franchise and marriage.

At a more sophisticated level of argument, the opponents of universal adult suffrage in Southern Africa contend that the system can work only where the electorate is homogeneous and has reached a fairly high common standard of civilization or responsibility. Reasoning along these lines has, of course, been stressed repeatedly in recent years in African territories which are reluctant to extend the vote to the non-whites on a basis that would give them a majority voice—at any rate at an early date.

In 1957 a Franchise Commission in Southern Rhodesia (the Tredgold Commission) investigated the matter and reached the conclusion that:

> It may be accepted that the ideal system for the government of a people is democracy based upon a universal suffrage, but . . . to operate satisfactorily it requires a homogeneous electorate, at a fairly high standard of civilization . . . and not confused by differences, such as race or colour, that tend to create artificial divisions cutting across the real issues. In a young country with a mixed population, at vastly different stages of development, it has yet to be proved that such a democracy can survive, and an objective approach to this possibility suggests grave doubts.[46]

A similar conclusion was reached by the South African Progressive Party's Franchise Commission, which considered that the demand

[45] *Democracy in America*, Vintage Books, vol. 1, p. 59.
[46] *The Tredgold Report*, pp. 2–3.

for adult suffrage among Africans was inspired, in part, by a spirit of nationalism and a desire to dominate. And 'on this basis', said the Commission, 'the Nationalist Party are right in seeking white self-preservation along the lines of dominance, or apartheid, or a combination of the two'.[47]

If this latter quotation reflects a correct analysis of the situation, then one may doubt whether there is any hope at all for building a common society in South Africa. However, for reasons which I have stated in an earlier chapter, I do not believe that basically non-whites in South Africa desire the vote to dominate or victimize whites. They desire the vote in order to live together, man for man, on terms of equal opportunity with the whites, in a community where skin-colour is irrelevant. Nor, certainly, do I believe that apartheid or white domination are preferable alternatives to adult suffrage.

Turning now to the main argument put forward by the supporters of a qualified franchise, we have seen that they contend that a parliamentary democracy can only work well when there exists a 'civilized' or 'responsible' electorate. What is meant by this? The explanation put forward in the majority report of the Progressive Party's Franchise Commission, is that the test of civilization for this purpose should be so devised as:

> to embrace those elements of the population that have attained an economic level or a degree of sophistication so as to enable them to feel sufficient identification with society as a whole—to possess sufficient stake in the country—not to fall prey to totalitarian illusions.[48]

Only in this way, it is argued, will one produce a stable and 'effective' democracy.

The first and most obvious comment that suggests itself is that the conditions of political instability are by no means removed 'by creaming off the educationally and economically more advanced' elements in the population.[49] On the contrary, it is almost a political truism that as long as there are large unenfranchised classes in a community there can be no stability.

Secondly, it is difficult to understand what is meant by the proposition that property qualifications or education give 'a feeling of identification with society as a whole'. Indeed Sir John Maud is more likely to be correct when he says:

> There are few occasions in history when a privileged section of any community has succeeded even in knowing what are the

[47] *The Molteno Report*, p. 15.
[48] Report, p. 13.
[49] A point made by Dr. S. Cooppan in one of the Minority Reports, op. cit., p. 33.

needs and just demands of the underprivileged, still less in satisfying them. Certainly it would be difficult to name a city in any part of the world in which the governing class has either known or done what justice demanded for the poorer and more needy sections of the community, so long as those sections have had no effective say in the government of the city.[50]

And, of course, as pointed out by Dr. Cooppan, what Sir John Maud had to say of city government is equally applicable to national government.[51]

Thirdly, it is invariably conceded that the application of any 'civilization' or 'responsibility' test resolves itself into an assessment of suitable property and educational qualifications—on which there is wide room for difference of opinion. Let us then briefly examine the relevance, if any, of property and educational qualifications.

Property qualifications

The foundation of property qualifications was the legal principle, until recently firmly established in English law, that the vote was an adjunct or incident of feudal status.[52]

J. S. Mill attempted to give this requirement a theoretically defensible foundation for modern representative government, by insisting that the payment of taxes was a necessary condition for the vote. Otherwise, he felt, it amounted to allowing people 'to put their hands into other people's pockets for any purpose which they think fit to call a public one'.[53] In order, however, to reconcile this condition with the desirability of universal suffrage, he insisted that some form of 'taxation in a visible shape should descend to the *poorest* classes'. And he suggested, therefore, that a small annual payment in the form of a capitation tax would suffice.[54]

In practice the limitation of the franchise to property-owners, or the economically advanced, proved to be 'disastrous to those who did not own property'.[55] And today property and income qualifications for the vote have been abandoned by almost the entire world. Indeed, as observed by Professor MacIver, the modern state has been advancing towards the ideal that 'personality *and not property* is the true basis of representation'.[56]

[50] *City Government*, pp. 209–10. To the same effect, J. S. Mill, *Representative Government*, Everyman edition, pp. 279–80.

[51] *Molteno Report*, p. 34.

[52] W. S. Shepard in *Encyclopaedia of the Social Sciences*, loc. cit., pp. 447–8.

[53] *Representative Government*, p. 281.

[54] Op. cit., pp. 281–2.

[55] H. J. Laski, *A Grammar of Politics*, p. 117.

[56] *The Modern State*, p. 144. My italics.

Education

J. S. Mill, who is probably the most distinguished protagonist of the idea that 'universal teaching must precede universal franchise',[57] set the requisite educational standard at a bare minimum. 'I regard it as wholly inadmissible', he said, 'that any person should participate in the suffrage without being able to read, write, and, I will add, perform the common operations of arithmetic.'[58] Theoretically, he felt that other kinds of knowledge were desirable as well, but he would not recommend them on the ground that 'there does not exist any trustworthy machinery for ascertaining whether they have been acquired or not'.[59]

Laski was more scathing. 'An historian', he said, 'whose expertness in the dissection of an early charter may be exquisite, may lack completely a sense of evidence when it is a question of deciding the merits of a tariff reform.'[60]

In the result, it seems difficult to resist Laski's conclusion that 'no test has been devised which enables us to limit the franchise in such a fashion as to equate civic virtue with its possession'.[61]

SUMMING-UP ON THE FRANCHISE

On a review of the theoretical considerations which I have outlined, I personally have no doubt that the supporters of universal adult suffrage have the better case. Nor, granted the kind of constitution which I shall elaborate in subsequent chapters, would I personally hesitate to see its early introduction in South Africa.

But from the point of view of strategy for integration, and solely in a spirit of compromise, it might be wise to accept certain qualifications, *on an interim basis*, in order to facilitate the eventual introduction of universal suffrage. Indeed, in the South African context, the sound conclusion might be that stated by the American jurist, Story:

The truth seems to be that the right of voting, like many other rights, is one which—whether it has a fixed foundation in natural law or not—has always been treated in the practice of nations as a strictly civil right, derived from and regulated by each society according to its own circumstances and interests. . . . The question is not susceptible of any simple solution which shall rigidly apply to the circumstances and conditions, the interests and the feelings, the institutions and the manners of all nations. What may best promote the public weal in one age or nation may totally fail in other circumstances which are essentially different.[62]

[57] *Representative Government*, p. 280.
[58] Op. cit., p. 280.
[59] Loc. cit., pp. 280–81.
[60] Op. cit., p. 115.
[61] Op. cit., p. 115.
[62] *Commentaries on the Constitution of the United States*, 5th ed., vol. 1, pp. 429–31.

If this is so, then our real problem is to determine what form of franchise is best calculated to foster the growth of non-racial democracy in the actual conditions of South Africa. And on these criteria it is possible, I think, to discern the broad principles which should govern.

The first guiding principle should be to extend the franchise as widely as possible and as rapidly as possible, compatibly with the general welfare; for as long as there are large unenfranchised classes there can be no real constitutional stability. This does not necessarily mean the *immediate* introduction of universal adult suffrage. But it does mean that, if a qualified franchise is adopted, right from the very start the qualifications should be so devised as to ensure that a really substantial number of non-whites are given an effective voice in the government of the country.

While non-whites may be content at the outset to regard universal adult suffrage as a goal to be aimed at, rather than an immediately realizable proposition, it would be quite unrealistic to expect any enthusiasm for a qualified franchise so 'loaded' or timorous that, in its practical operation, it virtually stifles the non-white voice.

In this latter regard it would be difficult to overestimate the importance of numbers, or the percentage of the non-white population to be enfranchised forthwith. Once one has faced up to the truth that 'qualifications' are based on expediency, then one's assessment of expediency should be open-eyed. What the whites may consider to be expedient is not necessarily what the non-whites will so consider. And from the non-white point of view, numbers are likely to be critical. Moreover, should events ever so develop as to allow non-whites to be fairly represented at any National Convention in which this issue is to be freely open to discussion, what the non-white delegates demand will matter no less than what the white delegates are prepared to concede.

However 'non-racial' a franchise may appear on the surface, however equally applicable to whites and non-whites its legal provisions may be, people will look at, and judge it by, its practical effects in operation.

Secondly, wherever possible, one should avoid stereotyping and perpetuating existing racial divisions and thinking. On the contrary, they should be broken down. This is, perhaps, the main reason for rejecting the principle of communal or separate representation whereby the community is divided into separate electorates registered on separate rolls in order that they may vote separately, either for candidates of their own or of any other race. In any event, communal representation has been given several trials—notably in India,

Ceylon and the Union of South Africa—and the results are generally regarded as unsatisfactory.[63]

If it is genuinely desired to break down racial politics and promote truly national representation, then the integration of the electorate on a common (as distinct from communal) roll is the answer. Moreover, within the broad framework of a common roll, there is much room for flexibility; and useful lessons are to be learned from the experience—happy and otherwise—of such countries as Tanganyika, the Federation of Rhodesia and Nyasaland, India and Ceylon.[64]

Thirdly, it is always preferable to have one voters' roll, not two; one class of citizens and their representatives, not a group of first class citizens who are separated from a group of second class or 'sub-responsible' citizens and the representatives whom they contrive to elect (despite their alleged inadequacies). In any event if, as a temporary expedient, there is to be a second roll in addition to an 'ordinary' voters' roll, it should be a roll for *all* those who are not represented, that is to say, it should be established on the basis of universal suffrage. Otherwise, a second roll may look very much like a device for raising the qualifications for the ordinary roll so as still further to reduce the number of non-whites who are given an effective voice in government.

But whatever expedient is adopted, it is, as I see it, essential to accept unequivocally the position that, in a country where the non-whites are in a majority, the day must come—and come fairly soon—when a majority of the electorate will be non-white; free, moreover, if they wish, to choose a government the majority of which is non-white. Any attempt to erect a permanent barrier against this, and to perpetuate the position of the white man as a privileged and dominant electorate, would, I think, be shortsighted, unjust, and, in the last analysis, futile and dangerous.

And this brings me to a final point in regard to the franchise. If the non-whites are progressively to win a voice in the government of the country, it may be essential for white men not only to commit themselves to a policy of gradually admitting more and more

[63] For penetrating and comprehensive discussion of communal representation, see the *Montagu-Chelmsford Report on Indian Constitutional Reform*, 1918, paras. 227–31; the report of the *Donoughmore Commission on the Constitution of Ceylon*, Cmd. 3131; and the *Hilton-Young Report on Eastern and Central Africa*, Cmd. 3234, 1929, p. 207 sqq.

[64] See also generally on the topics of multiple voting, proportional representation, the single transferable vote, and so on, Hoag and Hallett, *Proportional Representation*, 1926; Lakeman and Lambert, *Voting in Democracies*, 1955; *Report of the Indian Franchise Committee*, 1932, Cmd. 4086; *Report of the Southern Rhodesian Franchise Commission*, Salisbury, 1957; Gilchrist, *Principles of Political Science*, 7th ed., ch. XIV.

non-whites to the franchise, but also to envisage a time-schedule for periodic revision and advance. It may, for example, be wise to use the 'reserved seats' technique, in such a way as to allow for the phased but steady extension of representation from a basic minimum for non-whites to a basic minimum for whites, leading ultimately — and the sooner the better — to the entire abolition of reserved seats.

I am very well aware how reluctant people are to envisage a time-schedule; but, as Lincoln once pointed out in a similar context (when he offered 'the South' the chance of a gradual abolition of slavery), a time-schedule would have the advantage of acting as a spur to an immediate and dedicated effort to increase the opportunity for the general economic and educational advancement of non-whites; and so allow as many more as possible to qualify. Moreover, quite apart from acting as a spur to opening opportunities for the economic and educational advancement of non-whites, a time schedule could operate as a wholesome token of bona fides — by no means an unimportant consideration when one remembers the non-whites' previous disillusioning experiences in this field.

Finally, the importance of increasing the non-whites' opportunities for economic advancement requires emphasis. Long ago Disraeli perceived that the extension of the suffrage would not necessarily injure and might end by strengthening the Tory party. Long before the Act of 1867, which further extended the suffrage in England, he discerned that economic and social influence would in parliamentary elections count for more among the masses 'than the traditions of constitutional Whiggism or the dogmas of abstract Radicalism'.[65] In short, not to put too fine an edge on this point, the extension of the suffrage need *not* lead to totalitarianism.

THE MAJORITY PRINCIPLE

If, as we have seen, it is difficult to determine who shall have a voice in controlling the government, the problem of ascertaining how group decisions shall be reached, and what limits, if any, there are to their authority, is no less perplexing.

We are so accustomed to deciding questions by a majority vote that we seldom realize how very remarkable the majority principle is; yet the idea that the majority should represent the whole was once described by Edmund Burke as 'the most violent fiction of law that ever has been or can be made'.[66] Not only is the history of the

---

[65] Bryce, *Studies in Contemporary Biography*, p. 58.
[66] *Appeal from the old to the new Whigs*, Works, 1852, vol. 4, p. 463.

idea complex and in part obscure,[67] but the grounds on which it has been justified are notoriously conflicting.

The earlier and more fundamental principle in most societies requires group decisions to be reached unanimously. Though the majority principle was familiar to both the Greeks and the Romans,[68] only gradually and with difficulty did it come to be recognized throughout Europe. In English law to this day unanimity is required of jury decisions;[69] and in the field of international relations the majority principle is still struggling for recognition.[70] Again, until comparatively recent times, unanimity was required in the Russian Mir, and in the Diet of the Polish Kingdom the *liberum veto* of a single member could prevent the passage of any measure, even though it were approved by all the rest.

Moreover, even as it came to be recognized in the western world that political decisions within a state may validly be reached by a majority vote,[71] the extraordinary variety of reasons that were, and still are, put forward to justify the principle are an indication of its artificiality. These include arguments based on superior force and the ability of the majority to coerce the minority; various post-medieval theories of natural law; theories concerning the social contract; a large number of legal fictions; and, in more recent times, a frank avowal of convenience.

The ability of the majority to coerce the minority by superior force is, of course, the sense of Sir James Stephen's remark: 'We count heads instead of breaking them.'[72] This, however, is not a persuasive argument. No doubt men are, broadly speaking, fairly

[67] See, generally, Carlyle, *Medieval Political Theory*, vol. 6, p. 11; S. B. Chrimes, *English Constitutional Ideas of the 15th Century*, p. 133; O. Prausnitz, *Representation and the Majority Principle*, *Politica*, 1934, pp. 215 sqq. And for a good general survey, S. G. Heinberg, *History of the Majority Principle* (1926), vol. 20, *American Political Science Review*, pp. 52 sqq.

[68] For references, see Heinberg, loc. cit. For the position in Roman law, see Buckland and McNair, *Roman Law and Common Law*, 1936, pp. 83 sqq.; Duff, *Personality in Roman Private Law*, pp. 132-3.

[69] In Germanic legal systems the unanimity principle has, it would seem, tougher and more durable roots than in Romanistic ones. See, generally, T. Baty, 'The History of Majority Rule', *Quarterly Review*, 1912, pp. 19 sqq.; Otto Gierke, 'Uber die Geschichte des Majoritatsprinzips', *Oxford Essays in Legal History*, 1913, pp. 312 sqq.

[70] See Riches, *Majority Rule in International Organization*, Johns Hopkins, 1940, Introduction.

[71] For the history of the principle with special reference to political institutions, see S. B. Chrimes, op. cit.; Redlich, *The Procedure of the House of Commons*, 1907, vol. 2, p. 261; O. Prausnitz in *Politica*, 1934, pp. 215 sqq.; Haskins, *English Representative Government*, pp. 31 sqq.

[72] *Liberty, Equality, Fraternity*, p. 31. See also Locke, *Second Treatise of Civi. Government*, Bk. 2, ch. 8, sec. 96.

equally matched in physical strength; and from this point of view a majority might be expected to prevail in a contest. But when one considers the subtle ways in which power, including economic power, may influence decisions, this argument loses much of its cogency. Moreover its force has been further diminished since the invention of modern armaments. Indeed, the history of South Africa affords what is perhaps its best refutation.

Grotius was of the opinion that a majority 'naturally' has the authority of the whole, and he declared that 'it was manifestly inequitable that a majority should have to abide by the wishes of the minority'.[73] By Grotius' time, however, 'natural law' thinking, on which his statement was based, had begun to cut itself adrift from the sources which gave meaning to the great tradition of the Middle Ages. Its premises were beginning to be articulated in conflicting ways, with the result that, in its light, men often claimed justification for conflicting conclusions. The jurist Puffendorf, for example, unlike some of his contemporaries, denied that the majority principle had any foundation in natural law, as he understood it.[74]

Among the various 'Social Contract' justifications of the majority principle, an influential line of reasoning was that men must be presumed to have agreed (more or less unanimously) *before* associating together, or by virtue of joining an association, that their common will should in future be ascertained by a majority vote, subject to any conditions specified in the original contract; for example, subject to a fair opportunity being given to the minority to have its views heard.[75]

It would take us too far afield to analyse the many varieties of legal fiction which, at various times, have been invoked to justify the majority principle. However, it may be of interest to mention three of the main ones. At one period in Germanic law, a legal duty was attributed to the minority to acquiesce in the majority decision so that the appearance of unanimity might be maintained. In Roman law the decision of the majority was, by fiction, deemed to be the decision of all: *refertur ad minores quod publice fit per majorem partem*. But the Roman jurists never attempted any justification of this fiction.[76] And in this regard the Canon lawyers, who also resorted to a fiction, were more interesting. They justified the majority principle on the ground that the majority were more likely to approach 'the true and the good' than the few.[77]

[73] *De Jure Belli ac Pacis*, 2.5.17.
[74] *Droit de la Nature et des Gens*, VII, 2.15.
[75] For a modern statement of this view, see *The Round Table*, June, 1952, p. 197.
[76] J. G. Heinberg, *Theories of Majority Rule*, p. 455.
[77] J. G. Heinberg, op. cit., p. 456.

Unhappy, however, with the idea that the value of each vote should be assessed equally, the Canonists for a while attempted to evaluate votes qualitatively as well as count them numerically; they required decisions to be concurred in not merely by the *maior pars* (the more numerous part) but by the *sanior pars* as well (that is, by the sounder or wiser part). But this procedure broke down in practice; for at a papal election in A.D. 1159 the three cardinals who supported Victor IV declared themselves to be saner than the rest of the College who elected Alexander III. The Canonists thereupon invented the fiction that the *maior pars* was, in fact, likely, more often than not, to be the *sanior pars*. And hence the electoral decree of A.D. 1179 which made the numerical test of a two-thirds majority presumptive evidence of *sanitas*.

Among all these various explanations of majority rule, probably the least controversial is that based on convenience.[78] At the same time it leaves a great deal unexplained. Thus, to say that the views and wishes of a group may conveniently be ascertained by a majority decision is a very different thing from saying that the majority view is necessarily right or wise. Again, an argument based on convenience might appeal to any government—whether it be democratic, or oligarchic, humane or tyrannical. But what we really want to know is whether it be true that all who believe in democracy and, indeed, in good and humane government, must also believe in majority rule. And more particularly, must they believe in it unqualifiedly.

DEMOCRACY AND MAJORITY RULE

Now it cannot be doubted that, in the eyes of practical statesmen, and of most writers on democracy, the majority principle is, in fact, regarded as essential to democracy. 'A majority is the only true sovereign of a free people', said Lincoln. 'Whoever rejects it does of necessity fly into anarchy or despotism'.[79] 'The very essence of democratic government', declared de Tocqueville, 'is the absolute sovereignty of the majority.'[80] And scores of statements to the same effect can be found in works of high authority.[81] Indeed, even those who criticize the proposition more often deplore its possible consequences than deny its validity. When, for example, Lord Acton said that 'the one pervading evil of democracy is the tyranny of the

[78] Sir Carleton Allen, *Democracy and the Individual*, 1943, p. 41.
[79] *Works*, vol. 2, p. 5 (ed. Nicolay and Hay).
[80] *Democracy in America*, Vintage Books, vol. 1, p. 264.
[81] See, for example, Commager, *Majority Rule and Minority Rights*, p. 8; Lord Cromer: 'The essence of democratic rule is that the voice of the majority should prevail' (Cited Hearnshaw, *Democracy at the Crossways*, 1919, p. 345); The Rt. Hon. G. Lansbury: 'All who believe in democracy must also believe in majority rule. This is the essence of democracy.' *The Clarion*, 21 April 1934.

majority, or rather that party, not always the majority, that succeeds by force or fraud in carrying elections', he was, of course, implicitly recognizing that the majority principle is an axiom of modern democracy.[82]

The advocates of the majority principle in a democracy generally concede that unanimity would be the ideal, on the ground that what concerns all should be approved by all;[83] but they say that as unanimity can seldom be achieved in practice, the next best solution is the majority principle; and they claim, moreover, 'that on the whole, though no doubt with many exceptions, majority opinion does reach a sensible and workable solution of most practical problems of social life'.[84]

These are propositions which, I think, must be accepted by all who believe in democracy. And nothing is to be gained by grandiloquent (and often shallow) tirades against the majority principle, like T. Baty's:

> Like other superstitions, it was cradled in uncritical carelessness, and brought to its modern pitch of luxuriant rankness through indolence. Never deliberately or of set purpose adopted as a principle, it has drifted into casual acceptance through loose political thinking.[85]

If one shares Baty's views, it is much simpler and more effective to say: 'I don't like democracy.'

At the same time it is essential to realize that the majority principle (a) rests on certain assumptions, (b) presupposes certain conditions; and (c) that the authority of a majority decision is subject to certain limitations. These assumptions must be borne in mind, and the conditions and limitations observed, if democratic government is also to be sane government, and not degenerate into tyranny. Long ago Aristotle reminded us that majority rule was not confined to democracies;[86] and in recent times MacIver has again emphasized that, unless certain conditions are observed, 'majority rule may hold in the most intolerant and anti-democratic system of government'.[87]

The particular version of the majority principle which champions of democracy envisage, is that whereby the vote of 50 per cent plus one carries the day.[88] The underlying assumption, however, on

---

[82] *History of Freedom*, p. 87.
[83] McIlwain, *The Growth of Political Thought in the West*, 1932, p. 302, note 3.
[84] Allen, *Democracy and the Individual*, p. 40.
[85] *Quarterly Review*, 1912, p. 27.
[86] *Politics*, IV, iv. 1, 1290a.
[87] *Leviathan and the People*, p. 153.
[88] There are, of course, several other versions, e.g. two-thirds, three-quarters, and so on, either of the total membership or of those present and voting.

which the validity of this technique is based is that each member of the group is approximately equal in judgment and skill: each, in Bentham's phrase, is to count for one and nobody for more than one. McIlwain brings this out very clearly when he says that 'equality is the essential doctrine of modern democracy, and is implied in the principle of majority rule'.[89] And it is precisely this assumption of approximate equality in value that has so often proved a stumbling-block in modern democratic theory.[90]

It would, indeed, be of interest, but beyond the scope of this book, to trace the historical origins of what Maritain has called 'pseudo-Christian egalitarianism', in which, of course, the influence of Hobbes and Descartes has been great.[91] Here, however, we may avoid taking sides on the issue of equality and deal with our subject in a more practical, if more pedestrian, way.

Readers of Ibsen will remember Dr. Stockmann's round assertion that 'the majority is never right'. On the other hand, the most ardent democrat would hardly claim that the majority is always right. That the truth lies somewhere between these two extremes is indeed obvious. Accordingly, modern advocates of democracy, and of the rule of 50 per cent plus one, have wisely refused to make democracy the worship of mere quantity by insisting that what distinguishes democracy from dictatorship, and what distinguishes good from bad government, is not so much

> the number of citizens consenting but the conditions under which the consent is elicited; the vital point being the presence or absence of freedom not only in the process of voting, but also — and much more important — in the preceding process of discussion.[92]

Those who take this view rightly attach more weight to the conditions under which a majority decision is valid than to the question whether a democracy would cease to be such if some technique other than the ordinary majority principle were used. They emphasize that it is of the very essence of democratic government to use persuasion rather than compulsion; and so they rightly contend that a majority has no moral claim to require a minority to submit to its decisions, unless the minority is given full and free

[89] Op. cit., p. 304. The point is also made with lucidity by W. Konopczynski in 'Principe Majoritaire', *Oxford Legal Essays*, 1913, p. 338.

[90] Cf. Plato's caustic reference to donkeys jostling with their owners in supposed equality: *Republic*, VIII, 562d–563d.

[91] The opening sentence of Descartes' *Discourse on Method* (1637) reads: 'Good sense is of all things in the world the most equally distributed'. To the same effect, see Hobbes, *Leviathan* (1651), ch. XIII.

[92] Bassett, *Essentials of Parliamentary Democracy*, 1937, p. 117. And see, generally, Allen, op. cit., pp. 47 sqq.

opportunity of expressing its views, and, further, only if the minority is at liberty to use its energies to become a majority in its turn. It is, indeed, the observance of these conditions *inter alia* that makes the majority principle a tolerable and reasonable method of reaching group decisions.

THE TYRANNY OF THE MAJORITY

But when all this has been said, the danger of tyrannical use of power by a majority still remains one of the great problems of government.[93] What guarantee, for example, is there that the majority will respect the essential prerequisites for a valid majority decision, and allow criticism and full discussion? Again, may a government not seek to entrench itself by curbing free elections? And, even more important, should the majority be free to deal with all subjects at will; are there not *any* limits to the obedience which men must give to majority decisions?

Men have shrunk from the possible consequences of leaving their basic rights and freedoms at the mercy of a majority decision. They have sought to find criteria of right and wrong by which majority decisions may be judged; and they have devised barriers to protect them against the abuse of power of a majority. In fact, one of the most striking features of modern government is the dearth of examples where men have given their full assent to the idea of unqualified majority rule.

The United Kingdom is, of course, the main example of a country where the most precious freedoms—where Magna Carta itself—are at the mercy of an electoral and parliamentary majority; and other countries which approximate most closely to the British model are New Zealand, Israel and the Union of South Africa. This is a way of doing things which presupposes a remarkable degree of self-restraint among majorities; moreover it has in Britain been a slow growth aided by many favourable factors, not least of which is the homogeneity of her peoples and a fundamental unanimity among them on basic issues of government. But quite apart from these considerations, most other countries, no matter how deeply and genuinely they may be committed to the ideals of democracy, have refused to leave the basic freedoms and rights to a majority vote. They have preferred to act on the principle that:

> One's rights to life, liberty, free speech, a free press, freedom of worship and assembly, and other fundamental rights, may not

[93] Perhaps the most cogent expositions are still to be found in the classic pages of Mill, *Representative Government*, ch. VI, and de Tocqueville, *Democracy in America*, ch. XV.

be submitted to the vote; they depend on the outcome of no elections.[94]

This is the principle of government under law, a principle which limits the legal authority of majority decisions. Acceptance of this principle is, I believe, essential if democratic government is also to be sane government; and its acceptance may yet mitigate—and ultimately help to remove—some of the main tensions and fears now at work in Africa.

The principle itself, it should be noted, has not, in practice, been inspired by the peculiar difficulties confronting multi-racial societies; nor is its utility confined to such societies. On the contrary, it has been accepted wherever men have felt it wise to erect barriers against an abuse of power by *any* majority—quite irrespective of the question whether or not it be a racial majority.

And it is perhaps hardly necessary to add that acceptance of the principle of adult suffrage on the ground of the legitimate interest in government of all citizens, is in no way incompatible with refusal to accept the notion that what a majority of men (or even all men) may say, is necessarily right, or just, or good.

THE PROSPECTS FOR DEMOCRACY

We are now in a position to pose a question hinted at at the beginning of this chapter. What are the prospects for democracy, especially in Africa? In answering this question there is no room for any facile optimism. Democracy, in the ideal form which we have outlined, has not often occurred in the history of men, and seldom for long periods. Nor are the reasons far to seek.

In the first place such a democracy postulates a certain minimum of economic security. In times of grinding scarcity democracy always will have hard going.[95]

Secondly, there must be freedom from fear—fear of the disruption caused, for example, by war or the threat thereof; for war by its very nature requires the suspension of democratic principles.[96]

Thirdly, the people themselves must have confidence in the integrity and general beneficence of their government. And it is precisely at this point that constitutional guarantees and the techniques for taming power, which we shall discuss in subsequent chapters, assume importance.

[94] *West Virginia State Board of Education* v. *Barnette* (1942) 319 U.S. 638, per Jackson J.
[95] R. L. Calhoun, op. cit., p. 39.
[96] Calhoun, op. cit., p. 40. Also Mr. Nehru, in his opening speech at the Rule of Law Conference in New Delhi on 5 January 1959. *The Rule of Law in a Free Society*, Geneva, 1960, pp. 39 sqq.

But in themselves constitutional guarantees are not enough. 'Nothing is more fertile in prodigies', wrote de Tocqueville,[97] 'than the art of being free; but there is nothing more arduous than the apprenticeship of liberty.' Or again, to quote Walter Lippmann, government under law is 'a precarious and tentative thing like the clearing for a garden in a jungle, which has to be tended continually if it is not to be quickly submerged in the primeval forest'.[98]

And the reason why this is so is plain. In the ultimate analysis, no community can maintain a system of constitutional government unless a sufficient number of its citizens are clear as to the nature of man and the nature of human authority. As Walter Lippmann so rightly emphasized:

> To maintain a constitutional order men must be much more truthful, reasonable, just and honourable than the letter of the laws. There must be an habitual, confirmed, and well nigh intuitive dislike of arbitrariness; a quick sensitiveness to its manifestations and a spontaneous disapproval and resistance. For only by adhering to this unwritten higher law can they make actual law effective or have criteria by which to reform it.[99]

These, however, are topics to which we shall return in the last chapter of this book.

[97] *Democracy in America*, Vintage Books, vol. 1, p. 256.
[98] *The Good Society*, London, 1937, p. 343.
[99] *Op. cit.*, pp. 346–7.

6

Constitutional Safeguards

It will be recalled that Alexis de Tocqueville described the inclusion of a judicially enforceable Bill of Rights in the American Constitution—which took place at the end of the eighteenth century—as 'one of the most powerful barriers that has ever been devised against the tyranny of political assemblies'.[1] The historical antecedents of the American experiment go back far into the ethical and political thought of the ancient world,[2] but it is only now in the mid-twentieth century that the constitutional protection of human rights has, with the exception of a few countries, become a cardinal and generally recognized feature of government.

Throughout the nineteenth century and, indeed, up to the Second World War, there was in many countries—especially those under British influence—a marked distaste for the constitutional protection of basic human rights. And it is appropriate that we should remind ourselves of this attitude and of the reasons given to justify it.

These reasons fall into two broad categories. In the first place, the very need for, and value of, constitutional and legal limitations upon government have been questioned. Secondly, strong objections have been raised against assigning to the judiciary a role in the enforcement of constitutional guarantees. The first category of objections will be dealt with in this chapter, the second in the chapter following.

Writing at the end of the First World War, Professor Hearnshaw challenged the need for any constitutional safeguards when he said:

There is no remedy for the tyranny of the majority—and there is need of none—save the purification of public opinion, the elevating of public life, the rousing of public spirit, the education of public conscience, and the developing of a sense of public responsibility. ... Not in futile attempts by means of subtle devices to curb and check majorities, but by a magnanimous use of their omnipotence lies the way of deliverance.[3]

[1] *Democracy in America*, Reeve-Bradley text, Vintage Books, vol. 1, p. 107.
[2] Below, chapter 10.
[3] *Democracy at the Crossways*, London, 1919, p. 325.

During the period between the First and Second World Wars commissions were frequently appointed to consider the desirability of introducing Bills of Human Rights in countries of the British Commonwealth, but they invariably decided against them. One of the most explicit statements of the reasons for rejection was given by the Simon Commission on Indian Constitutional Reform, which reported in 1931 that:

> · Many of those who came before us have urged that the Indian constitution should contain a definite guarantee of the rights of individuals in respect of the exercise of their religion and a declaration of equal rights of all citizens. We are aware that such provisions have been inserted in many constitutions, notably in those of European states after the war of 1914–18. Experience, however, has not shown them to be of any great practical value. Abstract declarations are useless unless there exists the will and means to make them effective.[4]

Commenting on this, a Joint Select Committee said:

> With these observations we entirely agree, and a cynic might indeed find plausible arguments in the history during the last ten years of more than one country for asserting that the most effective method of ensuring the destruction of a fundamental right is to include a declaration of its existence in a constitutional document. But there are strong practical arguments against the proposal. Either the declaration of rights is of so abstract a nature that it has no legal effect, or its legal effect will be to impose an embarrassing restriction on the powers of the legislature.[5]

Two separate points are here involved; and as I wish to state the case against a Bill of Rights at its full strength before attempting to answer the objections, I propose to elaborate them somewhat.

In the first place, the valid point is made that in the ultimate analysis the only effective safeguard of liberty in any state is the character of its people. In the case of *Liversidge* v. *Anderson*, Lord Wright stated this conclusion as follows: 'The safeguard of British liberty is in the good sense of the people and in the wisdom of the representative and responsible government which has been evolved.'[6] And in the United States the same view was expressed even more forcefully by the late Mr. Justice Jackson:

> I know of no modern instance in which any judiciary has saved a people from the great currents of intolerance, passion, usurpation, and tyranny which have threatened liberty and free institutions.

---

[4] *Indian Statutory Commission Report*, vol. 2, para. 36.
[5] *Joint Select Committee Report*, vol. 1, para. 366.
[6] [1942] A.C. 206.

8

. . . It is not idle speculation to enquire which comes first, an independent and enlightened judiciary or a free and tolerant society. . . . It is my belief that the attitude of a society and of its organised political forces, rather than its legal machinery, is the controlling force in the character of free institutions.[7]

Laymen—and sometimes lawyers too—who sense the force in this view, often seek to illustrate it with what they regard as telling examples. Pointing to the 'entrenched sections' of the South Africa Act, they ask, as an ex-Chief Justice of South Africa, Mr. Fagan, has asked: what use were these guarantees in the end against a determined parliamentary majority backed by the electorate?[8] Others, again, point to the Constitution of the U.S.S.R. They remind us that in the Russian Constitution we find 'guarantees' of such rights as freedom of speech, of the press, of assembly and of meetings—yet what, in practice, does it all amount to?

Then too, it is said that when men place limitations upon the power of the legislature they betray a lack of faith in democracy. In South Africa this point of view was often expressed at the time of Union, notably by Lord Brand. Thus he wrote in his book *South Africa:*

> The supreme power given to the Parliament of the Union has been criticised in some quarters as excessive and dangerous to liberty. The criticism is not well founded. There is no more curious phenomenon in modern politics than the distrust of representative government which some forms of democracy have engendered. In the United States this feeling has gone to extreme lengths, and in the newest constitutions the legislature is hedged about by innumerable restrictions, and in some cases may not meet oftener than once in two years—surely a strange commentary on the power of public opinion to control the people's representatives.[9]

A topical variant of this argument is often voiced in the settler areas of Africa by non-whites who suspect that the advocates of a Bill of Rights are really concerned to palm off a second class democracy by circumscribing the sovereignty of the people. It is said that the real reason why some whites favour a Bill of Rights is not primarily because they desire to guarantee those rights for non-whites; but because they do not trust non-whites, and feel that if the non-whites were an enfranchised majority they would prejudice the whites. Therefore, so it is contended, the whites wish to erect a barrier, in the shape of a Bill of Rights, against the democratic expression of non-white desires and aspirations.

---

[7] *The Supreme Court in the American System of Government*, pp. 80–1.
[8] Cf. *Our Responsibility*, Stellenbosch, 1959, pp. 61, 64.
[9] Oxford, 1909, p. 48.

Turning to the second point involved in the Indian Commission's rejection of constitutional guarantees, this, too, merits elaboration. It is said that in so far as constitutional limitations upon legislative power succeed in being effective, they are an embarrassment to the legislature. Why, it may be asked, should this be so? And the answer usually given is that the constitutional guarantee of individual rights often obstructs the attainment of desirable social and economic objectives. This is an objection which, nowadays, tends to be emphasized by supporters of the idea of the 'welfare state', and more particularly by politicians in underdeveloped territories. It is pointed out that the traditional civil rights, like the right to own property free from arbitrary deprivation, freedom of movement and of association, freedom of speech and of the press, and so on, which were embodied in the American Bill of Rights, and which subsequently found a place in the constitutions of other countries, all reflect the *laissez faire* political philosophy of an earlier age—a philosophy which now stands, it is said, in need of revision. A feature of the traditional Bill of Rights is that they are negative in structure; they demarcate the field in which the state is required not to interfere with the individual. But what is needed, it is claimed, is more emphasis upon the positive duty of the state to provide social and economic benefits.

Some African leaders beyond the borders of the Union have developed this point in the following way. They argue that in countries where (*a*) men and animals and plant life are stricken by disease; (*b*) where lack of capital and grinding poverty afflict most people; (*c*) where communications are embryonic; and (*d*) where basic educational and civic amenities are either lacking or in a primitive state—in short, where these deficiencies are present on a massive scale, they contend that whatever importance attaches to the nineteenth-century rights of non-interference, equal if not greater importance attaches to the provision by the state of economic and social security.

It is plain that to the extent that this argument finds favour in underdeveloped territories, it raises a delicate problem of adjustment; for the two sets of interests, the traditional civil liberties on the one hand, and the claim for social and economic services, on the other, are sometimes in conflict. The provision of social and economic amenities may well involve the cutting down or invasion of some of the traditional liberties. For example, one cannot provide compulsory education without interfering to some extent with several freedoms (e.g. the child's personal freedom, a parent's right to choose the kind of education which his children shall enjoy, and even the privacy of family life). Again one cannot make provision for compulsory vaccination without in some degree curtailing personal freedom and, in some cases, even freedom of conscience. Plainly the more ambitious is the state's programme of positive action in providing social and economic amenities, the less room is there for the traditional guarantee of civil and political liberties. And so, it is argued, let us leave the state free to provide social and economic benefits unembarrassed and unfettered by legal restraints in favour of individual liberty.

It would be a great mistake to underestimate the appeal which attaches to this line of argument; and we would do well to take it seriously. As Professor Richard McKeon has rightly observed:

> Most of the fundamental opposition in the discussion of human rights is between those who hold that the preservation of civil and political rights is basic even before the establishment of economic and social rights and those who hold that unless economic and social rights are first secured, civil and political rights are an empty sham and pretence.[10]

Professor Laski was equally emphatic. Thus:

> Any attempt to formulate a declaration of human rights in individualistic terms would inevitably fail. It would have little authority in those political societies which are increasingly, both in number and in range of effort, answering the need to plan their social and economic life. It is indeed legitimate to go further and say that if the assumptions behind such a declaration were individualistic, the document would be regarded as a threat to a new way of life by the defenders of the historic principles which are now subject to profound change. Its effect would be to separate and not to unify the groping towards common purposes achieved through common institutions and common standards of behaviour which it is the object of such a declaration to promote.[11]

And one more quotation from Laski:

> Freedom of speech cannot be seriously said to exist in any political society (a) in the absence of economic security and (b) where the vital means of communication, the Press for example, the radio and the cinema are all of them departments of big business and tending increasingly towards monopoly in each instance. Without economic security, only the very exceptional citizen will speak his full mind for fear of losing his job. Freedom of speech is largely a function of economic power; even more so, the right to freedom of association especially in the context of industry. The right to strike, for example, is of necessity severely limited in any vital area of a complex economic community. A government is compelled to intervene wherever a strike endangers food or health,

---

[10] *Unesco Symposium on Human Rights*, New York, 1949, p. 45.
[11] *Unesco Symposium*, pp. 88–3.

communication or transport. If the services which provide these goods are privately owned, the inevitable result is that government intervention, save in the most exceptional circumstances, renders the power of the strike, as a weapon of effective protection for the worker, largely null and void.[12]

Laski's remarks may serve to emphasize a point of view which is certainly widely held among African intellectuals, and by not a few of Africa's leaders. And if we are realistic we must come to terms with this view; and attempt to meet it. Already several of the countries which adopted Bills of Rights after the Second World War have suspended them in favour of strong-man rule, ostensibly during an interim period while economic stability is being built up, and provision is made for basic educational and social amenities. The Sudan, Pakistan and Burma are examples of this.

Let me now attempt to deal with the various objections and difficulties which I have thus far outlined.

In regard to the first point, namely, that *ultimately* the only safeguard of liberty and of the decencies of life is the character of the people, I should be very slow to cry down the importance of this contention. Indeed I feel very strongly that the character of the people for whom it is made is ultimately more important than any constitution. But it does not follow from this that one should go to the opposite extreme and deny all efficacy to written constitutions and entrenched Bills of Rights. Merely because no constitution can possibly provide a complete and impenetrable defence against human passion and artfulness, it does not follow that one may legitimately deduce from this the virtue of necessity of leaving everything to the unfettered will of the legislature—or, let me add, of the people.

In these matters I start with the premise that when entrusting power to human hands, it is essential not to believe in the sweet reasonableness of man.[13] And of course this is the fundamental act of faith—or, if you prefer, the fundamental act of Whiggish cynicism —which the American people made when they established their Government. Thus in the Draft of the Kentucky Resolution we read:

> Free government is founded in jealousy, and not in confidence, it is jealousy and not confidence which prescribes limited constitutions, to bind down those we are obliged to trust with power; . . . our Constitution has accordingly fixed the limits to which and no further, our confidence may go. . . . In questions of power, then,

---

[12] *Unesco Symposium*, p. 89.
[13] Cf. Butterfield, *Christianity and History*, 1949, p. 47.

let no more be heard of confidence in man, but bind him down from mischief by the chains of the Constitution.[14]

The argument that constitutional guarantees are no certain defence because a determined government, backed by the people, can always find loopholes, has always seemed to me to be a superficial argument. No knowledgeable person has ever suggested that constitutional safeguards provide in themselves complete and indefeasible security. But they do make the way of the transgressor, of the tyrant, more difficult. They are, so to speak, the outer bulwarks of defence.

But then it is said: what is the use of such a bulwark, is it not too weak to take pains to erect? 'Look what happened to the entrenched sections of the South Africa Act', the critics say. The answer, of course, is twofold. The entrenched sections of the South Africa Act took six years of stratagem and manipulation to batter down; the glare of world publicity was on the whole sorry performance; and I venture to believe that there are very few people in South Africa today who are really proud of the ultimate achievement. But, in any event, the South Africa Act was in fact very loosely drafted, and—as I shall show presently—it would not be difficult to devise safeguards which would offer even sterner resistance to those who would circumvent a constitution.

In regard to the argument that all constitutional guarantees are likely to be as hollow as those in the Constitution of the U.S.S.R., I would say this is almost a disingenuous argument. The so-called rights 'guaranteed' in the Constitution of the U.S.S.R. differ from the kind of rights guaranteed in the American constitution in fundamental respects. Firstly, the Russian 'guarantees' are not limitations upon state action. On the contrary, they purport to be state policy objectives, undertakings of what the state will do for its citizens. It is, I repeat, almost disingenuous to quote side by side the words 'freedom of the press' in, say, the constitutions of the U.S.A. and of the U.S.S.R., and then argue 'there, what does it all add up to?' In the U.S.A. the emphasis is upon what the state may not do; and, secondly the limitations upon government are guaranteed in the U.S.A. by a right of recourse to the courts in the event of an infringement. In the U.S.S.R. there is no such guarantee; only an undertaking that the state will provide benefits; and no recourse to the courts. Thus the Constitution of the U.S.S.R. specifically states that freedom of the press 'is ensured by placing at the disposal of the working people and their organizations printing presses, stocks and paper, etc.' It must be obvious to all who are not deliberately blind

[14] Draft of the Kentucky Resolution, 1798, quoted by Hayek, *The Political Ideal of the Rule of Law*, 1955, p. 15.

that this differs as heaven does from hell from the sort of constitutional guarantee with which people in the western tradition are familiar.

As regards the contention that the demand for constitutional guarantees by whites in the settler areas of Africa is a hypocritical thing, prompted by a desire among privileged whites to preserve their privileges against democratic invasion by non-whites, I would say that this need not be so. No doubt the motives with which white people in Africa put forward a case for a Bill of Rights are very conflicting. But it is important to recognize that in recent years Bills of Rights have been sought in areas of Africa where no black-white problem exists, and also in countries which previously would have nothing to do with them. In fact since the last world war a revolution has taken place in world thinking about the formulation and protection of basic human rights. And presently I propose to give some attention to the reasons why there has been this revolution in thought.

Of course all this would be no answer to non-white critics if in fact a Bill of Rights were so timorously drawn up, or were so hedged about with exceptions, as to bear little resemblance to a true Bill of Rights. This, however, is an aspect which we shall discuss more fully presently.

Turning now to the objection that the constitutional protection of individual human rights might prove to be an embarrassing obstruction in the way of social and economic projects, I would say that the alleged difficulty has been much exaggerated. No doubt in particular cases it may be a difficult question to assess the relative importance of the negative civil rights and liberties, on the one hand, and the positive duty of the state to provide amenities, on the other hand. But the real question is whether one can secure an adequate minimum of both interests.

Writing on this point ten years ago, an Indian philosopher and poet, Humuyun Kabir said:

The problem of the 20th Century is to reconcile the conflicting claims of liberty and security. A new charter of human rights must secure to each individual, irrespective of race, colour or sex or creed, the minimum requirements for a bare human existence, namely, (a) the food and clothing necessary for maintaining the individual in health, (b) the housing necessary for protection against the weather and for allowing space for relaxation and enjoyment of leisure, (c) the education necessary for developing the latent faculties, (d) the medical and sanitary services necessary for checking and curing disease and for ensuring the health of the individual and the community. These are the four basic rights on which all other rights depend. It will be noticed that they appertain to the security rather than the liberty of the individual. The demands of security must take precedence over the demands for liberty in respect of the minimum human needs.[15]

He goes on to suggest that totalitarian systems have enriched our conception of human rights to the extent that they have compelled recognition of this fact. But the fundamental error of totalitarian systems, according to Kabir, is that they have drawn no limit to the precedence of social security over liberty for the individual. He contends that both theory and experience indicate that once the basic minimum of security is reached, human beings rightly place greater value on the rights and claims associated with the concept of liberty.

With due respect to Kabir's moderate and lucidly stated views, I feel that more stress needs to be placed on individual freedom. While I do not for one moment deny the great importance of providing social and economic security, I would suggest that there is an area of individual liberty which should necessarily, and in all circumstances, be safeguarded.

There are, in my view, certain fundamental rights with which the state should not ordinarily interfere—and if it may do so, then only in very exceptional circumstances which should be closely defined. These rights, in my view, take priority even over the need to provide social and economic services; they include what in the United States have sometimes been called the 'preferred freedoms'; and among them are personal liberty and the right to a fair trial; freedom of association and of assembly; freedom of religion; freedom of the press and freedom of speech.

I utterly repudiate the notion that the provision of social and economic security should be given pride of place above all other freedoms. In fact, as I see it, we are faced here with what is precisely the deepest issue between Russia and her satellites, on the one hand, and the free world, on the other. In my view the basic objection to the Russian method of 'guaranteeing human rights', as they call it, is that the Russian Constitution does not recognize any fundamental rights in the true sense. The state is professedly the universal provider, with the result that the individual ceases to count at all.

In any event the safeguarding of individual liberty and the provision of social and economic security are not mutually exclusive ideals. They are, in fact, complementary; without some amenities the traditional freedoms are small comfort, and without freedom the amenities are not worth having. The question—and I do not deny its difficulty—is how to strike a wise balance; where to draw the line? And on this I should like to say two things.

[15] *Unesco Symposium*, p. 192.

Probably no hard and fast answer can be given; for in part the drawing of the line depends upon the practical virtue of prudence.[16] Much no doubt depends upon the needs of time and place, and this is particularly the case in underdeveloped countries, like Africa. I have little sympathy for the point of view of those who would attempt to force African realities Procrustes-fashion into western political moulds, and who criticize newly independent African states on the ground that their polities are not exact replicas of British Parliamentary democracy. But while it may not be possible to draw up a comprehensive and *detailed* code of conduct for the guidance of rulers in all communities at all times, and while there is room for flexibility at many points, it is possible—as we shall see presently—to formulate the basic principles which will ensure that the provision of social and economic services does not take place only at the cost of the obliteration of human freedom.

Secondly, without intending to minimize the difficulty of a real problem, I believe that the extent to which the two groups of interests come into conflict is often exaggerated. The provision of social and economic services is not incompatible with most of the really basic rights and freedoms. I have, for example, yet to learn how the right to personal freedom and a fair trial, freedom of speech and the press, and freedom of worship, stand in the way of economic and social security in a given state. And if it is felt in a particular state that they do, then the state in question, I would say, is not worth living in.

Thus far I have dealt with arguments for the constitutional guarantee of human rights without reference to the verdict of history. If, in addition, one examines the post-war trends in world practice and opinion, it is found to be strongly in favour of Bills of Rights.

In the Far East, after the Second World War, India, Malaya, Burma and Pakistan all incorporated Bills of Human Rights in their constitutions; and very recently tentative steps in the same direction have been taken in Canada.[17]

In Africa today we are on the threshold of a great new venture in this field. North, East, West, Central and Southern Africa are increasingly concerning themselves with Bills of fundamental human rights. In 1959 a comprehensive Bill of Rights was incorporated in the Nigerian Constitution, including special provisions for the enforcement of those rights by the courts. Moreover, both the Nigerian Bill, and the procedure for its enforcement, were made 'entrenched' provisions, unalterable except by special majorities

[16] On the virtue of political prudence, see, generally, Gilby, *Between Community and Society*, 1953, p. 295; *Principality and Polity*, 1958, p. 283.

[17] As yet, somewhat hesitant steps. See, generally, (1959) 37 *Canadian Bar Review* 1 sqq. And below, p. 133.

in the federal legislature with the concurrence of two Regions. Similar provisions have been included in the new constitution which has just become operative upon the declaration of Nigeria's independence. And according to all reports, the Nigerian provisions, or something like them, will be included in the constitutions of the other emergent territories of British Africa, notably in Sierra Leone, Nyasaland, Tanganyika and Uganda. In 1960 agreement was reached in principle at Lancaster House for a Bill of Rights in Kenya. The Monckton Commission recommended the incorporation of a Bill of human rights and fundamental freedoms in the Rhodesian Federal Constitution;[18] and there are many who wish to see the idea implemented in the Union of South Africa.

Why is it that so radical a departure is now being made in the previously obtaining practice? Several explanations may be offered. In the first place, men are most concerned with the assertion and definition of human rights when they are threatened or denied. 'Bills of Rights', it has been said, 'are always monumental indictments of regimes in the past, as well as promised safeguards against the same abuse by regimes of the future.'[19] The atrocities and excesses of Nazi Germany towards her own nationals as well as against the occupants of conquered territories during the last war, caused a change in the climate of world opinion on the subject of Bills of Rights, and led to the inclusion in the Charter of the United Nations of a declaration that one of its purposes should be international co-operation in encouraging respect for human rights and fundamental freedoms.

In December 1948 a comprehensive Declaration of Human Rights was approved by the United Nations General Assembly. But while Britain and other adherents of this Declaration were prepared to treat the observance of human rights as a matter of international obligation, they were not yet convinced of the need to incorporate provisions of this kind in their own internal laws so as to make Bills of Rights enforceable in the domestic courts. Moreover, in several countries, among them Great Britain, more precision was demanded than is to be found in the Universal Declaration, especially in regard to enforcement. This led to the drawing up of the more modest, but more closely defined, European Convention of Human Rights in 1951; though here again, this Convention has not carried with it the consequence that Bills of Rights are necessarily to be enforced as part of the domestic laws of the adhering countries.

[18] Cmd. 1148 (1960), p. 80. It is not quite clear, however, what exactly the Monckton Commission had in mind. The Commission referred by way of illustration to the Canadian precedent; but if it was intended that the Canadian precedent be followed, it is doubtful if this would be adequate. See below, p. 133.

[19] A. G. Lien, in the *Unesco Symposium on Human Rights*, p. 24.

But despite all this caution, the fact remains that modern states have with increasing frequency introduced Bills of Rights into the framework of their domestic government. And they have done so because they felt that some such safeguards were called for by the particular facts of their own social and political life. Nigeria is a case in point. And as I believe that the carefully drafted Nigerian Bill may serve, in part at least, as a model in other territories, it may be useful to inquire a little more closely into the reasons which led to its introduction; we may find that they are applicable elsewhere.

In 1957 a Commission was appointed in Nigeria to inquire into the facts about the fears of minorities in any part of Nigeria and to propose means of allaying those fears. The Commission ascertained that fears were in fact entertained by the minorities in Nigeria,[20] and proposed the inclusion in the constitution of fundamental human rights as one of the methods of allaying those fears. To quote the Report:

> Provisions of this kind in the constitution are difficult to enforce and sometimes difficult to interpret. Nevertheless we think that they should be inserted. Their presence defines beliefs widespread among democratic countries and provides a standard to which appeal may be made by those whose rights are infringed. A Government determined to abandon democratic courses will find ways of violating them, but they are of great value in preventing a steady deterioration in standards of freedom and the unobtrusive encroachment of a Government on individual rights.[21]

Apart from the desire to protect minorities, the opinion was also expressed throughout Nigeria that the reasons which rendered a constitutionally entrenched Bill of Rights unnecessary in homogeneous communities, which had inherited long traditions of constitutionalism, did not apply in Nigeria; for there the structure of independence was being erected on parliamentary institutions which had had little time to grow, and the conventions which make for security and stability in countries like Great Britain had not yet fully evolved.

These, as it seems to me, are very solid advantages to be gained from a judicially enforceable Bill of Rights. And much of this reasoning is widely applicable in other African communities, not least of which is the Union of South Africa.

---

[20] In each Region one ethnic group exceeds numerically all other groups in the Region; the population of the Moslem North exceeds that of the two other Regions together. The franchise is universal adult suffrage save in the North where women are not entitled to vote.

[21] *Report of the Willink Commission*, July 1958, p. 97.

If, however, constitutionally guaranteed rights are to be the powerful barriers against tyranny which de Tocqueville and their more modern advocates have in mind, they must conform to certain criteria in regard to (*a*) their contents; (*b*) the method of their enforcement; and (*c*) the method of their adoption into the constitutional structure of the country.

Each of these topics merits a chapter to itself. In this chapter I shall deal with the contents of Bills of Rights. What rights should be guaranteed, and what do they include. Which particular rights are appropriate for incorporation in a particular constitution, say, in South Africa? What qualifications, if any, should be attached to such rights? In what circumstances, if any, may they be suspended? And—most important—in what circumstances, if any, may the constitution itself, which contains the Bill of Rights, be amended?

In the following chapter, it will be appropriate to discuss the problem of enforcement, with special reference to the case for and against entrusting the duty of enforcement to the courts. And thereafter we shall consider the problem of incorporating a Bill of Rights into the constitutional structure of a country, with special reference to the difficulty which presents itself where—as in South Africa—there already exists a sovereign Parliament and no Bill of Rights.

THE CONTENT OF CONSTITUTIONAL GUARANTEES

Professor K. C. Wheare has observed that in drafting a constitution containing guarantees of human rights, two essentials must be observed. First, the draftsman should confine himself to essentials. And secondly, though wide and general terms may often have to be used, the draftsman should, as far as possible avoid the ambiguous, the emotional and the tendentious.[22] What, then, are these essentials, which require to be drafted clearly, unambiguously, and unemotionally?

1. *The structure and organization of government*

At the very outset decisions are, of course, necessary in regard to the question whether the state is to be organized on a unitary or federal basis; whether bicameral or unicameral legislatures are to be favoured; what the composition and powers of the legislature should be; how the executive is to be chosen, whether it is to be responsible to the legislature; and the method of appointing judges —their powers and tenure of office.

In regard to these aspects, we shall have occasion later to discuss the value of federalism and of a second chamber (or senate) in

[22] *Modern Constitutions*, pp. 72–3.

preventing the abuse of power; and we shall also deal with certain necessary safeguards in regard to the appointment and tenure of office of the judiciary.

Here it may be helpful, however, to mention (though very briefly) two vital points—leaving further elaboration for a later stage.

In the first place, the idea of constitutional safeguards presupposes that limits are to be imposed upon the powers of the legislature, the limits being that the legislature is prevented from infringing certain human rights which are defined and articulated as fundamental. There can therefore be no room in such a system for the continued existence of a sovereign Parliament free to do what it likes. On the other hand, the system in no way interferes with state 'sovereignty', that is to say, the autonomy or freedom from external interference of the state itself.[23] The United States of America, for example, is a sovereign state but it has no sovereign legislature.

Secondly, it is necessary to ensure that those provisions in the constitution which deal with the composition and powers of the legislature, and with any other vital matters which may tempt the gerrymanderer, should *themselves* be placed beyond the reach of the ordinary legislative process. It would not be good enough, for example (as we now know so well), to provide that franchise rights can only be amended by a two-thirds majority in the legislature if the legislature is left free to enlarge its composition by an ordinary majority. However, these are matters to which we shall return later.

2. *Basic human rights*

It is plain that there are certain rights and freedoms which are necessarily presupposed by any democratic system and without which it cannot exist. What these are becomes manifest upon a reading of the Universal Declaration of Human Rights, the European Convention on Fundamental Human Rights, and representative constitutions among leading democracies in the modern world (like the U.S.A., Switzerland, West Germany, India, Nigeria and Eire).

Subject to certain qualifications and provision for suspension, which will be mentioned presently, each and every one of the following rights and freedoms require guaranteed protection:[24]

    (i) The right to life.
    (ii) Freedom from inhuman or degrading punishment.

---

[23] For fuller discussion see (1952) 15 *Modern Law Review* 292 sqq.

[24] In terms of modern legal phraseology, they could be more closely analysed as belonging to several different juristic categories: rights in the strict sense, liberties, powers and immunities. But this is not the occasion to undertake the analysis.

(iii) The right to personal liberty, including freedom from slavery and forced labour.

(iv) Freedom of speech and the press.

(v) Freedom of religion.

(vi) The right to marry and found a family.

(vii) Privacy of domestic and family life.

(viii) Freedom of movement.

(ix) Freedom of assembly.

(x) Freedom of association.

(xi) Freedom of residence.

(xii) Freedom to acquire and dispose of property.

(xiii) The right to fair compensation for property expropriated for public purposes.

(xiv) The right to work and of free choice of occupation.

(xv) The right of parents to choose their children's education.

(xvi) Freedom of correspondence.

(xvii) The right to a fair and public hearing by an independent and impartial tribunal in the determination of a person's rights and obligations and of any criminal charge against him.

(xviii) The right to an effective remedy for acts violating fundamental rights or freedoms.

(xix) Equality before the law, and equal protection of the law against any discrimination on the ground of race, colour, creed or national origin.

And, in addition, the following political rights:

(xx) The right to participate in government which is accountable to the people, and the right to vote in free and periodic elections.

And finally it is necessary to guard against certain abuses of executive power, notably in regard to delegated legislation; though full discussion of this somewhat more technical topic would take us beyond the scope of this book.[25]

QUALIFICATIONS AND SUSPENSION

Professor Wheare has pointed out that 'no realistic attempt to define the rights of the citizen can fail to include qualifications'. 'Yet when we see the result, it is difficult to resist asking the question: "What of substance is left after the qualifications have been given full effect?" '[26] I am disposed, however, to think that the difficulty has perhaps been rather too strongly stated by Professor Wheare.

[25] See, generally, *The Rule of Law in a Free Society*, Geneva, 1960, issued by the International Commission of Jurists, pp. 217 sqq.

[26] *Modern Constitutions*, p. 57.

The Constitution of the United States lays down basic human rights and privileges in unqualified terms, and makes scant provision (at any rate, expressly) for their qualification; yet, on the whole, it has worked well.

It is, however, plain that there must be some qualifications. The right to life, to take an obvious example, does not give an immunity from being executed for proved murder; nor should freedom of speech confer a licence to defame people with impunity. Again, to take less obvious examples, does freedom of speech include the right to disseminate opinions by dropping broadsheets on a city from the air so as to clutter up the streets; does it include the right to broadcast opinions at all hours in the public streets by loud-speaker? Again, does it include the right to advocate communism? Would legislation be valid if it sought to place limits upon the right of free speech in these circumstances?

The difficulty, of course, is to devise a formula which is flexible enough to prevent freedom from becoming licence; yet not so wide as to nullify the guaranteed freedoms and rights. When Professor Wheare says that qualifications make the rights themselves meaningless, he has in mind 'guarantees' coupled with phrases like 'save in accordance with the law'; and inasmuch as the law envisaged in such a phrase generally includes an ordinary legislative enactment, it is clear that the qualification takes away as much as is given.

This is the formula for qualification found in the Constitution of Eire. But one need not resort to the Irish formula. In the Nigerian Constitution the protected rights and freedoms have been grouped into two broad classes to which different values are attached. The first group might almost be described as absolute rights; for they may only be abrogated or suspended in a time of war or national emergency and then only to a limited extent, that is to say to the extent necessitated by the war or emergency, and it is for the courts to judge the necessity. Among the rights in this category are the following: the right to life, protection against cruel and inhuman punishments, protection against slavery, the right to personal liberty and the right to a fair trial.

On the other hand, the Nigerian Constitution includes a group of 'qualified' rights; these may be limited by any law 'reasonably justifiable in a democratic society' and in furtherance of the state's normal functions of ensuring 'national defence, public safety, public order and public morality'. Rights in this class include the right to private and family life, freedom of conscience, freedom of speech, freedom of assembly and freedom of association.

The key words, of course, are 'reasonably justifiable in a democratic society'; and seizing upon these words, critics of a judicially enforceable Bill of Rights, argue that the scope for qualifications which they afford is very wide.

It would be folly for me to minimize the difficulties which the Nigerian courts are likely to face in the concrete application of this clause. How is the judge to guide himself? Is he to be guided by the standards of democracies like Great Britain? Is he to take into account special local needs? What, in short, are democratic standards? Is there a lowest common denominator of democratic behaviour in non-totalitarian countries?

But again, the difficulties and dangers are apt to be exaggerated. Those who are anxious about the scope for discretion (both legislative and judicial) afforded by such formulas as 'reasonably necessary in a democratic society', may take comfort in the fact that at New Delhi, two years ago, a meeting of nearly 200 distinguished lawyers, from some sixty countries (excluding totalitarian countries but including Asian and African countries) were agreed that it is possible to formulate a lowest common denominator of democratic behaviour; and actually formulated their conclusions in the Declaration of Delhi.[27]

The separate but equal doctrine

There remains one topic in regard to the qualification of guaranteed rights which is particularly relevant to South Africa. I said earlier that a Bill of Rights would be no answer to those who suspect it of being an attempt to palm off a second-class democracy, if in fact the guaranteed rights were so qualified as to deviate materially from sound democratic practice. And in this regard it is necessary to give some attention to the 'separate but equal' formula.

In South Africa, as we saw in chapter 3, the Appellate Division, in 1934, laid down the rule (by a majority decision) that separate amenities might be provided by regulation for the different races provided that the amenities were substantially equal in quality. This, however, proved an uncomfortable and very expensive doctrine to live with. In fact, during the early years of the implementation of the policy of apartheid the courts ruled that several regulations providing separate facilities were invalid on the ground that the amenities given to non-whites were not substantially equal to those available to whites. Thereupon the Government, by Act 49 of 1953, laid down that separate amenities provided for one race might not be declared invalid merely on the ground that they were not substantially similar to, or of the same standard as, those reserved for another race.

In short, 'separate but equal', which is the theoretical ideal of

---

[27] See, generally, *The Rule of Law in a Free Society*, Geneva, 1960, pp. 3–14.

apartheid, was abandoned by the Government because in practice it proved too expensive.

In my view it would be folly for those who wish to build up a common society on the basis of merit and not race or colour, to attempt to re-establish the 'separate but equal' doctrine in South Africa. The doctrine is in fact an utterly discredited one. And to appreciate this fact fully it is only necessary to look back briefly into the history of its operation in the United States of America, where expense did not seem to matter so much.

The historical origin of the separate but equal doctrine is to be found in the judgment of Chief Justice Shaw in the Massachusetts case of *Roberts* v. *The City of Boston*, upholding segregated education for negroes and whites in the public schools of Boston.[28] Interpreting the constitutional guarantee of 'equal protection of the law' in a purely formal way, the learned Chief Justice held that all that this meant was that all men without exception (i.e. equally) were entitled to the protection of the law; but the extent of the protection depended on the provisions of the law itself—a piece of reasoning which reminds one of the more succinctly stated proposition put forward by the pigs in George Orwell's *Animal Farm:* 'All animals are equal but some are more equal than others.'[29]

Charles Sumner, who represented the negroes in the *Roberts* case, argued that the separate but equal doctrine was indefensible and unreasonable on the grounds, *inter alia*, that race was not a reasonable basis upon which to classify human beings for legal purposes; that in the nature of the case the doctrine could not operate fairly; and that, in any event, it would promote a caste system. By 1855 Sumner's views proved to be of greater weight in Massachusetts than the opinion of its Chief Justice. For in that year a statute was enacted by the legislature of Massachusetts which rooted out the doctrine, and laid down that:

> in determining the qualifications of scholars to be admitted to any public school or any district school in the commonwealth, no distinction shall be made on account of the race, color or religious opinions, of the applicant or scholar.[30]

Nevertheless, Chief Justice Shaw's opinion found other support. In 1896 in the case of *Plessy* v. *Ferguson*[31] the Supreme Court of the United States gave formal approval to the separate but equal doctrine in a case involving the provision of separate railroad

[28] 1849. See Levy and Phillips 'The *Roberts* Case: Source of the "Separate but Equal" Doctrine', vol. 56, *American Historical Review*, pp. 510 sqq.
[29] Levy and Phillips, op. cit., p. 516.
[30] St. 1855. ch. 256, sec. 1.
[31] 163 U.S. 537.

facilities. In a dissenting judgment, however, Mr. Justice Harlan made the following memorable statement:

> The white race deems itself to be the dominant race in this country. And so it is, in prestige, in achievements, in education, in wealth and in power. So I doubt not, it will continue to be for all time, if it remains true to its great heritage and holds fast to the principles of constitutional liberty. But in view of the Constitution, in the eye of the law, there is in this country no superior, dominant, ruling class of citizens. There is no caste here. Our Constitution is color-blind, and neither knows nor tolerates classes among citizens. In respect of civil rights, all citizens are equal before the law. The humblest is the peer of the most powerful. The law regards man as man, and takes no account of his surroundings or of his color when his civil rights as guaranteed by the supreme law of the land are involved. It is, therefore, to be regretted that this high tribunal, the final expositor of the fundamental law of the land, has reached the conclusion that it is competent for a State to regulate the enjoyment by citizens of their civil rights solely upon the basis of race.
>
> In my opinion, the judgment this day rendered will, in time, prove to be quite as pernicious as the decision made by this tribunal in the *Dred Scott* case. It was adjudged in that case that the descendants of Africans who were imported into this country and sold as slaves were not included nor intended to be included under the word 'citizens' in the Constitution, and could not claim any of the rights and privileges which that instrument provided for and secured to citizens of the United States.[32]

Time has proved Mr. Justice Harlan right. Year after year inroads have been made upon the separate but equal doctrine by the Supreme Court as the United States increasingly realized that the doctrine was basically incompatible with the ideal of a common integrated society.

1917: the Court declared invalid the provisions of a city ordinance which denied to coloured persons the right to occupy houses in blocks in which the greater number of houses were occupied by white persons, and which imposed similar restrictions on white persons with respect to blocks in which the greater number of houses were occupied by coloured persons.[33]

1927: the Court declared invalid an ordinance which forbade any negro to establish a home on any property in a white area or any white person to establish a home in a negro area 'except on the written consent of the majority of the persons of the opposite race inhabiting such area or portion of the city to be affected'.[34]

[32] The judgment is reprinted in Emerson and Haber, *Political and Civil Rights in the United States*, 1958, vol. 2, p. 1279.
[33] *Buchanan* v. *Warley*, 245 U.S. 60.
[34] *Harmon* v. *Taylor*, 273 U.S. 668.

1948: the Court ruled that the judicial enforcement of private covenants or agreements designed to restrict the sale or occupation of immovable property to persons of a particular race, was an infringement of the equal protection of the laws guaranteed by the United States' constitution.[35]

1954: The Court ruled that 'in the field of public education the doctrine of "separate but equal" has no place. Separate educational facilities are *inherently* unequal.'[36]

1955: the Court upheld the right of negroes to admission on the same basis as white persons to a municipal golf course;[37] again the right to use public bathing facilities was established,[38] and there have been similar rulings with respect to parks, public housing, and other public facilities.

In a recent and penetrating study, Professor Paul Kauper of the University of Michigan exposed the fallacy of the separate but equal doctrine. Thus:

> The claim to equal protection is a personal claim, not one to be considered by matching race against race. . . . The basic vice of the doctrine is that it permits classification by race or color and measures equal protection by reference to groups rather than individuals. . . . The repudiation of *Plessy* v. *Ferguson* is a triumph for Justice Harlan's view that the Constitution is color-blind and that classification on the basis of race is in itself arbitrary and irrational. Although legislatures have a wide power of classification consistent with the equal protection limitation, and although courts will indulge in the presumption that classification has a rational basis, classification based on race no longer has a place under our Constitution.[39]

And to quote John Courtney Murray:

> The doctrine of separate but equal facilities which never had any status in morals, no longer has any status in law.[40]

In short, the separate but equal doctrine is now dying in America.[41] In practice, the whole history of that country has shown that despite

[35] *Shelley* v. *Kraemer*, 334 U.S. 1.
[36] *Brown* v. *Topeka*, 347 U.S. 483.
[37] *Holmes* v. *Atlanta*, 350 U.S. 879.
[38] *Dawson* v. *Baltimore*, 350 U.S. 877.
[39] *The Frontiers of Constitutional Liberty*, Michigan, 1956, pp. 204, 223, 224.
[40] J. C. Murray, S.J., *We Hold These Truths*, New York, 1960, p. 146.
[41] See Kauper, op. cit., pp. 187 sqq.; Mason and Beaney, *The Supreme Court in a Free Society*, 1959, pp. 256 sqq.; J. Greenberg, *Race Relations and American Law*, New York, 1959; Ransmeier, 'The Fourteenth Amendment and the Separate but Equal Doctrine', 1951 *Michigan Law Review* 244 sqq.; and for an earlier survey, Frank and Munro, 'The Original Understanding of "Equal Protection of the Laws" ', 50 *Columbia Law Review* 131 sqq.

the enormous wealth available to try to implement it, 'separate but equal' has meant 'separate but unequal'.[42] Moreover, quite apart from the difficulty of making separate facilities substantially equal in physical terms, there is the psychological injury that is sustained when a person wishing to use facilities is debarred from doing so on the ground of his race or colour. Separate but equal is the mark of a segregated or caste society: within the confines of a single state it implies discrimination, however fine sounding it may be, and ultimately can only be maintained by force. Indeed, as Dr. Liston Pope rightly says, there is no acceptable middle course between integration and segregation.[43]

PROBLEMS OF ENTRENCHMENT

I turn now to a major point involved in the safeguarding of a Bill of Rights, namely the incorporation of the Bill in a rigid constitution. This is indeed a critical step; for it is only by incorporation in a rigid constitution that the basic rights and freedoms can be effectively put out of reach of an ordinary legislative majority. The reason why this is so becomes manifest when one considers the definition of a rigid constitution. A rigid constitution differs from a flexible one in the way in which it can be amended or repealed. Whereas a flexible constitution can be amended, or repealed, by the ordinary process of legislation (normally, by a majority vote of 50 per cent plus one, in exactly the same way as will do for enacting, say, a dog-licensing Act), a rigid constitution can only be altered by a special procedure.

There would not be much point in introducing a Bill of Rights while leaving the legislature free to repeal it by *express* enactment to the contrary—the unusual formula which Canada has recently employed in 'An Act for the Recognition and Protection of Human Rights and Fundamental Freedoms'.[44] No doubt this Canadian 'Bill of Rights' (so-called) will afford some protection as a consolidation of familiar common law rules for the interpretation of ambiguous statutes, and will obviate an *implied* repeal of fundamental rights; but it gives no protection against an express invasion of such rights—which is precisely what Bills of Rights are ordinarily intended to do.[45]

Not only is the process for amendment (including repeal) the key to the difference between a flexible and a rigid constitution, but it is

---

[42] The point has been made by practically every American critic of the doctrine; most recently by Dr. Liston Pope, *The Kingdom Beyond Caste*, p. 81.

[43] Op cit., pp. 82–3. And see Kauper, loc. cit.

[44] 8–9 Elizabeth II, 10 August 1960; sec. 2.

[45] The Canadian Bill as passed in 1960 is substantially the same as the original draft which was fairly widely criticized in the Canadian Bar Review for March 1959.

also the kernel of sound constitution-planning, making big demands on technical skill and foresight. The ideal solution is to ensure that the amending process is neither so difficult as to make amendment virtually impossible nor so loose as to facilitate circumvention. And here it is necessary to emphasize that the South African Constitution has never been rigid in the strict sense. Whereas a rigid constitution is one *all* of whose provisions require a special amending process, the framers of the South Africa Act chose a compromise technique of 'partial rigidity': that is to say, only some of the clauses required a special amending procedure, whereas others, including the vital clauses dealing with the composition of the legislature itself, did not.

In the result, this proved to be the Achilles heel of the so-called 'constitutional safeguards' in regard to the franchise. But the proven weakness of the South African Constitution as originally drafted— however damaging it has been to the faith of many people in the efficacy of constitutional guarantees—should not blind one to the fact that it is possible to devise far more effective safeguards.

Basically, the requirements for an effective entrenchment are:

(1) to ensure that, as far as possible, *all* the topics of fundamental constitutional significance are expressly dealt with in the constitution itself; and, having confined attention to essentials,

(2) to lay down a special and difficult procedure for the amendment of each and every clause in the constitution.

Let us assume, for example, that the constitution deals specifically with such vital matters, among others, as the composition and powers of the legislature; the appointment and powers of the judiciary; the franchise, the delimitation of the constituencies, and the composition and powers of the executive; and that it also includes an equal protection and non-discrimination clause. It is easy to see that if a special amending procedure—say, a two-thirds majority vote— were made applicable to all the provisions of the constitution, it would not be possible to circumvent the constitution and by-pass the special amending procedure by using such stratagems as 'packing' the legislature or the courts. Nor, in fact, could such a constitution be circumvented, at any rate without difficulty, by other stratagems.

It should be observed, however, that to require a two-thirds majority in a legislature operating under such a constitution, is by no means the only way of devising a stronger safeguard than that established by the framers of the Act of Union. Another useful method—which might well be appropriate for the circumstances of South Africa—would be to decentralize legislative sovereignty from

Parliament to the various Provincial Councils, and to require for a valid constitutional amendment the concurrence of a specified number of provinces in addition to a special majority in the central legislature.[46] This is the current Nigerian formula.

There are some who prefer not to make all the provisions of a constitution subject to a special amending process on the ground that this may entail too high a degree of rigidity. But the great danger about resorting to the technique of 'partial rigidity' is that one may omit to safeguard a particular feature which may be tinkered with in such a way as to nullify, by indirect means, the 'safeguards' themselves. This, in fact, is precisely what happened both in the case of the South African Constitution, and, slightly less blatantly, in the case of Ceylon.[47]

In passing, it should be noted that although the expression 'rigid' (originally coined by Bryce) is in general use, Lord Birkenhead's alternative expression 'controlled' seems preferable. Rigid carries the misleading and incorrect inference of unalterability, but in the modern world there are few, if any, constitutions which make no provision for their amendment.[48]

It has been suggested that to incorporate constitutional safeguards of human rights, and require in addition a special procedure for constitutional amendment, involves—strictly speaking—a departure from normal democratic procedures.[49] Up to a point this is true; but it is a deviation which has been proved by experience in order to safeguard the very ideals of democracy itself.

[46] See below, p. 173.
[47] See *Pillay* v. *Mudanayake* [1953] 2 W.L.R. 1142; Jennings, *The Constitution of Ceylon*, ch. 5.
[48] See, generally, Bryce, *Studies in History and Jurisprudence*, vol. I, pp. 196 sqq.
[49] Sidgwick, op. cit., p. 612.

7

The Courts and the Constitution

THE PROBLEM OF ENFORCEMENT

Constitutionally guaranteed Bills of Rights are enormously weakened unless there exists provision for their effective enforcement. It is not sufficient to frame a satisfactory Bill of Rights: it is not enough to devise a satisfactory special procedure for constitutional amendment, and to determine with accuracy the particular clauses to which it applies. In addition, the rights guaranteed by the constitution must be enforced; and the most effective method, so far devised, of providing for their enforcement is to empower the judiciary to interpret the constitution and to strike down legislation or executive decrees which conflict with its provisions.

In the course of our discussion of this subject we shall be using a few more or less technical terms which occasionally obscure understanding, but about which there really ought not to be any mystery. However, to ensure clarity, and to avoid possible misunderstanding, it may be useful to devote a few words to preliminary definition. I have in mind such terms as the 'testing right', or to use a synonymous expression, the 'power of judicial review'.

The 'testing right', in the context of constitutional guarantees, means the solemn *duty* entrusted to the courts to interpret the constitution and decide whether in a particular case the legal restraints placed upon the legislative and executive organs of government have been transgressed.

This doctrine is sometimes called the American doctrine of judicial review or judicial supremacy;[1] and if it is meant by this phrase to pay tribute to its outstanding importance and successful development in the United States, the description is both apt and just. But it is not an exclusively American institution. Indeed, as we have seen, it is fast becoming a cardinal feature of government the world over.

The United States is, of course, a country possessing a federal government and a rigid constitution; but one should not fall into the error of believing that the idea of a judicially enforceable Bill of Rights is necessarily bound up with the difference between federal and unified government, or even with the distinction between

[1] C. G. Haines, *The American Doctrine of Judicial Supremacy*, 2nd ed., 1932.

flexible and rigid constitutions. And in this connexion let us begin by putting on one side the distinction between federal and unified government. The point to note is that a judicially enforceable Bill of Rights is not incompatible with a unitary constitution. However desirable it might be to change the South African Constitution into a federation, a judicially enforceable Bill of Rights could be introduced without a federal structure. For example, Ireland, Ceylon, Portugal, Greece and Norway all have unitary constitutions; yet their courts have power to decide upon the validity of legislation. On the other hand, though the testing right is usual in federations, it is not indispensable. For example, Switzerland is a federation, but the judiciary has no power to test the validity of federal legislation.[2]

The distinction between flexible and rigid constitutions, which we discussed in a previous chapter, brings us closer to our subject. Obviously, where a country has chosen a flexible constitution there is little, if any, room for the courts to say whether or not the constitutionally prescribed limits of Parliament's power have been transgressed; precisely because flexible constitutions (unlike rigid constitutions) do not prescribe such limits.

Now although in modern times there is hardly any scope for judicial review under a flexible constitution, it would be a mistake to imagine that it is impossible to do without judicial review where the constitution is rigid. For example, Belgium, France and Holland all have rigid constitutions, yet the courts have no say in regard to the question whether the legislature has infringed the constitution. It is felt in these countries that this great power should be left to some other body, either the legislature itself (thereby making the legislature judge in its own cause), or some special tribunal, or the people.

It is precisely because practice in regard to judicial review differs from country to country, and also because sharp differences of opinion exist upon its merits and demerits, that it deserves our close attention.

As regards South Africa there is, perhaps, an additional reason why the subject merits attention. The country's historical experience of the judicial review of legislation enacted by superior legislatures has, on the whole, not been a happy one. On the contrary, with the brief and comparatively insignificant exception of the late Orange Free State Republic,[3] this experience has been stormy and unhappy. In the Transvaal Republic, under the Kruger regime, it led to

[2] G. Solyom, *La jurisdiction constitutionelle aux Etats-unis et en Suisse*, Paris, 1923; Bryce, *Essays in History and Jurisprudence*, vol. 1, p. 231.

[3] See L. M. Thompson, 'Constitutionalism in the South African Republics', 1954 *Butterworth's S.A. Law Review*, pp. 50 sqq.; Bryce, *Studies in History and Jurisprudence*, vol. I, pp. 430 sqq.

the dismissal of the Chief Justice, Sir John Kotzé;[4] and, it will be recalled, during the years 1952–6 there was another ugly clash between Parliament and the courts—with the victory on the side of Parliament.

Moreover, under the South Africa Act, and also under the former Cape Constitution Ordinance, the area in respect of which it has been competent for the courts to declare legislation void, on the score of its being *ultra vires*, has always been comparatively small. In practice this power has been confined, substantially, to setting aside the legislation of subordinate bodies, and then only on a few specified grounds.

There can be no doubt that the wide sphere in respect of which a parliamentary majority in South Africa has hitherto enjoyed undoubted legislative supremacy, has had the effect of appreciably reducing the onerousness of the judicial office. The South African judiciary, like the British, has been able to stand aloof from questions of high political import, and the possibility of unpleasant conflicts with the legislature has been negligible. The result has been to produce in South Africa a professional legal tradition of satisfaction with the existing system. Thus, in *Rex* v. *McChlery*,[5] Sir James Rose-Innes said:

> Having regard to the fact that a subordinate legislature is (within the limits of its subjects and area) in a similar position to the British Parliament, it is impossible that the Colonial courts should have an overriding authority to say when measures are, and when they are not, in the general interests of peace, order and good government. Such a task would be in the highest degree invidious and difficult, *and it is fortunate that the spirit of our constitution does not impose it upon the judges.*

Admittedly the duties which face judges who have to exercise powers of judicial review under a well-drafted constitution are, or should be, more definite and clear-cut than the determination of what is, and what is not, 'in the general interests of peace, order and good government'. But it is quite clear that however carefully a Bill of Rights may be drafted, the responsibilities of the judiciary would be very greatly increased. Accordingly, it is no more than realistic to suppose that an influential body of professional opinion in South Africa (not least among the judges themselves) might regard any extension of responsibility in the direction of judicial review, as being 'in the highest degree invidious'.

[4] For a balanced account, see the Hon. B. A. Tindall's introduction to Kotzé's *Memoirs and Reminiscences*, vol. 2. Gen. Smuts, then at the Bar in the Transvaal, supported Kruger and was probably the author of an anonymous pro-Kruger article in (1898) *Cape Law Journal* 94–108.

[5] 1912 A.D. at 200–1. My italics.

But these points, substantial as they are, are not of the essence of the case against judicial review. The real opposition to a judicially enforceable Bill of Rights would, presumably, be based not only on local historical experience, but on arguments of far more general application and significance, to which we shall turn presently. Here it may suffice to say that if the more general arguments against judicial review can be effectively answered, and if in time to come the popular demand for a judicially enforceable Bill of Rights becomes sufficiently strong, there is no reason why previous experience and professional habits of thought should present too difficult an obstacle.

At the same time, the present content of South African legal education in constitutional law would require radical revision — which might well be a very good thing.

THE CASE AGAINST JUDICIAL REVIEW

The case against judicial review may be stated under five heads:

1. *Defeating the will of the people and their representatives*

In the first place, it is often argued that when a court declares the enactment of a legislative body to be unconstitutional and void, it thereby defeats the will of the people as expressed through their representatives in the legislature. It is claimed to be undemocratic that the final word in government should rest with judges who are neither elected by nor answerable to the people. If Parliament makes a mistake, it is said, the people may always turn them out and put another Parliament in their place; but the judges are not accountable to the people.

That eminent names may be found to support this line of attack, I should be the last to deny. It is, for example, one of the grounds on which the judicial review of legislation was opposed by General Smuts and others when the South African Union was formed; and it is one of the grounds upon which Smuts supported Kruger against Chief Justice Kotzé during the 'judicial crisis' caused by Kotzé's exercise of the testing right in the former Transvaal Republic. Let me quote Sir Edgar Walton's account of a speech by General Smuts on the subject at the National Convention:

> Was the Convention — asked Smuts incredulously — to leave the supreme power of government in the hands of an unrepresentative body such as a court of justice; and shall it be made possible for a court of justice to override an Act of Parliament? That, however, was what was happening in Australia where the Supreme Court was giving judgment against the Parliament of the country.[6]

[6] Walton, *The Inner History of the National Convention*, pp. 60–1. It would be easy to multiply similar quotations.

In the United States the same point of view is sometimes expressed; and, in support of it, reference is made, *inter alia*, to Bishop Hoadley's statement that:

> Whoever hath an absolute authority to interpret any written or spoken laws, it is he who is truly the lawgiver, to all intents and purposes, and not the person who first spoke or wrote them.[7]

Occasionally the same line of attack is put forward in terms of the emotionally charged concept of sovereignty, it being assumed that sovereignty, like some gift of Divine grace, is precious beyond price. Thus it is said that to incorporate a judicially enforceable Bill of Rights means the abandonment of the sovereignty of Parliament, and it is claimed, in addition, that the judges would thereby be given power to override the sovereign will of the people.

2. *Are the judges better guardians than the legislature?*

Secondly, it is said that there is no good and sufficient reason why the courts should be regarded as better guardians of liberty, and interpreters of constitutional guarantees, than either the legislature or the executive.[8] For example, Professor Commager, the eminent American historian, says that most of the important questions that arise when the power of judicial review is exercised are not strictly legal questions, but really questions of social or economic policy in regard to which a legal training may be more of a hindrance than an advantage.[9]

Pointing to the United States Constitution, the critics show, for example, how over the years the Supreme Court reached conflicting decisions on the validity of various laws dealing with minimum wages and maximum hours in industry; and they contend, not without justice, that these decisions did not turn upon the exercise of a lawyer's skill in interpreting legal phrases, but upon economic policies which the court read into the Constitution by giving an arbitrary meaning to such broad concepts as 'property' and 'due process of law'. In essence, therefore, the economic policies favoured by the court were allowed to override those approved by the legislators.[10]

[7] Quoted by Mr. Justice Holmes in 6 *Harvard Law Review* 33; also Thayer's *Legal Essays*, 1908, p. 33. See, generally, L. B. Boudin, *Government by Judiciary*, New York, 1932, 2 vols.

[8] One of the earliest and still one of the most forceful statements of this point of view is to be found in the American case of *Eakin* v. *Raub* (1825). The judgment of Gibson J. in that case is highly critical of Marshall C.J.'s judgment in *Marbury* v. *Madison*. See Thayer's *Cases on Constitutional Law*, vol. 1, pp. 133 sqq.; Freund, Sutherland, Howe and Brown, *Constitutional Law*, vol. 1, pp. 11 sqq.

[9] *Majority Rule and Minority Rights*, Oxford, 1943, pp. 79–80.

[10] See, generally, Jackson, *The Struggle for Judicial Supremacy*, 1941; R. K. Carr, *The Supreme Court and Judicial Review*, 1942, p. 99 sqq.

The critics have no difficulty in showing how for two long years the judges of the Supreme Court ruled against the Roosevelt 'New Deal' legislation, and then proceeded to reverse their decisions after President Roosevelt had threatened to appoint new judges.[11] All this is wrong, say those who are opposed to a judicially enforceable Bill of Rights, and should be avoided by leaving the final word with the legislators. Moreover, even assuming that limitations upon legislative power should be written into a constitution, what right or reason, the critics ask, have we to say that the people's representatives are any less fit to interpret the limitations and provisions of the constitution than the judges?[12] And in support of this view they are able to quote several continental precedents.[13]

One might sum up the objections under this head in one sentence: a constitution should not be considered as an ordinary legal document to be interpreted by the ordinary courts, but primarily as a political document to be interpreted by political or specially constituted tribunals.[14]

3. *Political appointments to the Bench*

Thirdly, it is said that a major defect of a judicially enforceable Bill of Rights is that it leads to political appointments to the Bench: the Government finding its legislation overruled by the courts, proceeds to appoint judges whom it believes will be favourable to its own political bias. And this brings the Bench into disrepute.

Here again, names of weight and authority may be invoked to support the attack. This, for example, is what General Smuts said on the point at the South African National Convention:[15]

A natural result of a system [giving the testing right to the courts] was that the appointments to the courts were political, for a political party was likely to take such precautions as were possible to ensure itself and its measures against adverse judgments.

And it would not be difficult to multiply authority to the same effect.

4. *Uncertainty in the law*

Fourthly, it is claimed that where one leaves decisions upon the validity of legislation to the judges, this causes great uncertainty in the law; and in elaborating this contention, three main lines of argument are adduced.

---

[11] Jackson, *The Struggle for Judicial Supremacy;* C. H. Pritchett, *The Roosevelt Court*, New York, 1948.

[12] See, generally, the judgment of Gibson J. in *Eakin* v. *Raub*, note 8 above.

[13] See below, p. 143.

[14] See Haines, *The American Doctrine of Judicial Supremacy*, 2nd ed., ch. 1; and vol. 16, *Modern Law Review*, p. 284.

[15] Walton, op. cit., p. 61.

First, it is pointed out that great constitutional issues are made to depend upon whether a private litigant raises the issue in a court of law; and if he does bring the matter to court, there is the risk that statutes that have stood for many years, and have been widely acted upon, may be set aside. In the United States, for example, the Smith Act of 1940 and the Alien Registration Act, also of 1940, were challenged for the first time after the lapse of ten years.[16]

Secondly, it is claimed that the judicial enforcement of human rights encourages a 'flood' of constitutional litigation, with all the uncertainty which that entails; that human rights are, in short, primarily a gold-mine for lawyers.[17]

Thirdly, it is argued that in these cases judges often go back upon their previous decisions because of some technical reason, or because they have changed their minds. The judges tend to regard the doctrine of *stare decisis*, i.e. the authority of the binding precedent, as less persuasive in great constitutional cases where the liberty of the subject may be involved, than in ordinary commercial litigation.[18] And all this, it is alleged, leads to grave uncertainty in the law. Why not, then, leave it to the legislature to say authoritatively what the law shall be; leave them free to decide on these matters from day to day, and everyone will know where he is: what the legislature says will be the law of the land, and there is an end of the matter.

5. *Debilitating the people in the exercise of responsibility*

Fifthly, there is an objection which I think may best be stated in the words of a great American constitutionalist, the late Professor J. B. Thayer. This is what he says:

> Great and indeed inestimable as are the advantages in a popular government of this conservative influence (that is to say, the power of the judiciary to disregard unconstitutional legislation), it should be remembered that the exercise of it, even when unavoidable, is always attended with a great evil; namely, that the correction of legislative mistakes comes from the outside, and that people thus lose the political experience and the moral education and stimulus that come from fighting the question out in the ordinary way and correcting their own errors. The tendency of an easy resort to this great function of the courts, now lamentably too common, is to dwarf the political capacity of the people and to deaden their sense of moral responsibility.[19]

[16] Jackson, *The Supreme Court in the American System of Government*, pp. 24–5.

[17] See Gledhill, *Fundamental Rights in India*, 1956, pp. 128–9; 'The First Decade of the Indian Constitution'; in *Journal of the Indian Law Institute*, 1960, pp. 157 sqq.

[18] See the cases cited by Mason and Beany, *The Supreme Court in a Free Society*, New Jersey, 1959, pp. 22 sqq.

[19] Cited by Commager, op. cit., p. 73.

Much the same sort of thing has been said in the United States in more recent times, notably by Mr. Justice Frankfurter. 'Education in abandoning foolish legislation', he says, 'is itself a training in liberty'.[20] And in quoting this passage, Professor Commager adds this:

> If our democracy is less educated in this respect than we might wish, if our legislatures are less alert to constitutional principles than might be desirable, a heavy responsibility rests upon the courts. For these, by taking over to themselves the peculiar guardianship of the constitution, have discouraged the people's active and intelligent interest in such matters.[21]

Thus far I have gathered together and restated arguments which are more or less familiar among political scientists in the English-speaking world. Similar arguments, however, have been used, and have found acceptance, on the continent of Europe. Thus, although constitutional guarantees have long found a place in continental constitutions, until comparatively recently they have not (broadly speaking) been court-enforced, for a variety of reasons which may be summarized under three heads.

In the first place there are certain historical reasons, which have operated mainly in France. The climate of French thought in this field has been strongly influenced against judicial review by the obstructionism of the old 'Parliaments' (courts) during the pre-revolutionary period.[22]

Secondly, continental lawyers interpret the doctrine of the separation of powers far more strictly than do their Anglo-American colleagues; and they regard adjudication upon legislative acts by the ordinary courts as an infringement of that doctrine.[23]

And thirdly, they have hitherto tended to hold the view that problems of government are so entirely different from those of private and commercial intercourse, that the law relating to them should 'breathe a different atmosphere', and not be dealt with in the same courts.[24] For these reasons constitutionalists on the Continent, while purporting to place 'legal' restrictions upon the legislature, have hitherto tended to make the legislature the sole interpreter of the constitution and the judge of its own powers; or, alternatively, to entrust this task to some specially constituted tribunal. In short, on this view, the constitution is not regarded as a legal document in the ordinary sense.

[20] Quoted by Commager, op. cit., pp. 74–5.
[21] Op. cit., p. 75.
[22] See, generally, (1953) 16 *Modern Law Review* 283 note 50.
[23] See previous note.
[24] See the discussion in Stephen's *Commentaries on the Laws of England*, 21st ed., vol. 3, p. 341.

THE CASE FOR JUDICIAL REVIEW

This then is the case to be met; and I am not disposed to deny that at first sight it seems a very formidable one. Moreover, I certainly do not dispute that there is a degree of truth in several of the objections. But I believe that it is possible to answer all the objections fairly and effectively; and that, on balance, despite several dangers which may attend it, the case for a judicially enforceable Bill of Rights is the sounder one.

1. *The judges do not override the will of the people*

Two answers have been given to the first line of attack—namely, that in declaring an unconstitutional statute to be void, the courts defeat the will of the people. And both answers give full weight to the idea that, in the ultimate analysis, the people are entitled to establish the framework of government under which they live.[25]

In the first place, it is necessary to distinguish between 'the people' (*a*) considered as a community consisting of the entire living population together with their predecessors and successors; and (*b*) the voters who from time to time elect representatives to act as legislators.[26] In other words, it is necessary to distinguish between the people, considered in their constitution-making or constituent capacity, and the people considered in their electoral capacity.

And the relevance of this distinction, in this context, is itself twofold. One approach, which is perhaps the best known, is to ascribe more weight to the will of the people, in their sovereign constitution-making capacity, than to their will as declared in periodic general elections. This point of view has been so well explained by Willoughby, the author of one of the older but still very useful text-books on the American Constitution, that I cannot do better than quote his words:

> In truth what is done is this. The people acting solemnly and deliberately in their sovereign capacity declare that certain matters shall be determined in a certain way. These matters, because of their great and fundamental importance, they reduce to definite written form and declare that they shall not be changed except in a particular manner. In addition to this, they go on to say, in substance, that so decided is their will and so maturely formed their judgment upon these matters, that any act of their own representatives in legislation inconsistent therewith is not to be taken as expressing their true will. When, therefore, the courts declare void acts inconsistent with constitutional provisions, the

[25] A doctrine which is more fully discussed below, pp. 185 sqq.; 232–3.

[26] Walter Lippmann, *The Public Philosophy*, 1955, pp. 38–41; A. K. Brohi; *The Fundamental Law of Pakistan*, 1958, p. 44.

judges are giving effect to the real will of the people as they had previously solemnly declared it.[27]

The classical exposition of this point of view in the American courts was given by Chief Justice Marshall in the famous case of *Marbury* v. *Maddison*.[28] After asserting that the people have an undoubted right to establish their future government, he went on to say that 'the exercise of this right is a very great exertion; nor can it, nor ought it, to be frequently repeated'. The constitution then is the *basic*, maturely considered, mandate of power from the people to all organs of government, including the legislature. More recently Mr. Justice Owen Roberts summed up this point of view as follows:

> There should be no misunderstanding as to the function of this Court. It is sometimes said that the Court assumes a power to overrule or control the action of the people's representatives. This is a misconception. The Constitution is the supreme law of the land ordained and established by the people. All legislation must conform to the principles it lays down. When an act of Congress is appropriately challenged in the courts as not conforming to the constitutional mandate, the judicial branch of the Government has only one duty—to lay the article of the Constitution which is invoked beside the statute which is challenged and to decide whether the latter squares with the former. All the Court does, or can do, is to announce its considered judgment upon the question. The only power it has, if such it may be called, is the power of judgment. This Court neither approves nor condemns any legislative policy. Its delicate and difficult office is to ascertain and declare whether the legislation is in accordance with, or in contravention of, the provisions of the Constitution; and, having done that, its duty ends.[29]

From another, and even more direct point of view, the superior binding authority of the people's will, as contained in the constitution, may be justified as follows. The people in establishing a constitution generally include a clause defining the method in which the constitution may be amended or repealed. This method is invariably a difficult one—more specifically, the amending process is ordinarily, by the people's express intention, made far more difficult than a popular vote at a general election. The United States Constitution, for example, cannot be amended by a mere majority vote at an election. Now, once the people in establishing their fundamental

[27] The Constitution of the United States, 2nd ed., vol. 1, p. 9. To the same effect, Bryce, *The American Commonwealth*, 3rd ed., vol. 1, p. 256.

[28] (1803) 1 Cranch.

[29] *United States* v. *Butler*, 297 U.S. 1 at 62, cited by Curtis, *Lions under the Throne*, p. 16.

law (i.e. the constitution) have laid down the method for repealing or amending that law, then, in Professor Wheare's words, 'the constitution binds thereafter not only the institutions which it establishes, but also the people itself'.[30] They cannot thereafter, without resorting to a revolution or a break in the established legal order, amend the constitution except by the methods which it provides. And, of course, the reason for this is obvious. The law in force for the time being, including the law on the subject of constitutional amendment, must be observed; to deny this is to deny the authority of *all* law and to resort to mob rule.[31]

Thus far we might summarize the argument by saying that the people's wishes, as solemnly declared on behalf of the whole nation in their constitution-making capacity, are deemed in law to have superior force to the people's wishes as declared from time to time in general elections. And so far, I venture to think, so good. Admittedly there is no room here for the sovereignty of the legislature; nor for the sovereignty of electoral mandates from time to time. But then it is precisely to abolish such sovereignty that Bills of Rights are established. This point could hardly be better expressed than it was by Mr. Justice Jackson in the case of *West Virginia State Board of Education* v. *Barnette:*

> The very purpose of Bills of Rights was to withdraw certain subjects from the vicissitudes of political controversy, to place them beyond the reach of majorities and officials and to establish them as legal principles to be applied by the courts. One's rights to life, liberty and prosperity, free speech, a free press, freedom of worship and assembly, and other fundamental rights, may not be submitted to the vote, they depend on the outcome of no elections.[32]

Moreover, it is not irrelevant to add, for the comfort of those who are so much concerned about maintaining the power of the legislature, that Bills of Rights may on occasion even operate to safeguard the legislature from the encroachments involved in delegated legislation; for in modern states it is, regrettably, becoming more realistic to speak about the sovereignty of ministers than the sovereignty of Parliament.

I turn now to the second argument that is sometimes employed in answering the objection that judicial review allows the judges to override the will of the people. It was usual for an older generation of lawyers to raise a second line of defence by emphasizing that all the judges do in these cases concerning the constitution is to

---

[30] *Modern Constitutions*, pp. 89–90.
[31] For further elaboration see pp. 232–3 below.
[32] 319 U.S. 638 (1942).

'interpret' the law; and attempts were made to play down the creative role of judges in the process of interpretation. There is, indeed, a trace of this attitude in the statement which I have quoted by Mr. Justice Roberts. And a far more typical pronouncement of this once fashionable point of view is the following, by Lord Bryce:

> It is therefore no mere technicality to point out that the American judges do not as Europeans are apt to say 'control' the legislature. They simply interpret the law. The word 'control' is misleading, because it implies that the person or body of whom it is used possesses and exerts a discretionary personal will. *Now the American judges have no will in the matter.* The will that prevails is the will of the people as expressed in the constitution which they have enacted.[33]

Ever since Mr. Justice Cardozo published his now famous pioneering essays on the *Nature of the Judicial Process*,[34] few serious lawyers would contend that the judges have *no will* in the matter of interpreting a constitution. The judicial function is no mere automatic slot-machine process. On the contrary, the judges occasionally have very wide discretion in interpreting constitutional guarantees, and in some cases, as for example when interpreting the phrase 'due process of law' in the United States Constitution, they have appeared to their critics to read into them virtually what they liked. As Mr. Justice Holmes put it, at one time in the United States it seemed as if the sky was the limit in the matter of judicial discretion; and he once found it necessary to warn his colleagues that the United States Constitution did not embody Mr. Herbert Spencer's *Social Statics*. In the result one heard critics allege that the United States was saddled with government by judiciary, rather than government by the people's representatives.[35] Or to quote Chief Justice Hughes (as he later became): 'We live under a constitution; but the constitution is what the judges say it is.'[36]

Here again, however, we must guard against exaggeration. Much depends upon how a constitution is drafted. The idea is to fix the outside limits of reasonable legislative action; and for this purpose comparatively few guarantees are, or need be, as vague as the 'due process' clause. Indeed, I am convinced that the role of judicial discretion in these matters has often been exaggerated. It should

---

[33] *The American Commonwealth*, 3rd ed., vol. 1, p. 252. My italics. There is a passage to precisely the same effect in the judgment of Marshall C.J. in *Marbury v. Madison*.

[34] *The Nature of the Judicial Process*, Yale, 1921.

[35] One of the most vigorous presentations of this point of view is L. B. Boudin's *Government by Judiciary*, 2 vols. New York, 1952. The literature on the subject is vast.

[36] Quoted by Corwin, *The Constitution and What it Means Today*, 1948, p. xiii.

never be forgotten that, on the whole, when judges interpret and enforce the traditional civil liberties, they give effect to established traditions, traditions with a long ancestry in religious, ethical and political thought. I do not say that the process of applying 'the law' is a mechanical one, a judicial slot-machine process; far from it. But the area of discretion is apt to be caricatured by the critics; as, for example, when one writer sees in a long line of decisions by the South African Appellate Division an ill-concealed plot by a 'liberal' court to strike down the Government's apartheid legislation because they did not like it.[37] The critics have overstated a good point which needed stating.

Again, the quotation from Bishop Hoadly that 'whoever hath an absolute authority to interpret laws is truly the lawgiver', is misleading. If by 'absolute' is meant final, the judge's interpretation is not necessarily final. Most constitutions provide for their amendment, even though the process may be difficult; in fact, the United States Constitution has more than once been amended to reverse the effect of a decision of the Supreme Court.

If, on the other hand, by 'absolute' is meant 'arbitrary', it suffices to note that judges do not possess arbitrary power. Admittedly they should exercise self-restraint;[38] but they are very materially helped to do so by the accepted convention that they must give reasons for their decisions. It is not sufficiently realized, I think, how substantially the need to give reasons helps to make judicial decisions principled.[39]

2. *The judges are the appropriate guardians*

We should have no difficulty with the second argument against judicial review—namely, that even where limitations upon the powers of government and guaranteed rights are written into a constitution, the duty of interpretation should not be entrusted to the courts, because (so it is contended) there is no good and sufficient reason why the legislature or the executive should not themselves be left to interpret the constitution.

This is really to deny that the constitution is a legal document. But to deny that the constitution is a legal document is to deny what it normally specifically purports to be. Constitutions like the United States Constitution, when established by the people, normally declare specifically that their provisions are 'the supreme *law* of the

[37] Edward McWhinney, *Judicial Review in the English-speaking World*, Toronto, 1956.

[38] For a recent statement on the subject, see Learned Hand, *The Bill of Rights*, Harvard, 1958.

[39] Legislatures used to give reasons for making laws, namely in preambles, but unfortunately the practice is waning. See, generally, Taylor's introduction to Plato's *Laws*, pp. xvii–xviii, where the value of preambles is discussed.

land'. And once this is appreciated, then, as Marshall C.J. pointed out in *Marbury* v. *Madison*, 'it is emphatically the province and duty of the judicial department to say what the law is'.[40]

There is, too, yet more to be said against the objection with which we are now concerned. Summarizing arguments which were once used by Alexander Hamilton, Professor Willis has pointed out that to entrust the interpretation of the constitution to the judges is the 'natural and appropriate' thing. And these are the reasons which he gives:

> It is the natural and appropriate thing, first, because the limitations in the constitution are mostly limitations upon the executive and legislative branches of the government and not upon the judiciary; and since a branch with such limitations should not measure its own power, it is appropriate for the judiciary to do this. Secondly, it is the natural and appropriate thing because the judiciary is the weakest of the three departments. It has no control over the sword, nor over the purse, and its members are less likely to be influenced by momentary passion.[41]

This quotation does not need lengthy elaboration, but three points may perhaps usefully be made.

In the first place, if further argument be needed on the point that an assembly or tribunal should not be the judge of its own powers, attention should be directed to that remarkable phenomenon—the South African version of the High Court of Parliament. The moral of the judgment which struck down that tribunal is well stated in the following passage in the judgment of Mr. Justice Greenberg:

> The high standard of impartiality necessary for a judicial determination of questions both of fact and of law is a cornerstone of [the judicial] system; and is preserved by the undoubted principle that no one should be a judge in his own cause, and that the litigant can ensure the preservation of this principle by the right of recusation. The constitution of the High Court of Parliament which appoints as its judges the legislators who themselves have been responsible for the passing of the legislation, the validity of which is the question in issue before that Court, and the denial to the litigant of a right of recusation on this ground, accord ill with the fundamental requirement of judicial impartiality.[42]

Secondly, it is important to give emphasis to Willis's point that the judges, by the very nature of their training, are less likely than any other body to be influenced by passion or prejudice. And on this

[40] (1803) 1 Cranch; reprinted in Freund, Sutherland, Howe and Brown, *Constitutional Law*, vol. 1, p. 9.

[41] *Constitutional Law*, Indiana, 1936, p. 78.

[42] 1952 (4) S.A. at 786. See also Bryce, *American Commonwealth*, 3rd ed., vol. 1, p. 256.

point I would quote another South African judicial pronouncement. Mr. Justice Schreiner has said:

> The Superior Courts of South Africa have at least for many generations had characteristics which, rooted in the world's experience, are calculated to ensure, within the limits of human frailty, the efficient and honest administration of justice according to law. Our courts are manned by full-time judges trained in the law, who are outside party politics and have no personal interest in the cases which come before them, whose tenure of office and emoluments are protected by law and whose independence is a major source of the security and well-being of the State. The jurisdiction of these courts is general as to subject-matter, they are available to all disputants who claim that they have legal rights to maintain and before them all interested parties are entitled to present their evidence and their arguments.[43]

And thirdly, it is not always realized, to quote Willis, how comparatively powerless as an organ of government even a great court like the United States Supreme Court really is. Its jurisdiction in a wide field is subject to such exceptions as Congress may make:[44] the President may increase its size;[45] it can only settle law-suits brought to it by litigants and has no power to take the initiative in checking what the judges may know to be violations of the Constitution.[46] And it has no power to enforce its judgments.[47] As President Jackson once said of a decision which he disliked: 'John Marshall has made his decision; now let him enforce it.'[48] But such an attitude of open defiance is extremely rare.

Some of these attributes of judicial impotence should, in my view, be regarded as defects and not as merits, if the judiciary is to be entrusted with the great responsibility of safeguarding a constitution. They cannot, and no doubt should not, all be remedied; but some of them both can and should be.

Thus, for example, if the judges are to discharge their function as guardians of the constitution effectively, it is very desirable—and in most countries necessary—that the composition and jurisdiction of the Supreme Court, the method of making judicial appointments and the tenure of the judges, should be placed beyond the reach of legislative or executive manipulation. Long ago, Lord Bryce

[43] 1952 (4) S.A. at 789. To the same effect, Hughes, *The Supreme Court of the United States*, p. 241.

[44] Jackson, *The Supreme Court in the American System of Government*, p. 11, quoting *Ex parte McCardle*, 7 Wall 506.

[45] Jackson, op. cit., p. 25.

[46] Jackson, op. cit., pp. 11–12.

[47] Jackson, op. cit., p. 11.

[48] Quoted by Jackson, *The Supreme Court in the American System of Government*, p. 11.

revealed an inadequacy in the existing Constitution of the United States of America in this connexion; and he showed how, by the device of 'court-packing', a president could make the protections of the Constitution disappear 'like a morning mist'.[49] In the intervening years, however, the whole question of judicial tenure has been intensively studied, and marked progress has been made in effecting greater security.

One of the most recent and, in my view, soundest methods of dealing with the subject is to be found in the law of Israel, under which members of the Bar, the existing judiciary, as well as members of the Government, are all given a voice in judicial appointments.[50]

3. *Political appointments—an inconclusive argument*

As regards the dangers to be feared from political appointments, I think that these have been heavily exaggerated. Of course, as long as judges continue to be appointed by the Government, the risk is there. No one denies it. But the risk would largely disappear if the method of judicial appointment suggested in the preceding section were introduced.

And, in any event, there is another side of the picture which largely offsets the present danger. We must not discount the force of legal training and professional tradition. It must not be forgotten that even though appointments are sometimes made to the Bench because of the political antecedents of the appointees, nevertheless when these men go on the Bench they take with them the restraints of their legal training, and they cannot entirely ignore the professional opinion of their colleagues—on the Bench, at the Bar, at the Side-Bar, and in the universities.

There are stories attributed to both the late Mr. Tielman Roos and the late Mr. Oswald Pirow (when they were Ministers of Justice in previous South African governments) about certain South African judges whose appointments were made on political grounds; and the Ministers found to their chagrin that the particular judges then proceeded to give decisions against the government that appointed them. 'The trouble about these judges', said Roos and Pirow, 'is that they get delusions of grandeur. Having acquired security of tenure, they imagine that they were appointed on merit!' There are, in fact, numerous cases in the history of the United States Supreme Court where appointments, obviously political in character, have proved to be completely impartial, the judges in question fre-

<hr />

[49] *The American Commonwealth*, 3rd ed., 1900, vol. 1, p. 276.

[50] For details, see Judges Law 5713 of 1953 (Israel). The Israeli law has been influenced by the Missouri system in the United States.

quently giving judgment against the administration that appointed them.[51]

And finally, on this point, it is relevant to invoke the experience of Professor Wheare. Dealing with the argument that the 'testing right' brings judges into the field of political controversy, and thereby tends to discredit the judiciary, he says:

> There can be little doubt that there is some truth in this opinion, though it is interesting to notice that in the United States, Canada, and Australia, the supreme tribunals are regarded with respect, though often with sympathy for their difficulties in the task laid upon them.[52]

4. Uncertainty—What is certainty?

In regard to the fourth objection, namely the alleged uncertainty which a judicially enforceable Bill of Rights brings into the law, Professor Wheare has rightly pointed out that much depends upon the actual way in which the constitution is drafted. When the guarantees written into it are simple and clear-cut, and designed primarily to protect the traditional liberties like personal freedom, freedom of speech, freedom of association, freedom of conscience, the right to a fair trial, and so on, and where the qualifications, if any, are carefully drafted, there is not nearly as much risk of uncertainty being introduced into the law as is sometimes suggested. After all, these are ideas which have been given precision by centuries of tradition; their scope is comparatively clear-cut and deeply ingrained in both the lay and the professional mind. And these, moreover, are the freedoms that most need protection in the modern world.

Turning now to the more specific objections under this head, there is clearly substance in the objection that enactments may be nullified in private litigation after the delay of many years. In part, however, the difficulty may be met by making provision for declaratory judgments on a stated case immediately after the enactment of legislation. Another suggestion sometimes put forward in this regard, is that the court should, at the request of the government, be empowered to give an advisory opinion upon the introduction of any Bill *before* it is passed. But this is an altogether more dubious procedure.

There would also appear to be substance in the contention that where one allows the judicial review of legislation, the volume of constitutional litigation is likely to be heavy. Though this has not been the Irish experience, it has been the Indian experience, and is likely to be the experience of countries—like India or South Africa—

[51] Hughes, op. cit., p. 48, quoting Warren, *The Supreme Court of the United States*.

[52] *Modern Constitutions*, p. 175.

with considerable internal stresses. On the other hand, litigation is discouragingly expensive; though it must be conceded that if judicial review were introduced, an increase in litigation is one of the hazards to be faced.

The objection that the judges introduce uncertainty by changing their minds and overruling themselves is not convincing. Indeed, it is difficult not to be a little impatient with this talk about certainty. To begin with, judges are slow to depart from established precedents. And why should they not change their minds upon mature reconsideration? They are fully alive to their responsibilities, and will not lightly overrule themselves. Surely it is better for them to be right, even if inconsistent, than to be consistently wrong? It is true that Lord Hardwicke once said—and every tyro repeats it—that certainty is the mother of repose and therefore the law aims at certainty.[53] But is this not mere rhetoric? Certainty is always a matter of degree. Absolute certainty in law is an illusion. And, in any event, what is the alternative? The alternative is that the legislature should be given unfettered power to tamper with fundamental values at will— responsive to every gust of popular emotion, and to every surge of an impatient majority. The only certainty here, in countries without long established and ingrained traditions, is the certainty of instability and possible tyranny.

5. *Public opinion is not thereby debilitated, but rather educated*
The fifth argument against a judicially enforceable Bill of Rights is that it tends to transfer responsibility from the public to the courts and so debilitates public opinion. This, I think, is unconvincing and inconclusive. Indeed, I would suggest that the exact contrary is the case. Not only is public interest positively stirred when great constitutional issues come before the courts, but, in addition, the critics of judicial review would appear to overlook the great educative value of a set of written criteria serving as the measure of governmental conduct. A properly drafted Bill of Rights, which is actually enforced, becomes part of the political education of the community; the values which it embodies are taught in the schools in civics classes; and, if properly taught, may open the way to an understanding of the natural law. Moreover, these values, by becoming a common heritage, serve as a cohesive factor in society. In the result, notwithstanding the respect which is due to opposite opinions, it is submitted that the conclusion reached by Lord Bryce is sound:

> The rigid Constitution of the United States has rendered, and renders now, inestimable services. It opposes obstacles to rash

[53] *Walton* v. *Tryon* (1753) 21 English Reports 262.

and hasty change. It secures time for deliberation. It forces the people to think seriously before they alter it or pardon a transgression of it. It makes legislatures and statesmen slow to over-pass their legal powers, slow even to propose measures which the Constitution seems to disapprove. It tends to render the inevitable process of modification gradual and tentative, the result of admitted and growing necessities rather than of restless impatience. It altogether prevents some changes which a temporary majority may clamour for, but which will have ceased to be demanded before the barriers interposed by the Constitution have been overcome.

It does still more than this. It forms the mind and temper of the people. It trains them to habits of legality. It strengthens their conservative instincts, their sense of the value of stability and permanence in political arrangements. It makes them feel that to comprehend their supreme instrument of Government is a personal duty, incumbent on each one of them. It familiarises them with, it attaches them by ties of pride and reverence to, those fundamental truths on which the Constitution is based. These are enormous services to render to any free country.[54]

IMPACT UPON EXISTING LEGISLATION

In countries, like South Africa, where the Statute Book is riddled with legislation which infringes most provisions of any reasonably comprehensive Bill of Human Rights, it is necessary to be clear as to the effect which the introduction of such a Bill would have on existing legislation.[55] And on this point it is clear that it would be useless to preserve the *status quo*, leaving the Bill to operate only on future legislation—either without qualification or (as is sometimes suggested) to the extent that future legislation may involve 'a deterioration in the existing position'. Quite apart from the impossible burden of interpretation which such a formula would place upon the judiciary, it would hardly be acceptable to Africans.

Indeed it would seem that concurrently with the introduction of any new constitution containing a Bill of Rights—or as soon thereafter as possible—it would be necessary to embark upon a ruthless pruning from the Statute Book of all discriminatory legislation. For as long as such legislation remains, the doors of the courts would indeed be open to a flood of litigation. In short, committal to a policy of introducing a genuine Bill of Rights in Southern Africa must carry with it, of necessity, a committal to repeal a vast quantity of legislation. There will, to mention one point only, have to be few, if any, references in the law to race and skin colour.

[54] *The American Commonwealth*, 3rd ed., vol. 1, pp. 406–7.
[55] Cf. *The Report of the Monckton Commission*, Cmd. 1148, p. 151.

A SUMMING UP

We are now in a position to attempt a brief assessment of the respective merits of the arguments for and against judicial review. In any fair assessment it is relevant, I think, to keep two points in mind.

First, once it is conceded that some restraints upon legislative and executive power are necessary, it is difficult to think of any alternative to judicial review which does not have graver defects of its own. This, too, was the considered opinion of Professor Dicey.[56]

A brief but lucid survey of alternative procedures for enforcement is to be found in Professor Wheare's book on Modern Constitutions.[57] None of them seems to offer as strong a safeguard as the American doctrine of judicial review; and some of them—like the Swiss technique of submitting a law challenged by 30,000 citizens to a referendum—are very much hit-and-miss affairs.

Secondly, in the affairs of men one seldom, if ever, finds a flawless institution. It is always a question of weighing advantages and disadvantages. Judicial review may well have the defects of its qualities, but in my view its merits outweigh its defects.

[56] *The Law of the Constitution*, 9th ed., pp. 175–9.
[57] Chapter 7.

8

Federalism and other Safeguards

Against the abuse of governmental power, a judicially enforceable Bill of Human Rights, entrenched in a rigid constitution, provides a measure of legal protection for the individual by placing a *check* upon state power. Federalism gives a different kind of safeguard by *dividing* power at its very core. In Sir Robert Garran's words, it is 'a form of government in which sovereignty or political power is divided between the central and local governments, so that each of them within its sphere is independent of the others.'[1]

We have seen that one of the aims of good government is to accommodate the variety and complexity of social life, so that both individuals and groups may flourish. This ideal is constantly threatened, however, by the power of the big centralized state, which tends increasingly to treat individuals and smaller groups as cyphers. Indeed, as Professor Wheare has said:

> One of the most urgent problems in the world today is to preserve diversities . . . and at the same time to introduce such a measure of uniformity as will prevent clashes and facilitate co-operation. Federalism is one way of reconciling these two ends.[2]

Federalism, however, does more than provide a framework within which the power of the state may, perhaps, most satisfactorily be tamed:

> . . . in its broadest and most general sense it is a principle which conceives of the federation as the ideal form of social and political life. It is characterised by a tendency to substitute co-ordinating for subordinating relationships, or at least to restrict the latter as much as possible; to replace compulsion from above with reciprocity, understanding and adjustment, command with persuasion and force with law. The basic aspect of federalism is pluralistic, its fundamental tendency is harmonization and its regulative principle is solidarity.[3]

[1] *Report of the Royal Commission on the Australian Constitution*, 1929, p. 230. And see, generally, K. C. Wheare, *Federal Government*, 3rd. ed., p. 15.

[2] *Federal Government*, 3rd ed., pp. 259–60.

[3] Max Boehm, quoted by A. K. Brohi, *Fundamental Law of Pakistan*, 1958, p. 209.

There are those who say that these ideals are all very well, in fact admirable, but that federalism is not the way to achieve them. Pointing to a tendency in some modern federations for power— especially economic power—to become concentrated in the hands of the central government, they argue that logically the ideal would be to split the world into a multiplicity of small and wholly independent states, without attempting to make any provision for division and co-ordination within the framework of a federal structure; and they remind us of Plato's view that, ideally, a state should be small enough to enable the rulers to maintain personal contact with the citizens.

No one would deny that even in a federation there is the danger of a concentration of power which may well be inimical to freedom; but experience has shown that this danger can be guarded against much more easily in a federal than in a unitary state. Again, no one pretends that federalism is a perfect protection, or an impenetrable barrier against the abuse of power; but without it, there is much *less* protection for individuals and groups.

Then, too, the value of the unifying and co-ordinating functions of federal government should not be lost sight of; for in federations— as in other forms of government—these functions have a role to play, though under federalism it is a carefully defined role; for, as far as possible, barriers are erected against the tendency of power to become centralized. Federalism, in short, means more than mere diversity: it means diversity in unity.

Not only should the co-ordinating function of the federal government disarm fears, antagonisms and jealousies which would be greatly increased by a multiplicity of small sovereign states (antagonisms which, during the foreseeable future, cannot wisely be made the sole responsibility of the United Nations Organization); but, in addition, federalism—as opposed to a multiplicity of small wholly independent states—offers powerful economic advantages, especially in regions where differences in natural wealth are marked. For example, the advantage of a politically organized common market, such as that afforded by the federal structure of the United States of America, is one of the reasons why the less richly endowed states have been able to share in the wealth and prosperity of the whole.[4]

FEDERALISM IN SOUTHERN AFRICA

But for a federation to be a practical success, it—like any other system of government that wishes to conform to democratic and

---

[4] For some economic arguments in favour of federalism in Central Africa, see *The Report of the Monckton Commission*, Cmnd. 1148 of 1960, chapter 4. At the same time, it is clear that the economic case for Central African Federation can be exaggerated. See A. Hazlewood and P. D. Henderson, *The Economics of Federation*, Basil Blackwell, 1960.

not authoritarian standards—must be based on acceptance by the people; and must allow full and fair participation by the people in its functions. And this is just where the Rhodesian or Central African Federation has hitherto been fatally defective. It was apparently felt by those who brought it into being that the increase in wealth which would result from the alliance to Southern Rhodesia of Northern Rhodesia's mineral wealth and Nyasaland's labour, would make the political framework of secondary importance. But this has not been the case. Indeed the argument of economic advantage, without political and social rights, is worthless.[5] Experience, especially African experience, has shown very clearly that men prefer to suffer great economic privation, even to starve, rather than be denied elementary political and social rights.

It is, of course, obvious that in African eyes the record of the Rhodesian Federation has hardly made federalism a popular concept; and I must not be thought to be a supporter of the existing Rhodesian structure in anything like its present form. Nor, indeed, is it at all likely that it will survive in anything like its present form. But whatever the future of the Rhodesian Federation may be,[6] it remains true that federal constitutions can be devised which do not allow discrimination and domination of one group by another; which—on the contrary—could help materially to prevent these evils. And it is perhaps hardly necessary to add that where the political and social aspirations of a people *are* genuinely and fully met, they would not—indeed could not—reasonably object to economic prosperity as well.

It is instructive to note that whereas opposition to federalism in Central Africa comes mainly from non-whites, in South Africa the federal idea is often most strongly opposed by the whites—and in both cases 'the colour question' is at the root of the objection.

In South Africa the argument usually put forward against the idea of territorial federation is that 'it is ruled out by the colour problem', and it is said to be so ruled out for the following reasons. Starting with the assumption that it is essential to deal with race relations throughout the Union in a uniform way, and pointing to the fact that each and every aspect of government may involve a question of race relations; the critics of federation argue that the provinces could not be given exclusive authority over any matter, without endangering the requirements of a uniform method of dealing with race relations.

[5] See the Minority Report of Messrs. W. M. Chirwa and H. G. Habanyama; *Report of the Monckton Commission*, Cmd. 1148 of 1960, pp. 139 sqq.

[6] This was written early in December 1960, when the future of the Federation was obscure.

In 1910 this was widely felt to be the decisive argument in favour of South Africa's decision to adopt a unitary rather than a federal system.[7] But there is an answer to this argument, based as it is on the outworn notion that it is the function of the 'White races to govern the vast Native population of South Africa'.[8] If this notion were abandoned—as in my view it must be—and replaced by the more wholesome idea that colour should be no bar to full participation in government, this obstacle would fall away, and one could then both advocate territorial federation and concede the desirability of a uniform policy in regard to race relations. But this would be a very different uniform policy from that which actuated the majority of the founders of the South African Union in 1910; the policy would, in short, be one of over-all non-discrimination, leaving the provinces free to regulate many important matters as they like—subject always to the proviso that their legislation shall be non-discriminatory.

What is needed is a rigid federal constitution, containing a genuine and judicially enforceable Bill of Rights, binding on both the central and the territorial governments. If in addition—and this is essential—whites and non-whites were each given full and fair opportunities to participate in government on a basis of merit only, such a federation would, I believe, not only be acceptable but welcomed in Southern Africa. At one stroke one would meet the point about a uniform policy in regard to race relations, and also allay fears that have been expressed by Africans in Central Africa that federalism is likely to be yet another instrument of white domination.

It has also been objected, both in Central and in Southern Africa, that federalism is not an economical form of government, and that African communities by and large are not rich. Like many of the good things in life, however, federalism is expensive. But it is worth the cost and the sacrifices that may be entailed.

At a more fundamental level it has been objected (especially in South Africa) that because of growing nationalism of an aggressive kind, whites and non-whites simply cannot live together in peace, and that federalism is therefore no answer because it would merely reflect in the federal structure the inner conflict in society itself. But for reasons which I have stated in an earlier chapter, I do not believe that it is necessary yet to confess to such abject failure. If, of course, the white 'bearers of civilization' have in fact so completely failed in their mission, if whites and non-whites are in

[7] See, in particular, the speech of the Under-Secretary of State for the Colonies (Colonel Seeley) during the passage of the South Africa Act through the British Parliament: quoted by A. P. Newton, *The Unification of South Africa*, 1924, vol. 2, p. 259.

[8] I quote Colonel Seeley's words during the debate on the South Africa Act; Newton, op cit., p. 259.

fact too greedy and too prejudiced to live together in peace; then—as these critics suggest—the ultimate resort of partition, of strategic withdrawal, is indeed all that is left.

I do not deny that before the ideal which I have put forward can be achieved, the existing political structure will require the most drastic revision—indeed a fresh start will have to be made. But again for reasons which I have stated fully in previous chapters,[9] this is a preferable alternative to partition, apartheid—or civil war. In any event, I am here concerned with the direction in which alone, as I see it, political and economic health lies; not with predictions as to the course which events may yet have to follow before the goal is achieved.

In a federal structure the powers of the existing provincial councils in South Africa should, I think, be very widely extended, and safeguarded from interference by the central government. This is not the place to go into details concerning the exact allocation of functions between the central and the territorial governments, but one point does require emphasis. Such allocation is always difficult; and, it would seem, especially difficult in countries where one is faced with the risk of racial discrimination.[10] If, however, racial tension is to be eased in a federation, the Monckton Commission are correct in their conclusion that no subject should be divided between the central and the territorial governments on a racial basis.[11] Again—as the history of the Central African Federation has shown—the subjects of defence, external affairs, trade relations, internal security, immigration and deportation, require particularly careful definition and vigilance, lest they become instruments of racial domination.[12] But these difficulties are not insuperable.

There are, however, many people who feel that even federation, coupled with a judicially enforceable Bill of Rights, would not be enough to withstand racial domination or discrimination; and that additional safeguards must be sought to bolster up white courage before a dive into the democratic pool can be attempted. The Monckton Commission, for example, came to the conclusion that because racial discrimination, open or disguised, may occur in so wide a range of laws and executive actions, the legal safeguards afforded by a Bill of Rights would not be completely satisfactory, and that in addition a safeguard of a political nature is needed.[13]

[9] See chapters 2, 3 and 4.
[10] See, generally, the *Report of the Monckton Commission*, Cmd. 1148, pp. 47–8; and especially the Minority Report, pp. 142, 152, 153.
[11] Op. cit., p. 48.
[12] Op. cit. *Minority Report*, pp. 142 sqq.
[13] Op. cit., p. 82.

ADDITIONAL POLITICAL SAFEGUARDS

Two kinds of additional political safeguards have in recent years been suggested in Southern Africa in order to prevent racial discrimination: (1) the introduction of a racially composed senate or second chamber; and (2) the establishment of a council of state.

1. *A senate or second chamber*

A strong advocate of the idea that groups as well as individuals should be represented in the political organs of a state was the American, John Calhoun, who felt that society should not be regarded merely as an aggregate of individuals. Though it was partly an aggregate of individuals, it was also, he felt, an aggregate of group interests. Thus:

> There are two different modes in which the sense of the community may be taken. One, simply by the right of suffrage, regards numbers only, considers the whole community as one unit, and deems the sense of the greater number of the whole as that of the community. The other (mode) . . . regards interests as well as numbers, considers the community as made up of different and conflicting interests so far as the action of the government is concerned, takes the sense of each through its appropriate organ, and regards the united sense of all as the sense of the entire community. The former of these I shall call the numerical or absolute majority, and the latter, the concurrent or constitutional majority.[14]

In Europe the idea of giving separate representation to various branches of industry and commerce and the professions was, of course, a feature of Mussolini's 'corporative' state: but it is not generally regarded as satisfactory.[15] The idea also has a fairly long history in regard to national and religious groups; the inspiration going back to the practice of 'voting by nations' which is still observed in some universities.[16]

In more recent times the most influential exponent of these ideas has probably been the Austrian scholar, Joseph Redlich. And as his views were developed specifically with an eye to constitution making in a multi-racial society (free, however, from the colour problem), they are perhaps worth quoting. According to Redlich, the technique

---

[14] *A Discourse on Government*, Gralle's ed. (1841), p. 28. cf. Alexander Hamilton in *The Federalist*, paper 51.

[15] For a convincing criticism of the principle long before its introduction by Mussolini, see Sidgwick, *Elements of Politics*, 2nd ed., pp. 395-6.

[16] See Rashdall, *The Universities of Europe in the Middle Ages*, vol. 1, pp. 412 sqq. Also Bryce, *Essays in History and Jurisprudence*, vol. 2, pp. 297-8, for an analogous practice in Republican Rome. And see Gierke, *Political Theories of the Middle Ages*, Maitland's translation, p. 67.

of a majority vote to ascertain the 'general will' has a very limited role in a multi-racial community. Thus:

> The fundamental problem of democracy is the formation of the 'general will' of the people, that is, the deciding of legislative enactments by the absolute majority. In cases where two or more nationalities inhabit one and the same country, a 'general will' can be constituted only if and when the specific national, racial or religious interest of each group is eliminated from the question to be decided by the people as a whole. Only so far as this can be done, is it possible to assure that by a direct vote of each citizen, or by the duly and equally elected representatives of all citizens, anything like their 'general will' can be ascertained. Any principle laid down in the constitution recognizing the full equality of both or more nationalities can be altered only by the voluntary agreement of the minority nationality and the majority people.[17]

One of the best examples of how these ideas may be translated into the practice of actual constitution-making is given by Redlich himself. In Moravia the Czechs and the Germans lived together in a numerical proportion of about 70 to 30 per cent; and each group wished to maintain its own identity. Accordingly, under the Constitution of 1905 membership of each of the two nationalities was made a formally acknowledged legal status, and a legal duty was placed upon every citizen to register in a particular national group—the enlisting taking place in accordance with his own declared will. The legislative assembly was composed of curiae or corporations representing the two nationalities; and they were given proportional representation.

The problem then remained of ensuring that the Czech majority could not use their voting power so as to violate the national, and especially the linguistic, rights of the German minority. The solution ultimately reached was embodied in clause 38 of the Constitution, under which certain special 'national interests of the German minority' were enumerated, *inter alia*: (*a*) any amendment of the constitution; (*b*) laws concerning the use of language; (*c*) laws concerning the disestablishment of schools; (*d*) grants of money to schools; and (*e*) the franchise. And in these matters the voting procedure was so arranged that the requisite majority for legislation could only be obtained *if both national bodies agreed*.

This technique has become known in Southern Africa as 'racial federalism'. And were it considered a wholesome and desirable technique, it could, no doubt, be adapted to the circumstances of

---

[17] 'Sovereignty, Democracy, and the Rights of Minorities', in *Harvard Legal Essays*, 1934, p. 391.

11

Southern Africa so as to give a power of veto to any racial (or religious or linguistic) group which might consider its vital interests to be jeopardized by the decision of any other group.

This could be done in various ways. One method (that has been fairly widely discussed) would be to begin by writing into a rigid constitution all the subjects which it is desired to place beyond the reach of an ordinary majority decision—including such matters as the basic human rights and freedoms; the composition and powers of the legislatures; the appointment, tenure and functions of the judiciary; the franchise; the delimitation of constituencies; the powers of the executive; and any other special topics (like the public service, conditions of employment, military service, housing, public amenities and so on). The next—and vital—step would be to use the notion of racial federalism in regard to the composition and powers of the second chamber. This would, for example, be made representative of all the significant racial groups in the country, and it would be provided in the constitution that no constitutional amendment, and no legislation touching any of the enumerated special subjects, might validly be passed without the concurrence of a majority (or a specified percentage) of each racial group in the second chamber, as well as an over-all majority of the members.

It would, however, be folly to imagine that a racially composed senate of this kind is not open to serious and forceful criticism.

To begin with, if in implementing the notion of racial federalism one were to divide the electorate into racial groups, each electing a quota of members of its own race, one would be open to all the criticism that has so often, and so cogently, been levelled against communal representation. Many years ago a proposal to establish a racially composed senate along the lines now being discussed was in fact made to the Donoughmore Commission on the Constitution of Ceylon. But it was rejected for the very reason that led the Commission to describe communal representation as 'a canker in the body politic'. This is what the Commission had to say on the subject:

> In surveying the situation in Ceylon we have come unhesitatingly to the conclusion that communal representation is, as it were, a canker in the body politic, eating deeper and deeper into the vital energies of the people, breeding self-interest, suspicion and animosity, poisoning the new growth of political consciousness, and effectively preventing the development of a national or corporate spirit. As we are suggesting in the following chapter, there can be no hope of binding together the diverse elements of the population in a realisation of their common kinship and an acknowledgment of common obligations to the country of which they are all citizens so long as the system of communal representa-

tion, with all its disintegrating influences, remains a distinctive feature of the constitution. *What useful purpose would be served by its abolition in the Lower and its perpetuation in the Upper House we confess that we are unable to appreciate.*[18]

In the second place, the implementation of the idea would, in my view, involve the perpetuation of some form of population register. However much one may seek to mitigate the asperities of the existing South African law on the subject, it would probably still be necessary to devise certain workable definitions of the various racial groups. It is sometimes said that one might leave the determination of racial identity entirely to the individual's discretion. However, having regard to the complex racial groupings in South Africa, I do not think it would be possible for the advocates of racial federalism to dispense entirely with arbitrary definitions—but these notoriously cause hardship, and, in any case, are deeply resented by many people.

Quite apart from the almost daunting difficulties involved in keeping a racial population register, if a real effort is to be made to build a common society in Southern Africa, the overriding consideration in principle should be to do everything possible to discourage the legal relevance of racial distinctions, and not to do anything to perpetuate them. And on this point I entirely agree with Dr. Kiano, of Kenya, when he says that the recognition of distinct racial groups, having a defined legal status, is not a sound solution for a multi-racial society.[19]

Thirdly, in the circumstances of South Africa, just precisely which racial groups would be represented in a multi-racial senate? Let us assume that the whites, both English-speaking and Afrikaans-speaking, are to form one group—though, if regard be had to the facts, it would not be illogical for the advocates of a multi-racial senate to divide them into two. But assume one white group. Are all the Bantu-speaking Africans to be lumped together in another group? Sotho with Xhosa, Sotho with Nguni and so on? More particularly, is any distinction to be drawn between Africans in the towns and those in the Reserves? Are the Asians to form one group, or are they to be divided into Hindu and Muslim? Again, are the Malays to be treated as part of the Cape coloured community, and what about the Griquas?

And there are, in addition, yet more formidable objections. Thus— fourthly—advocates of a racially composed senate with powers of veto, realize that the whole business of government might be brought to a standstill if the racially composed senate were to be given

[18] Cmd. 3131, 1928, p. 39. My italics.
[19] *Colonial Times*, Nairobi, 21 August 1958.

powers of veto in financial legislation; and certainly the whole question of cabinet responsibility would be vitally affected. And so they suggest that the veto in financial matters or money bills should be excluded from the range of powers to be given to the senate. But, again as the Donoughmore Commission very clearly pointed out, financial measures are precisely those which may be among the most racially discriminatory and oppressive. Here then is a dilemma; for if the power of veto is not given in respect of financial matters, the bottom is virtually knocked out of the alleged safeguard.

This particular difficulty was very present to the Monckton Commission; and for this reason, *inter alia*, it decided against recommending a racially composed senate for the Rhodesian Federation.[20]

Again, in a racially composed senate racial bias might be used to impede the passage of essential legislation on 'filibustering' lines — even though the legislation be entirely non-discriminatory. Indeed, it is necessary for constitution-makers not to assume that men always act in a sweetly reasonable way.

Fifthly, there is the objection that to the extent that a racially composed senate may in fact succeed in vetoing a discriminatory measure, this may serve to exacerbate racial animosity; every time the racial veto is exercised it will high-light racial divisions and rivet world attention upon them.

Sixthly—and finally—it is perhaps fair to say that a fundamental objection to a racially composed senate is that it is based on the erroneous assumption that the interests in a community which merit legal recognition and protection are the interests of race or colour groups. This is, basically, to confuse colour or race with culture; and to perpetuate racial thinking in the life of the community.

For all these reasons I believe that any advantage which a racially composed senate may have in, perhaps, affording maximum political security, is outweighed by the very dangerous defects which necessarily attach to the scheme.

2. *Councils of state*

Councils of state are relatively new institutions. Their constitutional position and functions have, however, been fully explained in the recent Report of the Monckton Commission. And it is convenient to quote the conclusions of that Commission:

> A Council of State would not be an integral part of the Legislature of the Federation or of any Territory. Its functions would be to deal with one aspect only of the Bills laid before the particular

[20] Op. cit., p. 83.

Legislature with which it was concerned. Its main task would be to distinguish between beneficial and harmful discrimination and to protect persons against the enactment of legislation unfairly discriminatory on grounds of race, colour or creed. The Councils of State would have no power to make, amend or annul any law. They would perform their protective task by drawing attention to any legislation which was in their opinion unfairly discriminatory in order that its objectionable features might be removed or modified. By an 'unfairly discriminatory' measure we mean any Bill or legislative instrument any of the provisions of which are, or are likely in their practical application to be, disadvantageous to persons of other communities, either directly, by prejudicing persons in that community, or indirectly, by giving an advantage to persons of another community. The Councils of State would intervene in the legislative process only when a proposed provision was discriminatory and might in its practical application differentiate unwarrantably, and with a disparity of advantage or disadvantage, as between persons of different communities. Discrimination should be the one concern of the Councils of State; the prevention and removal of unfair discrimination should be their sole, all-important duty. The defence of the liberties set out in the Bill of Rights should be left to the courts and the courts alone.[21]

Dealing with the composition of councils of state, as proposed for the Rhodesian Federation, the Monckton Commission said:

We have given a great deal of thought to the composition of the Councils of State, and we have reached agreement on several important points. We think that every member of the Federal Council of State must be a member of the Territorial Council of State and that none should be a member of any Legislature. We are convinced that members of the Councils of State should be selected solely on grounds of their personal eminence, experience and detachment, and we hope that they will act as wise and impartial men and not as spokesmen of their race or Territory. The Federal Council of State should, we believe, consist of twelve persons and have an equal number of members chosen from each of the three Territories. We recommend that the Governor-General and the four Chief Justices of the Federation should appoint the members of the Federal Council of State from the membership of the Territorial Councils of State, and additionally choose an independent chairman with a casting vote only.

We have not, however, been able to agree about the racial composition of the Councils of State. Appointments to the Councils could be made either without any necessary regard to race, or, alternatively, with the purpose of producing some kind

[21] Op. cit., p. 83.

of racial balance. There are three possible solutions of the problem, none of which is favoured by an overall majority of Commissioners. We set these out below:

(i) The chief purpose of the Councils of State is to prevent racial discrimination and to protect the interests of all races. Some of us believe that this purpose could be more certainly achieved if the composition of the Councils were to be racially balanced. Such a balance could take one of two forms; first, parity between the two principal racial communities, Europeans and Africans; or, secondly, a less exclusive parity which would not preclude the appointment of Asians and Coloureds. The first solution, which would divide the entire membership of each Council equally between Africans and Europeans, unquestionably possesses strong political advantages. It would provide the greatest possible security for both the main racial communities and, as a result, it would be most likely to win their confidence from the start. Those, however, who oppose this solution consider it undesirable in principle as being based upon a purely and rather narrowly racial approach to the problem. Moreover, it would not achieve the absolute parity desired. An independent chairman, with a casting vote, is a necessity for each Council of State, however composed; and the chairman might upset the racial balance.

(ii) The second solution is a modified version of the first. Here again equal numbers of Europeans and Africans would be appointed; but in this case such appointments would not necessarily complete the full membership of each Council of State and would therefore not preclude the appointment of members drawn from other races. Asians and Coloureds, Federal citizens qualified in other respects for public life, might thus have a place on the Councils of State; and representation could be given to minorities very likely to be affected by racial discrimination. This also is a racial solution of the problem—a less exclusively racial solution which would not, however, give quite as much sense of security to Europeans and Africans as the first scheme. Moreover, it has other weaknesses. If equality of Europeans and Africans in a Federal Council of twelve is to be maintained this would mean that representatives of other races would always have to be appointed in pairs. The same requirements would exist for the Territorial Councils of State from which the Federal Council of State is to be drawn. Those charged with the appointment of the members of the Councils of State might find it difficult to make these double appointments from the relatively small Asian and Coloured communities.

(iii) The third solution is that appointments to the Council of State should be made without a required regard to race. In principle this is obviously the most desirable solution. It would be one of the best means of ensuring that Councils which are created to prevent unfair racial discrimination should themselves rise above all considerations of race. It is the ideal solution for a genuine multi-racial state; but it is less politically acceptable, because less reassuring, than the two others. It would not, on the face of it, provide the same security for the two main racial communities; it might not inspire so much confidence.[22]

And, finally, dealing more specifically with the powers and functions of Councils of State, the Monckton Commission reported that:

The Councils of State would be charged with the continuing duty of reviewing proposed legislation with power under the different constitutions to delay its passage through the Legislature if it is unfairly discriminatory. They should also be required to recommend the introduction of legislation to remove existing unfair discrimination. We believe that the task of reviewing existing legislation for this purpose is one which they should be able to complete without great difficulty and in a comparatively short time. In addition the Councils of State should examine and report on any unfairly discriminatory trends that may develop. They should set up channels by which news of such trends may reach them. But they should not deal with the grievances of individuals as such. We recommend accordingly that the Councils of State should have the following functions:

(a) to consider proposed substantive legislation; and if this was found to be unfairly discriminatory to report accordingly to the Legislature;

(b) to consider existing legislation and subsidiary legislation, and if this was found in any respect to be unfairly discriminatory to report to the Government and the Legislature;

(c) to acquaint themselves with any unfairly discriminatory trends and to report thereon, while not dealing directly with individual complaints or grievances.[23]

What are we to say about all this? In my view councils of state set up along these lines have most of the defects of a racially composed senate with a power of veto, and none of the compensating advantages. Lacking real power over legislation they are hardly likely to inspire confidence among those who feel the necessity for a 'political safeguard'. And at the same time their very composition would tend to perpetuate racial thinking. Indeed the only real advantage which they enjoy over racially composed senates with a power of veto is that they do not run into difficulties in regard to such matters as 'financial legislation', and modifications of normal

[22] Op. cit., pp. 84–5.
[23] Op. cit., pp. 85–6.

cabinet responsibility, which are involved in the introduction of racially composed senates possessing the power of veto.

THE PROTECTION OF MINORITY OPINION

At the same time it must be recognized that a senate or second chamber, properly composed on non-racial lines, has a most useful role to play. Second chambers have long been recognized as useful institutions for providing minority protection; and a few words on this subject may, therefore, be appropriate.

At the outset two different kinds of minority problems must be distinguished. The first is that of giving adequate representation in the legislature to *minority opinion*. This problem exists in every community possessing representative government and an electoral system, and is not confined to communities with racial complications. The second problem is that of trying to ensure that in actual practice no group or groups in a heterogeneous society will unjustly discriminate against another group or groups. This is by far the harder problem, and—not unnaturally—the one which claims most attention in Southern Africa. I have already indicated why, in my view, racially composed senates and councils of state do not adequately solve this latter problem, and shall turn to the subject again—with certain positive suggestions—later in this chapter. But first it is convenient to deal with the question of protecting minority opinion.

The problem of giving adequate representation to minority opinion exists because of the difficulty that has been experienced in devising a fair method for organizing elections. General elections are, of course, among the most important of factors which go to the making of modern history. However, the results of an election depend not only upon the system of franchise which has been adopted but also, to an extent which is insufficiently realized, upon the electoral machinery which the state has adopted. In other words, the result depends not only upon the mind and will of the citizens who have the vote and exercise it, but equally on the method of voting. Let me now briefly elaborate this fact, and explain how it ties up with the subject of senates or second chambers.

Most countries of the modern world have bicameral legislatures consisting of a popularly elected lower house (like the House of Commons in the United Kingdom), and a senate or second chamber (like the House of Lords) which may be constituted in various ways. Moreover, as a general rule—though there are important exceptions —one of the two bodies in a bicameral legislature is more powerful than the other—the popularly elected lower house ordinarily being more powerful than the second chamber. And now for our problem.

In most countries today, including those which have adopted universal suffrage, the method of election to the dominant lower house is by majority vote in single member constituencies. This system, however, enables a victorious party to obtain a number of representatives far in excess of that to which their polling strength entitles them. It leads to an assembly which is not representative of the polling strength in the country as a whole, and to the complete obliteration of minority opinion.

The reason is plain; with a single member majority system the *whole* representation of a constituency must be awarded to a majority of the electors whether that majority be large or small. It follows that the results will depend not so much on the actual strength of the parties in the country but on the manner in which that strength is distributed. If, for example, the strength is evenly distributed throughout the constituencies, then a minority is crushed in every constituency; if unevenly distributed, then any result is possible and everything depends upon how the boundaries of the constituencies have been arranged.

An example[24] will clarify the importance of boundaries. Let us take an area with 25,000 electors, 13,000 Pinks and 12,000 Blues. And let us assume that this is to be divided into 5 electoral districts of 5,000 voters each. If, now, there is a part of the area where the Pink supporters are largely concentrated, say in a central area, the result of the election will depend on the way in which the boundary lines are drawn. With one set of boundaries, the area in which the Pink supporters predominate may be cooped up or enclosed in one constituency. They might then obtain a majority of 3,000 in this constituency but lose all four of the other seats. Thus:

BOUNDARIES

	PINK	BLUE	RESULTS
	4,000	1,000	Pink Win (1)
	2,400	2,600	Blue Win (1)
	2,300	2,700	Blue Win (2)
	2,200	2,800	Blue Win (3)
	2,100	2,900	Blue Win (4)
	13,000	12,000	

On the other hand, if the boundaries are so arranged that each constituency has a portion of the surplus Pink votes in the one pent up area, the Pinks might win all five seats. Thus:

[24] Taken from Humphreys, *Proportional Representation*, 1911, p. 28.

PINK	BLUE	RESULTS
2,600	2,400	Pink Win (1)
2,600	2,400	Pink Win (2)
2,600	2,400	Pink Win (3)
2,600	2,400	Pink Win (4)
2,600	2,400	Pink Win (5)
13,000	12,000	

Pink win   Pink win   Pink win   Pink win   Pink win

In both cases, it follows, the result of the election fails to give a true representation, a true reflection, of the state of party opinion in the area as a whole. How to remove these anomalies has been one of the most acutely discussed problems of government for the last 100 years.

It was the view of J. S. Mill that the best remedy was proportional representation. That is to say, in the example I have given of an area containing 25,000 voters, one would treat the whole area as a single constituency returning, say, 5 candidates, and the rules for counting the votes would be so devised that the candidates who won would reflect *proportionally* the main trends of opinion in the constituency.

There are several methods of working proportional representation so as to achieve this result, and it is not my purpose to spend time in explaining them. One may find them fully discussed in any standard textbook on the subject. The method known as the single transferable vote in a multi-member constituency is probably the most widely favoured. What I do want to stress is that the principle of proportional representation, to which Mill pinned his hopes, has not generally been favoured as a method of election for the *lower* or more powerful house in a bicameral legislature.

It has been argued, in the first place, that the rules governing the system are too complicated to be generally understood. But this is neither a fair nor a conclusive objection. The available evidence proves, on the contrary, that in those countries where proportional representation has been used the voters have experienced no real difficulty in learning how to use it.

A more cogent objection to proportional representation is based upon its possible effect on the party-system, and on cabinet government and responsibility. It has been argued that it tends to weaken party government, encourages the multiplication of parties, and leads to insecure government by coalition. It is said, more particularly, that where you have a cabinet or government that is primarily responsible to the lower house, all stability would disappear if the government were made answerable to a lower house constituted on the basis of proportional representation. This was the conclusion reached some fifty years ago by the Royal Commission on Electoral Systems.[25] And it has hitherto proved a major obstacle in the path of all who would advocate proportional representation as a method of constituting the lower house.

Now, I am not disposed to challenge the conclusions reached by the Royal Commission, but I would emphasize that whatever the objections may be to constituting the lower house on the basis of proportional representation, I can see no reason why the system should not be used in the composition of a second chamber. On the contrary, the Royal Commission was itself of the opinion that proportional representation was an excellent method for the election of members of a second chamber.[26]

Moreover, this was the solution favoured by the framers of the South African Constitution. They refused to recommend proportional representation for the lower chamber but did recommend it for the upper chamber. Unfortunately, however, in my view, they did not go far enough. Two courses were open to them. One course was to combine proportional representation in the senate with *direct* election by the voters in large constituencies using, for example, the provinces as constituencies. If this had been done, then—provided the franchise were wide enough so as to include, in particular, non-whites—it would have been possible for the various sections of political opinion throughout the country to be represented in the senate in proportion to their strength.

The second course—which the framers of the constitution preferred—was to accept the idea of proportional representation but instead of having direct elections for senators, the senators were to be elected *indirectly* by an electoral college consisting of members of the lower house and the provincial councils. However, as the electoral college is itself elected without proportional representation, it has all the defects of unrepresentative character which flow from the ordinary majority system in single-member constituencies. In the result the South African Senate came to be a reflection of an already distorted picture, the echo of a voice which had already drowned all minority opinion. And this is still the case.[27]

If, on the other hand, a second chamber for the Union were constituted in the way I have suggested, i.e. by a system of propor-

[25] Cd. 5163.

[26] Humphreys, *Proportional Representation*, p. 275.

[27] Both under the Senate Act, 53 of 1955, as amended by Act 53 of 1960, and under the proposed Republican Constitution.

tional representation coupled with *direct* elections on a wide non-racial franchise, the picture would be very different and much healthier. Such a senate could, as a pure question of fact, properly claim more influence and power than is the case at present, precisely because it could claim to be more widely representative, and not a mere echo of the lower house.

In my view it is desirable that a representative senate of the kind I have suggested should be established in South Africa. Not only could such a senate fairly claim more power than the present Senate —as a matter of pure fact—but, in addition, I am of the view that as a matter of law a senate reformed along these lines should be given far greater powers than are at present possessed by the South African Senate.

The powers at present accorded to the South African Senate are mere powers of delay and revision. There is, however, need for a strong senate which could be used, along with the courts and the federal structure, as one of the guardians of a rigid constitution containing a Bill of Fundamental Human Rights. Let me now develop this point.

As we saw earlier, the amending process is the very kernel of sound constitution-making. It is, however, directly related to the role of a second chamber as a guardian of the Constitution. Three methods of framing an amending clause may be suggested. Each involves, as an essential feature, the use of a second chamber; each would be workable and effective.

One method would be to lay down that constitutional amendments may only be validly made by a two thirds majority vote of both Houses sitting together. Another, more difficult method, would be to lay down that amendments require the concurrence of both Houses sitting separately, and by a two-thirds majority vote in each. And thirdly, one could make constitutional amendments still more difficult by providing that they may only be made if, in addition to a two-thirds majority vote in the two Houses sitting separately, the particular amendment receives the approval of the electorate at a referendum; and —where a federal structure has been introduced—of a specified number of the territorial legislatures as well. And it is this latter method (for which there are precedents) which I personally prefer.

CONCLUSION

It is difficult not to agree with the conclusion of the Monckton Commission that racial, colour and religious 'discrimination, open or disguised, is present in many kinds of human activity and may occur in a wide range of laws and executive actions'. But, as we

have seen, racially composed senates, and councils of states constituted and empowered along the lines suggested by the Monckton
Commission, may aggravate rather than help the situation.

Probably no country in the modern world has had greater experience of the very real practical difficulties involved in building a
common society and in avoiding racial discrimination than the
United States of America. It has been realized in that country that
in addition to judicially enforced Bills of Rights, other agencies are
useful—and perhaps necessary—for the avoidance in daily life of
such discrimination. Provision has, therefore, been made for the
appointment of 'anti-discrimination commissions', and 'fair employ-
ment-practices commissions', to aid compliance with the law.

These commissions, unlike the councils of state proposed in the
Monckton Report, are fairly numerous (they are to be found in the
major cities); and though they have no high-sounding names, they
do have considerable powers. They are empowered—again unlike
the councils of state—to investigate complaints. Indeed this is one
of their main functions. They then attempt to settle matters by
conciliation and persuasion;[28] and if these fail, there are other
remedies, one of them being the power to initiate court proceedings.
And in this latter connexion it is interesting to note that in their
Minority Report on the Rhodesian Federation, Messrs. Chirwa and
Habanyama recommended that councils of state should be empowered to initiate court action.[29]

The composition of such bodies should present little difficulty.
In the circumstances of Southern Africa they should, I suggest,
be appointed entirely on non-racial lines by senior members of the
judiciary assisted, perhaps, by a few representatives of commerce
and industry (who should, however, be in the minority).

On one point, moreover, there should be no doubt. If white
domination is to be outlawed, there is only one way to avoid black
domination, or alternatively a resort to territorial partition; and
that is to set one's face sternly against all racial classifications and
racial criteria. To erect institutions of government which themselves
embody racial classifications is, I believe, dangerously short-sighted;
and certainly not the way to build up a common society.

Surely the primary aim should be good government; that is to
say, government under law in a community in which all feel that
they belong. To achieve this end the requirements which alone
seem necessary are:

(1) A wide suffrage, preferably universal adult suffrage.

[28] See, generally, 'Equal Economic Opportunity', A Report of the President's
Committee on Government Contract Compliance, Washington, 1952.

[29] Op. cit., p. 152.

(2) A judicially enforced Bill of Rights containing, *inter alia*, a 'non-discrimination' and an 'equal protection of the laws' clause —along the lines suggested in Chapter 6.

(3) The appointment of anti-discrimination commissions—as suggested by the experience of the United States of America—to deal, *inter alia*, with the many subtle kinds of discrimination which operate in practice, and which cannot always be exactly defined in a legal formula.

In addition, as we have seen, two further safeguards might well be recommended as most desirable—though not strictly necessary; namely:

(4) Federalism.

(5) A Senate or Second Chamber constituted and empowered as suggested above.

Federalism is not strictly necessary because—contrary to a widespread but wholly fallacious notion—a rigid constitution containing a Bill of Rights enforced by the judiciary can be established under a unitary constitution.

If, however, all these safeguards are not deemed sufficient, then the question (which I imagine protagonists of apartheid would not be slow to ask) must be deeply pondered: is a single coherent society in South Africa (or in the Rhodesias) really a practical proposition?

Those who desire government under law, and who wish to avoid the failure—and suffering—of apartheid or partition, must have the courage of their convictions.

9

Establishing a Constitution

It is often said that quite apart from what a new constitution should contain, and how its provisions should be enforced (topics we have discussed in previous chapters), a major difficulty is to determine how to introduce or adopt a new constitution in an effective way. The problem is undoubtedly a difficult one, especially in a country where—as in South Africa—there already exists a sovereign Parliament. But the difficulties are not insuperable.

Four aspects of the problem may be distinguished. Firstly there is a problem of 'practical politics'. Plainly the question of introducing a Bill of Rights designed to place limitations upon the powers of a Parliament which is at present sovereign, just is not practical politics unless: *either*,

(1) a government is returned to power which intends to introduce such change,
   or,
(2) the existing political structure crumbles and an entirely fresh start has to be made in the national life in an atmosphere favourable to the introduction of a Bill of Rights.

I do not propose to speculate as to which of these courses is the more likely in South Africa. On either assumption, however, there are other aspects of the problem of general importance which require attention; and it is these other aspects which I propose to consider in this chapter. In an earlier chapter I gave reasons why one should not be deterred from careful investigation of the whole subject of the incorporation of constitutional guarantees, merely because this is a policy which, at present, is not supported by the Government or by the majority of the South African electorate.

Apart from what I have called the question of 'practical politics', three broad groups of problems are involved. They are raised specifically in the Report of the Constitutional Reform Committee which was appointed by the Government of New Zealand in 1952 to consider, *inter alia*, the procedure necessary for making durable and effective changes of a basic nature in the Constitution of New Zealand. The Commission reported as follows:[1]

In our view, there are three ways, and only three, in which a Constitution can be devised for a people and their Government. they are —

(i) A Constitution may be created for, and imposed upon, a subordinate legislative body by a sovereign and superior legislature. The British Parliament did this for New Zealand when it gave the power of self-government to the Colony: the New Zealand Constitution Act, 1852. The Imperial Parliament has at our request and with unqualified assent surrendered this power: the New Zealand Constitution Amendment Act, 1947. There now remains no external authority whatsoever that could or would create for us or impose upon us a Constitution of that kind.

(ii) A Constitution may have its origin in the assent or consent of those who are to be bound by it. Such a Constitution has its origin in contract and can be altered only in the manner that has been agreed upon by the constituent members. The outstanding examples of this kind are the federal Constitution of the United States of America and of the Commonwealth of Australia.

(iii) A Constitution could be created by a 'unitary' Legislature like our own and imposed upon itself by a kind of self-denying act of self-discipline; it could bind itself in a statute and hope that its successors would feel equally constrained to respect that enactment. But it could not easily bind them to observe it by any process that could be described as legally effective. Any Parliament can bind itself by its legislation, but in no way can a Parliament like ours by its own act bind its successors.

At the outset we may follow the example of the New Zealand Commission and put on one side, as out of the question, any idea of turning to the Parliament of the United Kingdom—in terms of the Statute of Westminster—for any radical revision of the South African Constitution. Clearly the position in regard to the introduction of a new constitution in countries like South Africa or New Zealand, which are already fully independent, is quite different from that which obtains in countries like Kenya or Northern Rhodesia, where the writ of the British Parliament still runs. It would, for example, hardly be practical politics for any South African statesman to take South Africa's problems to Westminster Palace for solution.

There remain, then, two other alternatives; and each raises its own group of problems.

[1] *The Bishop-Algie Report*, 1952, pp. 37–8.

In the first place, an attempt might be made to rest support for a new constitution upon the approval of 'the people'. If this is done, three basic questions have to be faced: (*a*) precisely who are 'the people' whose consent to a new structure of government should be invoked? (*b*) by what procedure should this be done—should it be done, for example, by a referendum or by the summoning of a constituent national convention? And if by a national convention, how should the convention be constituted; (*c*) and more important perhaps than either of the two previous questions, precisely what authority are 'the people' able to give to a constitution?

It has become customary to speak of constitutions 'ordained' or 'enacted' by 'the people' as being fundamental law. But precisely what is it that makes it fundamental law? To quote a recent book on the subject:

> Is it the fact that the 'people' in the fullness of their sovereign power have established it? Or is it that certain principles of government are *inherently fundamental*? If the latter is the case, what are the criteria of inherently fundamental principles and how are they discovered.[2]

More specifically, are the people free to establish human rights and to abrogate them all without regard to any consideration other than their declared will? Or are there standards of right and wrong binding on the people themselves? And if there are such standards, in what sense are they binding?

Secondly, and quite apart from the role of 'the people' in constitution-making, there is the interesting question of what can be done by Act of Parliament. In recent years, in countries within the British Commonwealth, thought has been given to the possibility of introducing Bills of Rights and constitutional rigidity, and other far-reaching changes, without resorting to constituent assemblies of the people or referenda. In short, the question has been asked: can the objective be achieved simply by Act of Parliament?

It is of course, possible to combine both techniques; that is to say, to use the machinery of Parliament, as well as to invoke the authority of the people either in constituent assembly or at a referendum. And, as I shall show presently, this combination of techniques is probably the course which might most effectively be followed in the event of a sufficiently peaceful change being brought about in South Africa. In what follows, however, it will help clarity of exposition if I deal with each of the two techniques separately.

[2] O'Rourke and Campbell, *Constitution-Making in a Democracy*, Johns/Hopkins, 1943, p. 27.

ADOPTION BY ACT OF PARLIAMENT

It will have been noted that in the summary of the conclusions of the New Zealand Constitutional Commission, quoted above, the view was expressed that a durable constitution could not easily be introduced by Act of Parliament in such a way as to prevent succeeding Parliaments from undoing the whole work. In the body of the Report, however, a distinction is drawn between two wholly different procedures, namely:

(1) the abdication or surrender of sovereignty by a sovereign Parliament; and

(2) attempts to redefine the legislative process without an abdication or surrender of sovereignty by Parliament.

In regard to the first procedure, the New Zealand Commission came to the conclusion that it could legally be resorted to with complete efficacy; but, for political reasons, the Commission felt that an abdication of sovereignty was not in fact practicable. Thus after quoting the opinion of Dicey that there is nothing in law to prevent a fully sovereign body from surrendering its sovereignty, or part of it, to another body, the members of the Commission went on to say:

> In New Zealand, for example, it would be quite competent for our Parliament to re-establish some form of provincial government in this Dominion and to create a federal system based upon a written constitution very like that in force in Australia. This plan was, in fact, suggested in evidence placed before the Committee. The members of the Committee felt that such a type of 'suicide Act' *was legally possible of enactment*, and there was indeed high authority in support of such a view. We reached the conclusion, however, that the plan was impracticable.[3]

In regard to the alternative procedure of redefining the sovereign law-making process, the New Zealand Commission gave much attention to a suggestion that a 'referendum clause' be incorporated in the Constitution by Act of Parliament, the idea being that no subsequent amendment of the constitution by Act of Parliament should be valid unless the amendment was first approved by the electorate at a referendum. The conclusion reached by the Commission on this aspect was that, notwithstanding such a referendum clause, the New Zealand Parliament could, in law, 'treat the need for a referendum with contempt and the courts would be powerless to intervene'.[4]

As both aspects of this subject—abdication of sovereignty as well as redefinition of the legislative process—may well become practical

---

[3] *The Bishop-Algie Report*, pp. 39–40. My italics.

[4] Op. cit., p. 41.

politics in South Africa, and in other parts of the Commonwealth, I propose to deal with them in rather more detail; for there has, as yet, been comparatively little modern discussion of these matters.

1. *Abdication*

Assuming that there were sufficient parliamentary support for the measure, I have no doubt that it would be legally competent for the Union Parliament to terminate its present status of undivided sovereignty by irrevocably transferring its law-making power in defined shares to new legislatures (including, for example, provincial legislatures) constituted along different lines and empowered in terms of a new constitution, whose enactment would—concurrently with an act of abdication—be the old Parliament's last act. If the act of legal abdication or legal suicide were clear, then, in my view, Parliament as previously constituted could have no power to repeal the new constitution; there would be no question of the old Parliament being unable to bind its successors, for the simple reason that the old Parliament would no longer continue to exist. Or, to state the same proposition from another point of view, the old Parliament would have *no successors of a like nature*.

One of the earliest and best discussions of this subject is to be found in Bacon's legal maxims.[5] Bacon drew a clear distinction between an attempt by a sovereign Parliament to prevent itself from repealing a law in the future, without a prior act of abdication, and the case where an act of abdication takes place. Thus:

> If an Act of Parliament be made wherein there is a clause contained that it shall not be lawful for the King, by the authority of Parliament, during the space of seven years to repeal and determine the Act, this is a void clause, and the same Act may be repealed within the years.[6]

The reason for this, says Bacon, is that a clause prohibiting repeal (*clausula derogatoria*) 'doth deprive men of that which of all other things is most incident to human condition, and that is alteration or repentance'. He proceeds, however, immediately to qualify the generality of his remarks as follows:

> And yet if the Parliament should enact in the nature of the ancient *lex regia*, that there should be no more Parliaments held, but that the King should have the authority of the Parliament; this act were good in law; *quia potestas suprema seipsum dissolvere potest, ligare non potest*. . . . It is in the power of Parliament to extinguish or transfer their own authority, but not, *whilst the*

---

[5] Regula XIX. Bacon's *Works*, ed. Spedding, Ellis and Heath, 1859, vol. VII, pp. 369–72.

[6] Op. cit., pp. 370–1.

authority remains entire, to restrain the functions and exercises of the same authority.[7]

Bacon will have no truck with the suggestion that, without an Act of abdication, an Act which purports to be irrevocable is good until repealed.[8] In his view the Act must either be void or valid. Thus:

> But the law is that the first law by the impertinency of it was void *ab initio et ipso facto* without repeal; as if a law were made that no statute should be made during seven years. If the first statute should be good, then no repeal could be made thereof within that time.[9]

The reasons given by Bacon for the voidity of a statute purporting to be irrevocable, unless accompanied by an abdication of sovereignty, are of wide application and by no means confined to English constitutional law. There are indeed several Roman texts, and a good deal of Romanistic and Roman-Dutch legal learning, to the same effect.[10]

The problem arose in a concrete way—giving rise to illuminating comment—in regard to Mr. Gladstone's Government of Ireland Bill, 1886.[11] It was proposed to 'reconstitute' the Parliament of the United Kingdom by setting up (*a*) a new Irish Parliament, (*b*) a British Parliament, consisting of the rump of the existing members after the subtraction of the Irish members; and (*c*) a 'special' Imperial Parliament—each differing in composition and authority from the previously existing Parliament of the United Kingdom.[12] Clause 39(1)(*a*) provided that after an appointed day, those provisions of the new Constitution which were within the exclusive competence of the Irish Parliament could not be altered by the

---

[7] Op. cit., pp. 371–2. cf. Bentham, *Works*, Bowring's ed. (1843), vol. 2, pp. 401 sqq. My italics.

[8] A view held by Dr. W. Jetho Brown, *The Austinian Theory of Law*, p. 161.

[9] Loc. cit.

[10] See, e.g. D. 32.22 pr. (*Hermogenianus*) . . . *nemo enim eam sibi potest legem dicere ut a priori ei recedere non liceat.* . . . Cf. D. 29.7.6.2. Girard, *Manuel Elementaire de Droit Romain*, 8th ed., p. 886, note 4. Windscheid, *Lehrbuch des Pandektenrechts*, 7th ed., vol. 3, p. 87. Cajacius, *Observationes*, XIV. 7 (*sub voce, clausula derogatoria*), discusses the texts, and applies the principle of D. 32.22 pr. (above) to legislation by the Princeps. Thus: *Princeps multo minus potest sibi legem dicere, ut a priori non possit recedere, quae omnia summe notanda sunt.* These questions were discussed and disputed by the Glossators; and the flow of writing has continued ever since. As Bijnkershoek, *Quaestiones Juris Privati*, 1774, Book 3, Ch. VI, observed: *De hac clausula multi multa disputant et circa hanc non una difficultas, nam ars deluditur arte.*

[11] Printed *in extenso* as an Appendix to Dicey's *England's Case Against Home Rule*, London, 1886.

[12] Dicey, op. cit., pp. 235–6.

British Parliament save 'with the consent of the Irish legislative body testified by an address to Her Majesty'.

For political reasons, however, the Bill was vaguely drafted and it was not clear whether it was the intention that the existing British Parliament should surrender part of its sovereignty. Not surprisingly, the legal effect of the proposal was keenly debated by England's leading constitutional lawyers; and opinion was divided. Dicey, Anson and Sir Robert Finlay, who considered that an act of abdication was involved, held the view that if the Government of Ireland Bill were passed, the British Parliament could not thereafter validly legislate for Ireland without the consent of the Irish Parliament. Bryce, who considered that no act of abdication was involved, took the opposite view.

Let us now look at the opinions a little more closely; for they are of enduring interest.[13] Speaking in the House of Commons on 21 May 1886, Sir Robert Finlay said:

> The measure destroyed the Imperial Parliament as it now existed. It created out of the materials which the Parliament provided two Parliaments, the British Parliament on this side of the water and the Irish Parliament on the other side of the water.[14]

He therefore entertained 'the very gravest doubt' whether the British Parliament could repeal the Act except in terms of it.[15]

Dicey summed up his views as follows:

(a) 'It was indisputable that a sovereign parliament could not, while retaining its sovereign character, limit its sovereign powers.'[16]

(b) 'No principle of jurisprudence is more certain than that sovereignty implies the power of abdication . . . no fact is more certain than that a sovereign Parliament has more than once abdicated, or shared its powers.'[17]

(c) Accordingly, 'if it were said that the body which passed this enactment could also repeal it, then the judge might consider that that body, namely the Parliament of the United Kingdom, had in effect ceased to exist, and that the successor to its sovereign powers, if any, was not the British Parliament . . . but the special Imperial Parliament.'[18]

---

[13] For fuller but rather more technical discussion see my article on Legislature and Judiciary (1953) 16 *Modern Law Review* 288–97.

[14] *Hansard*, col. 1680.

[15] *Hansard*, col. 1682.

[16] *England's Case Against Home Rule*, p. 242. *Law of the Constitution*, 9th ed., p. 68, *in notis*.

[17] *England's Case Against Home Rule*, pp. 244–5.

[18] Op. cit., p. 246.

Again in his standard work on the *Law of the Constitution* Dicey said:

A sovereign power can divest itself of authority in two ways only. It may simply put an end to its existence. . . . It may, again, transfer sovereign authority to another person or body of persons.[19]

Anson pointed out that the statement that Parliament cannot bind its successors may be taken to be true, subject to two exceptions: (i) where Parliament surrenders its sovereign powers over a certain area to another person or body; (ii) where a sovereign body divides itself into two—the terms of separation must then provide that one shall be subordinate to the other, or that both shall be independent, or that both shall be subordinate to the articles of their separation and to the written constitution so created.[20]

Bryce, who was at the time Under-Secretary of State for Foreign Affairs, was prepared to go part of the way with these authorities. He was, for example, prepared to concede the possibility of an act of legal suicide or abdication. Thus in his essay on 'Flexible and Rigid Constitutions', he wrote:

Upon the general question whether Parliament could so enact any new constitution for the United Kingdom so as to debar itself from subsequently repealing that constitution, it may be suggested, for the consideration of those who relish technicalities, that Parliament could, if so disposed, divest itself of its present authority by a sort of suicide, that is by repealing all the statutes under which it is now summoned, and abolishing the common right of the Crown to summon it, and thereupon causing itself to be forthwith dissolved, having of course first provided means for summoning another parliament, and the new constitution whatever it was, would therefore not be liable to be altered save in such manner as its own terms provided.[21]

At the same time, however, Bryce did not consider that the Government of Ireland Bill—on a true interpretation—was an 'act of suicide'. Accordingly, he said in the House of Commons: 'we cannot bind our successors; if we pass a statute annihilating our right to legislate it may be repudiated by our successors.'[22] It will be appreciated, therefore, that he differed from his colleagues not so much on the question of law involved, but as to the true interpretation of what was intended by the Government of Ireland Bill.

We may conclude, then, that there is clear authority for the view that a sovereign Parliament may by an act of abdication terminate

[19] 9th ed., p. 69 *in notis*.
[20] Vol. 2, *Law Quarterly Review*, p. 440.
[21] *Studies in History and Jurisprudence*, vol. 1, p. 207.
[22] *Hansard*, 17 May 1886, vol. 1220.

its sovereignty, and transfer either all or a part of its sovereignty to another person or body of persons. Indeed, in the opinion of many authorities the Unions between England and Scotland, and between Great Britain and Ireland, are examples of the former process and the English Declaratory Act of 1782, in regard to Ireland, is an example of the latter process. Thus, for example, Anson explained the Anglo-Scottish and the Anglo-Irish Unions as follows.

> In the first case the Parliaments of England and Scotland, in the second the Parliaments of Great Britain and Ireland, respectively, approved of terms by which their sovereignty and their existence came to an end. Each Parliament with all its sovereign powers passed into a new body, the united Parliament of the two countries concerned.[23]

Again, it was the clear intention of the Declaratory Act of 1782 (6 Geo. I, c. 5) to concede legislative independence to Ireland beyond recall; and both Anson[24] and Dicey[25] regarded that partial surrender of sovereignty by the British Parliament as being legally effective. Moreover, this would not be an unreasonable interpretation of the Statute of Westminster in regard to Britain's power to legislate for the other Commonwealth countries. Indeed, in a South African case, Mr. Justice van den Heever specifically referred to 'the Imperial abdication of Great Britain';[26] and a similar view was expressed in Australia by Dr. H. V. Evatt.[27]

2. *Redefinition of the legislative process*

Short of abdication or legal suicide, some interesting 'possibilities' depend upon whether it is legally competent for the South African Parliament to redefine the method of expressing its will in such a way as to preclude the members thereof from subsequently ignoring the new method and reverting to the old. If this can be done, then one solution of our problem might be to incorporate a Bill of Rights into the Union constitution by an ordinary Act of Parliament which would provide that subsequent amendments might be made only by a process more difficult than the vote of a bare majority. For

[23] *Law and Custom of the Constitution*, 5th ed., p. 8. See also Dicey, *The Law of the Constitution*, p. 69 *in notis*. And for fuller discussion, Dicey and Rait, *Thoughts on the Scottish Union*, pp. 19–23; W. L. Mathieson, *Scotland and the Union*; and T. B. Smith, *The United Kingdom: Development of its Laws and Constitutions*, 1955, pp. 641 sqq.

[24] 2 *L.Q.R.* 438–9.

[25] *A Leap in the Dark*, London, 1911, p. 29.

[26] 1952 (2) S.A. at 791.

[27] Evatt, *The King and His Dominion Governments*, pp. 308–9. See also the Report of the Bishop-Algie Commission for New Zealand. But cf. *British Coal Corporation* v. *The King* [1935] A.C. at 520 per Lord Sankey, and my comments on that case in 15 *Modern Law Review* 294 note 47.

example, it could be provided that before any amendment became law it would have to be approved by the electorate at a referendum.

This was, in fact, the recommendation put forward by the New Zealand Constitutional Commission in regard to a possible revision of the New Zealand Constitution. Despite the fact that the New Zealand Commission considered that such an expedient—unlike a surrender of sovereignty—would have no *legal* efficacy to prevent the New Zealand Parliament from ignoring the 'referendum clause', they nevertheless felt that such a clause afforded some *practical* protection (for it could not be ignored without adverse criticism); and for this reason they recommended it.[28]

This is probably not the place to develop the question of the legal efficacy of such a referendum clause. Ever since the subject was first raised seriously by Sir Owen Dixon in 1931 in the case of *Attorney-General for New South Wales* v. *Trethowan*,[29] there has been considerable legal interest in it, and a growing literature.[30] The question could arise under the existing law of South Africa in regard, for example, to the provisions of Act 45 of 1934 which provide that Parliament shall not alter provincial boundaries nor abolish provincial councils except on petition by the provincial councils concerned;[31] for this was an attempt to redefine the legislative process *without* a surrender of sovereignty. However, in the present state of the authorities, one cannot prudently give a clear-cut answer to the legal question; for this is where the fields of law and logic, politics and history meet and overlap, where their boundaries are fluid, elusive and obscure.

But whatever the answer may be in law to this particular problem, namely redefinition of the legislative process without a surrender of sovereignty, there are as we have already seen, and as we shall see more fully presently, other means of making a desirable and effective change in the South African Constitution, by terminating the existing sovereignty of Parliament.

ADOPTION BY THE PEOPLE

'*We, the people* of the United States, in order to form a more perfect Union, establish Justice, insure domestic Tranquility, provide for the common defence, promote the general Welfare, and secure the Blessings of Liberty to ourselves and our Posterity, *do ordain and establish* this Constitution for the United States of America.'

[28] Report, p. 42.
[29] 44 C.L.R. 394 at 424 sqq.
[30] See, especially, W. Friedmann, *Parliamentary Sovereignty and the Limits of Legal Change* (1950) 24 *Australian Law Journal* 103; also (1953) 16 *Modern Law Review* 294 sqq.
[31] Sec. 1.

Such is the famous preamble of the Constitution framed in 1787 by the Federal Convention over which Washington presided. Thus appeared in the fundamental law of a great modern state the axiom of the Roman law *lex est quod populus jubet atque constituit*.[32] But although in the modern world the establishment of a framework of government by the people is distinctively an American institution, it is now an accepted technique in most democracies.[33]

During the first years of America's independence constitutions were established by various procedures. In three states they were established by the existing legislative bodies without express authorization and without submission to the people. In five states they were drafted by legislative bodies expressly authorized by the electorate to perform this function, but were not thereafter submitted to the electorate. In four states a similar procedure was followed, coupled, however, with an 'informal' submission of the draft to the electorate in three cases, and with a 'formal' submission for approval in one case—that of Massachusetts.[34]

Indeed the establishment of the Massachusetts Constitution in 1780 is generally regarded as an American model of popular participation in setting up a framework of government. As its principal author, John Adams, wrote while the constitution was in preparation:

> There never was an example of such precautions as are taken by this wise and jealous people in the formation of their government. None was ever made so perfectly upon the principle of the people's rights and equality. It is Locke, Sidney and Rousseau and De Mably reduced to practice, in the first instance. I wish every step of their progress printed and preserved.[35]

And to this day the Massachusetts precedent is regarded as combining the normal steps to be followed in summoning state constitutional conventions, namely:

> the submission to popular vote of the question of calling a convention for the sole purpose of framing a constitution; the popular election of members to compose the convention; and the submission of the constitution to popular vote.[36]

---

[32] Gaius. Also Ulpian: *Leges nulla alia causa nos tenent quam judicio populi receptae sunt*. See Charles Borgeaud, *The Adoption and Amendment of Constitutions*, 1895, C. D. Hazen's translation, New York, p. 131.

[33] As regards similar doctrines in the Middle Ages, see Gierke, *Political Theories of the Middle Ages*, Maitland's translation, pp. 37 sqq.

[34] O'Rourke and Campbell, op. cit., p. 24.

[35] *Works of John Adams*, 1851, vol. IV, p. 216; quoted by Lobingier, *The People's Law*, 1909, p. 178.

[36] *The Encyclopaedia of the Social Sciences*, vol. 4, p. 245.

The Massachusetts example had an immediate echo in contemporary France as is manifest from the Declaration of the Rights of Man, adopted by the National Assembly in 1789:

Law is the expression of the general will. All citizens have the right to participate in its formation, either personally or through representatives. (Art. 6) . . . Sovereignty resides in the people; it is one and indivisible, imprescriptible and inalienable. (Art. 25.)[37]

And soon all this was to become a commonplace of political and legal theory in the United States and France, and, ever increasingly, in Europe. In 1803, for example, John Marshall, Chief Justice of the United States declared:

That the people have an original right to establish, for their future government, such principles as, in their opinion, shall most conduce to their own happiness, is the basis on which the whole American fabric has been erected.[38]

Though the idea of an original and inalienable right in the people to establish a framework of government was familiar to Cromwell's soldiers—and indeed may be said to be part of the political philosophy of the Puritan Reformation—it was not an idea which easily took root in the theory and practice of the British Commonwealth. Writing on this subject in 1951 Professor Wheare stated:

There is no doubt that the supremacy of the people as law-giver is recognized in the United States so far as the Constitution is concerned. It is accepted, indeed, in most countries. To introduce it into the law of the British Commonwealth, however, is an innovation. The people there, so far from being a supreme law-giver, is not, as was pointed out above, a law-giver at all.[39]

And there is abundant authority to support this statement.[40]

Professor Wheare went on to point out, however, that 'already the innovation has been made'. And after referring to the examples of Eire (1937) and India (1950), he continued:

Why should other members of the Commonwealth not follow this example? . . . Evidently, as a matter of politics, it can be done and it may be done again. As a matter of law, however, it is clear that it involves a break with the past.

There are authorities who contend that already the constitutional structure of South Africa, and her legal system, rest ultimately upon the will of the people. They hold that the formal break, dissevering the South African structure from its former British legal roots came

---

[37] See generally Borgeaud, op. cit., pp. 198 sqq.; Lobingier, op. cit., pp. 367 sqq.
[38] (1803) 1 Cranch.
[39] *Modern Constitutions*, p. 88.
[40] Dicey, *The Law of the Constitution*, 9th ed., pp. 59–60.

after the Statute of Westminster at the time of the Union Status Act in 1934.[41] And there is undoubtedly a great deal to be said for this point of view. But whether it is sound or not, is not a question which need detain us now. For we may accept the position that if sufficient popular support were forthcoming, the people of South Africa could, if necessary, break the continuity in their legal and constitutional structure, and make a fresh start by submitting a new constitution to 'the people'. This, on one view, would be a revolution in the legal sense, albeit a peaceful one; but it would be in accordance with modern democratic practice in a large part of the world, including several countries in the Commonwealth.

Such a course would, however, present its own difficulties, and it would also have far-reaching implications, to which we must now turn.

1. *Who are the people?*

In dealing with the question who are 'the people' for the purpose of ordaining or establishing constitutions, it is important to recognize that we are concerned not with a legal question but with a purely practical question; namely how much popular support is necessary to give the constitution a chance of general acceptance and survival?

There are instances in history where constitutions were established with remarkably little popular participation. For example, it is now well settled that no more than 5 per cent of the whole population of the United States 'ordained' and 'established' the American Constitution. Walter Lippmann has explained this as follows:

> On September 17, 1787, about forty members signed the draft on which they had been working since May 25, for one hundred and sixteen days. In ART. VII of their text they stipulated that if and when conventions in nine States had ratified it, then for those nine States *The People of the United States* would have ordained and established the Constitution. In this context a majority of the delegates elected to nine State conventions were deemed to be entitled to act as The People of the United States.
>
> The inhabitants of the United States who were qualified to vote for these delegates were not a large number. They included no slaves, no women and, except in New York, only such adult males as could pass property and other highly restrictive tests. We do not have accurate figures. But according to the census of 1790, the population was 3,929,782. Of these, 3,200,000 were free persons and the adult males among them who were entitled

---

[41] See, generally, R. T. E. Latham, 'The Law and the Commonwealth', ed. W. K. Hancock, *Survey of British Commonwealth Affairs*, 1, 1937, pp. 533–4. Cf. *Ndlwana* v. *Hofmeyr*, 1937 A.D. 229 at 237; *Minister of the Interior* v. *Harris*, 1952 (4) S.A. 769 (A.D.) at 791.

to vote are estimated to have been less than 500,000. Using the Massachusetts figures as a statistical sample, it may be assumed that less than 160,000 actually voted for delegates to all the ratifying conventions; and of those voting, perhaps 100,000 favoured the adoption of the Constitution.

The exact figures do not matter. The point is that the voters were not—and we may add that they have never been and can never be—more than a fraction of the total population. They were less than 5 per cent when the Constitution was ordained. They were not yet 40 per cent in 1952 when, except under the special conditions in the South, we had universal adult suffrage. Manifestly, the voters can never be equal to the whole population, even to the whole living adult population.[42]

Similar considerations apply to the French Constitution of 1871–5; indeed the Republican Law of 1875 was adopted by one vote in the Chamber of Deputies. It is surprising, too, to find by what a narrow vote constitutions like that of the Fourth French Republic (1946) or the Irish Republic (1937) were established. In Ireland, for example, the vote was 686,042 for, 528,362 against.[43] The Constitution of Pakistan, 1956, was adopted by an unrepresentative assembly against very heavy popular opposition.[44]

There are, however, obvious dangers in such inconclusive support. As Herman Finer observes 'the latent fissures and insincerities' of the French Constitution of 1871–5 'emerged with disastrous effect' in 1940.[45] Similarly the German Weimar Constitution of 1919 'suffered from the feebleness of its reception by the electorate'.[46] And, of course, the Constitution of Pakistan has also revealed the flimsy foundation on which it was built, and has crumbled.

It is, in fact, essential to recognize that the example of the American procedure in 1787 could not be exactly copied in Southern Africa in the mid-twentieth century; for the circumstances prevailing in the United States at the time were wholly different. Thus, again to quote Finer:

The United States was, indeed, fortunate to have established its constitution in the eighteenth century, for it enjoyed advantages not available to constitution-seeking nations in our own day. In the first place, it had the passion of a people recently emerged from ordeal by battle for their joint emancipation from alien rule. In the second place, neither political parties nor special

[42] *The Public Philosophy*, 1955, pp. 32–3. See also Charles Beard, *An Economic Interpretation of the Constitution of the United States*, 1913, p. 16.
[43] See, generally, Herman Finer, *Theory and Practice of Modern Government*, pp. 122–3.
[44] A. K. Brohi, *The Constitution of Pakistan*, p. 46.
[45] *Theory and Practice of Modern Government*, p. 124.
[46] Op. cit., p. 124.

interests had coagulated into hard organisations. No one would wish to minimize the factional and ideological differences prevailing, nor the strength of the regional and economic interests in collision. They were immense, and almost disastrous. But it will also be admitted that American colonial society was simpler, the general spiritual outlook more unified, and the functional and party organisations less conscious and firm and pressing and insistent than anything like what would have been encountered within fifty years from that time, and even more so, one hundred and fifty years afterwards. Even so, the great compromise between the small and the large states was made in a form which does injustice today (and could hardly be produced today, *de novo*) and made it impossible to settle the slavery problem inside the margins of the constitution.[47]

Indeed it is doubtful whether existing precedents have any real relevance. Today in South Africa, as we have seen, the Africans are disenfranchised; and to confine the right to make any new constitution to the existing electorate would, in my view, be wildly unrealistic. If 'the people' of South Africa are to 'ordain' or 'establish' a new constitution for the country as a whole, 'the people' will have to include Africans, and other non-whites, as well as whites. From this there neither can, nor should, be any escape.

How then, in practice, might the problem be solved on a peaceful basis? This question brings me to the problem of summoning a national convention or constituent assembly.

2. *A national convention*

The question of the composition of an effective national convention is, like the preceding question, a practical or political question, and not primarily a legal one: what will work is the criterion.

On this, O'Rourke and Campbell have rightly observed that:

> Whatever the legal powers of the constitutional convention, the empirical evidence on its peace-time operations makes it clear that any convention functions within very effective *practical* limitations. These limitations can be discerned by a study of the political forces and institutions which operate at the time of the convention. The notion that a politically organised society becomes a *tabula rasa* upon which a constitutional convention may write whatever may come to the minds of its delegates is scarcely a credible one.[48]

And again:

> Adequate criticism of a given constitutional convention must rest upon detailed analysis of its workings, within the context of

---

[47] Op. cit., pp. 122–3.
[48] *Constitution-Making in a Democracy*, p. 26.

forces and institutions of which it is a part. The realities of
democratic politics—of party politics, pressure politics, personal
ambitions, social needs—must be accepted as the raw materials
for study, much more than the abstract concepts which are too
often used to relieve members of a democracy of the responsibility
for its travail.[49]

The American practice has been to confine membership of national
or constituent assemblies to those who already enjoy the franchise,
with the result, as W. F. Dodd has pointed out, that

if the constitutional defect to be cured is one of under-representa-
tion of any group in the legislature, (this type of) constitutional
convention is not an effective instrumentality; because like the
legislature it will reflect the interests of the groups that are
over-represented.[50]

Here, too, the South African constitution-maker must largely
cut a new path, so as to do elementary justice to those who are
voteless, as well as take due account of their influence and power
in fact. How, then, should this be done?

Much, of course, will depend on the actual conditions prevailing
at such time as a national convention might become practical
politics; so that it would not be profitable to go into this aspect too
fully. Within the South African context, however, it would probably
be realistic for a government wishing to summon a national convention to make it equally representative of white and non-white
opinion. This could be done, for example, by allowing the whites to
be represented by say forty persons chosen by the present Parliament
and the provincial councils (which represent the whites), both
government and opposition parties being represented according to
their strength. The non-whites would have to be left free to organize
politically so that all parties having substantial support might
elect, say in equal numbers for each party, up to one-half (i.e. forty)
of a national convention of eighty members. The convention should
then elect its own chairman and frame its rules of procedure.

I have spoken of parties having 'substantial support': what this
amounts to is a question of fact and judgment which must be left
to the future. It is a question, moreover, which is likely to answer
itself.

3. *Scope of the people's authority*

It has become customary in the United States in modern times to
ascribe both the legality of the constitution, and its supremacy over
ordinary legislation by the people's representatives, exclusively to

[49] Op. cit., pp. 60–1.
[50] *The Encyclopaedia of the Social Sciences*, vol. 4, p. 246.

the fact that, in its own phraseology, it was 'ordained' by 'the people of the United States'.[51] This attitude reflects what has become known as a 'positivist' conception of law, that is to say a conception of law as being purely the embodiment of human will.

Two degrees of this 'positivist' conception of law are involved in this explanation of the authority and supremacy of the United States Constitution. In the first place the people's representatives make laws by a declaration of their will; but such declarations are inferior in force to the embodiment of the people's *more deliberate* will as expressed in the constitution. And, in this regard, as Professor Corwin has pointed out:

> The same two ideas occur in conjunction in the oft-quoted text of Justinian's Institutes: 'Whatever has pleased the prince has the force of law, since the Roman people by the lex regia have yielded up to him all their power and authority.' The sole difference between the Constitution of the United States and the imperial legislation, justified in this famous text, is that the former is assumed to have proceeded immediately from the people, while the latter proceeded from a like source only mediately.[52]

Professor Corwin has also shown how the attribution of supremacy to the Constitution as a legal document on the ground solely of its rootage in the popular will, represents a departure from an earlier tradition. Earlier the supremacy accorded to constitutions—at any rate to the extent to which they dealt with essential matters, like human rights—was ascribed less to their source in the people's will than to their content, to the idea that they embodied essential and unchanging justice.

The earlier theory stands of course in direct contrast to the positivist view. As Corwin explains the position, the earlier view assumed that there are:

> certain principles of right and justice which are entitled to prevail of their own intrinsic excellence, altogether regardless of the attitude of those who wield the physical resources of the community. Such principles were made by no human hands. They are eternal and immutable. In relation to such principles, human laws are, when entitled to obedience (save as to matters indifferent), merely a record or transcript, and their enactment is an act not of will or power but one of discovery and declaration.[53]

We might perhaps sum this all up by saying that, on the one view, man alone decides what is legally right and wrong, and especially

---

[51] Corwin, 'The Higher Law Background of American Constitutional Law', reprinted in *The American Law Schools' Selected Essays on Constitutional Law*, vol. 1, p. 3.

[52] Op. cit., pp. 3–4.

[53] Op. cit., p. 4.

what is proper or improper in the sphere of government; whereas according to the other view, there are eternal standards to which man must attempt to conform. The struggle between these two ideas is still unresolved; but it is man's responsibility to make a choice, and accept the consequences of his decision. What the implications of that choice are we must now proceed to examine.

10   Under God and the Law

REDISCOVERING THE MEANING OF LAW

Fifteen hundred years ago, in the fifth century of our era, there lived and worked in the North African town of Hippo a non-white bishop who decisively 'moulded the thought of Western Christendom so that our very civilization bears the imprint of his genius'.[1] St. Augustine lived in times of upheaval and ruin. Rome had just fallen to the Barbarian hordes; and to Pagan and Christian alike, it seemed the end of all things—in St. Jerome's words, 'the light of the world was put out'.[2]

There is an ominous parallel between the age of St. Augustine and our own. Pleasure-seeking and material progress marked the later years of the Roman Empire, yet—to quote St. Gregory—while superficially the world flourished, 'in men's hearts it had already withered'—*in cordibus aruerat*. Similarly, today, despite man's technological achievements, there is inner doubt and tension, and a groping for values and meaningfulness which mock at the achievements themselves.

In the West the very freedom implicit in true democracy is menaced with becoming licence, freedom of thought with becoming anarchy of thought; and there is danger that, taken at its face value, 'western civilization' will seem just as materialistic as, and considerably less cogent than, the communist philosophy to which it declares itself opposed.

If true democracy is to survive, those who would give it allegiance must become more fully conscious of the real significance and place in history of the values which it must serve. It is senseless to compete with Russian Communism on a materialistic basis—with bigger and better Luniks or production figures. And certain it is that the West will be in no shape for the struggle without a clear idea of what it does stand for. As Father John Courtney Murray puts it, 'the trouble is that even a damnable philosophy is more effective than no philosophy at all'.[3] The West, then, must rediscover itself.

[1] Christopher Dawson, 'St. Augustine and His Age' in *A Monument to St. Augustine*, London, 1945, p. 39.

[2] Quoted by Dawson, op. cit., p. 37.

[3] J. C. Murray S.J., *We Hold These Truths*, New York, 1960, p. 91.

194

13

In his masterly survey of St. Augustine's age, Christopher Dawson has observed that:

> to the materialist, nothing could be more futile than the spectacle of Augustine busying himself with the reunion of the African Church and the refutation of the Pelagians, while civilization was falling to pieces about his ears. It would seem like the activity of an ant which works on while its nest is being destroyed. But Augustine saw things otherwise. He looked beyond the aimless and bloody chaos of history to the world of eternal realities from which the world of sense derives all the significance which it possesses.[4]

While going about his daily task as a bishop and practical administrator, he was trying, in the face of the sternest adversity, to cope with the predicaments of his time in the light of eternal principles. He went on thinking, writing, and clarifying the principles and ideals which should guide individual and political life.

Dawson tells us that the Church of Africa, in the service of which Augustine spent his later life, was destined to be blotted out as completely as if it had never existed; nevertheless St. Augustine was justified in his faith. For his spirit and his insistence upon principle bore fruit in the moulding of western Christendom.[5] And this, as it seems to me, is the real message of St. Augustine today: conduct, both of individuals and governments, must be principled, and the principles must be sound.

If we are to see our contemporary predicament in true perspective it is essential to realize that we are living in great times—times every bit as full of significance as the fall of the Western Roman Empire, the Reformation, the American Revolution, or the French Revolution—and that Africa, for reasons which are plain, is right in the front line.

Let us keep in mind that since the end of the Second World War—

(1) more than forty new states, populated by more than eight hundred million people (one-third of the entire population of the world) have obtained independence, or freedom from external rule and the right to govern or misgovern themselves;

(2) atomic power has annihilated distance—even beyond the earth —and while giving promise of peaceful use, has added a new terror to war:

(3) necessity has given birth to new agencies of international government and co-operation, chief among these being the

[4] Op. cit., p. 38.

[5] Edgar H. Brookes, *The City of God and the Politics of Crisis*, 1960; Marthinus Versfeld, *A Guide to The City of God*, 1958—two recent books written by distinguished South Africans.

United Nations Organization; and now this organization has
come to the time of its great testing;

(4) upon attaining independence, many of the new states proclaimed
their belief in democracy; indeed, for many of them the clamour
for democracy was a powerful factor in the drive for independence.

At the same time, the experience of these fifteen years has taught
several hard lessons. It has become plain for all to see—

(1) that independence does not bring with it automatic well-being
and temporal felicity; there is still in the world today an
overwhelming majority of hungry and illiterate people. Increasingly it is being realized that independence is not an automatic
panacea, and that although the maxim 'seek ye first the political
kingdom and all other things will be added to you' may contain
powerful truth, yet it is not the whole truth;

(2) that the achievement of democracy was beyond the capacity of
several of the newly independent states (for example, Pakistan, the
Sudan and Burma), and in others it is still in issue (e.g. in Ghana);

(3) that the concept of sovereign state independence (with its
insistence on 'essentially domestic interests') is becoming
increasingly inapplicable, less and less suited for the maintenance
of peaceful co-existence. It is being realized that 'freedom from
external control' is sterile, and even dangerous, if it means
isolation. We are learning to come to terms with the paradox
that to maintain freedom even at a national level, it may be
necessary to surrender sovereignty (for example, to organizations like the European community or the United Nations);

(4) and it is also plain that we live in a time when certain potent
and druglike words are in constant and controversial use—often
without adequate, or any, appreciation of their meaning—*vox
et praeterea nihil*. To mention a few: democracy, colonialism,
a free society, a Christian country.

Amid all this welter and confusion, men are starved for a new
understanding, a sense of direction, a belief in the worthwhileness
of what they are doing. But if a start is to be made it is essential that
the perspectives of history be borne in mind. By this I do not mean
that one should rely on the passage of time to solve problems—the
'time heals all wounds' and 'tomorrow is another day' outlook.
In Southern Africa, for example, one often hears the cry 'give us
time'. It is not time that is needed but an immediate committal to a
policy of wholesome government; for as each year goes by the
canker of indecision, fear and hate eats more deeply into the fibre
of the people. Again, it is a fact that the underdeveloped countries,

particularly of Africa, are in a hurry to overcome their disadvantages and take an active and fully responsible part in the community of nations. They are not content merely to let things evolve, nor is there any sufficient reason why they should be; for it is possible to profit from other people's experience. If the West believes that it has anything to offer other than technology, it is therefore urgent that besides being able to train engineers and doctors, it be able to interpret the ideals of good government which it professes to stand for, and unfold the heart of the philosophy on which those ideals rest.

But before people can justify their beliefs to others, they must be able to justify them to themselves. In previous chapters attention was given to the procedures and techniques of democracy; and the main objectives of good government were briefly outlined. Now it is necessary to look deeper.

Perhaps the best known statement of what is essentially the theme of this book is that by Henry Bracton, a great lawyer of the thirteenth century:

> The king ought not to be under any man, but he ought to be under God and the law, since the law makes the king. Therefore let the king render to the law what the law has rendered to the king, namely dominion and power; for there is no king where will prevails and not the law.[6]

There, in words that have rung through the centuries, you have the fundamental antithesis between government under law and government by arbitrary will. These are, in fact, two opposite poles of political life. Government under law is the antithesis of unfettered power. It is the antithesis of sheer domination of man over man, of arbitrariness and caprice. And only where government under law exists, is it possible for human dignity to be maintained, and for men to be free to live the good life.

Now although there is a deep chasm between unfettered power and law, power must be reconciled with law; for there can be neither government nor law without the exercise of power. And freedom, too, must be under law; for otherwise it degenerates into licence and confusion. In short, unfettered power is despotism or tyranny; unfettered freedom is licence or anarchy. But between these two extremes there is a middle way, where power tamed by law guarantees true freedom.

The seat of power has, of course, largely changed since Bracton's day. It is no longer so much a question of taming the arbitrary will

---

[6] *De Legibus et Consuetudinibus Angliae*, 1.8.5. The Latin text is set out in R. W. and A. J. Carlyle, *A History of Medieval Political Theory in the West*, vol. III, p. 38, note 1.

of kings and emperors and popes, but of restraining the people themselves and their representatives. Today it is the tyranny of a majority which constantly threatens to pervert and destroy democracy; and this is a tyranny which can be as ferocious and evil as that of any other ruler—and more difficult to circumscribe.

But the ideal of government under law, which inspired Bracton and his contemporaries, is still true and strong, it still has a great role to play. In December 1948, at San Francisco, the major nations of the world subscribed to the Universal Declaration of Human Rights, the only significant abstentions being Soviet Russia, Poland, Czecho-Slovakia, Yugoslavia, the Ukraine, Byelo-Russia, Saudi Arabia—and South Africa. And, as we have seen, all over the world today men are seeking to realize the ideal of government under the law by means of judicially enforceable constitutions which place the fundamental human rights and freedoms beyond the reach of legislative majorities and executive decisions.

However, if these efforts are to succeed and be meaningful, a real appreciation of the nature of the rights themselves is called for. One must understand the philosophy on which they rest. One must know, too, the broad outlines of the history of their evolution; how, for example, it has come about that whereas Bracton and his contemporaries placed the emphasis on the authority of *law*, we in modern times put the stress on individual *rights*.

Again the signatories of the Declaration of Human Rights represented countries from all over the world and many different religious faiths; yet it is a fact that the whole idea of basic human rights and their protection stems directly from a specific philosophy—the philosophy of natural law. How, then, it may well be asked, can a philosophy which for centuries was regarded as embodying the highest ideals of Christianity—and what is more, of Roman Catholicism—be sincerely subscribed to by Hindus and Muslims and even by agnostics.

Presently I shall attempt an historical and theoretical discussion of what is meant by natural law, which will, I hope, show its universality. At the outset, however, we should be clear on two points. In the first place, as Father John Murray, S.J., has observed:

> It is sometimes said that one cannot accept the doctrine of natural law unless one has antecedently accepted 'its Roman Catholic presuppositions'. This, of course, is quite wrong. The doctrine of natural law has no Roman Catholic presupposition. Its only presupposition is threefold: that man is intelligent; that reality is intelligible; and that reality, so grasped by intelligence, imposes on the will the obligation that it be obeyed in its demands for action or abstention. Even these statements are

not properly 'presuppositions', since they are susceptible of verification.[7]

At the same time natural law is most congenial to people who look beyond man, to God, for the ultimate source of their values, though scientific humanists, and others of an agnostic frame of mind, can and do unwittingly often find shelter under its umbrella.

In the second place there is no room for a genuine Bill of Rights in a country which is committed to authoritarianism or communism; for genuine Bills of Rights are the antithesis of government by arbitrary will.

It is sometimes said that a constitution should not embody any particular philosophy; that it must be able to accommodate men of many different faiths and of different outlook. Up to a point this is true. Indeed, if the traditions of freedom in a particular country are strong enough, and firmly enough based on principle, there should be room within the framework of a Bill of Human Rights even for those who would *openly* and *fairly* advocate incompatible doctrines. Every country that would enjoy really free institutions has the task of demonstrating their superiority over the organs of government appropriate to a totalitarian communist state, and this may well mean that the peaceful and fair advocacy of political heresy must be allowed.[8] Indeed it is one of the marks of a true democracy that it *is* prepared to demonstrate its superiority by allowing the full and fair self-criticism implicit in freedom of speech and freedom of association. States like Russia, on the other hand, cannot face such internal criticism, and for this reason—among others—cannot admit a genuine Bill of Rights.

What must be emphasized, however, is that no nation which is committed to a genuine Bill of Rights can afford to dispense with a clear understanding of the philosophy on which it is based. Indeed, as I see it, the protection given by constitutionally guaranteed rights is likely to be dangerously weak without such understanding. In the ultimate analysis human rights can only be fully meaningful, and can only survive, when they are consciously based on a philosophy of life.

At this point the view expressed by Maritain will be recalled, that in regard to human rights men are today divided into two groups; those who to a greater or lesser extent explicitly accept,

[7] Op cit., p. 109.

[8] See, more specifically, in regard to the difficult problem presented by communism, Alan Gledhill, *The Republic of India,* British Commonwealth Series, 1951, p. 10; *Australian Communist Party* v. *The Commonwealth,* 1951 A.L.R. 129, and the literature on the Communist Control Act of 1954 in the U.S.A. cited by Emerson and Haber, *Political and Civil Rights in the U.S.A.,* vol. 1, pp. 421–2.

and those who to a greater or lesser extent explicitly reject, natural law as the basis of human rights.[9] And it is precisely on this issue that I believe that a firm committal is necessary. I am aware that non-committal and pragmatism (and even the evasion of issues) are claimed to be philosophies; but they are no match, in these times, even for a 'damnable philosophy'.

Committal to a Bill of Rights in a true democracy must carry with it committal to the values which such a democracy must serve. And if we would know how, in the last analysis, those values are to be understood, so that they may be effectively realized—then, as I see it, there is only one satisfactory answer. There must be a committal to the natural law—to the system which, stemming from the best thought of the Graeco-Roman world, flowered in the work of St. Thomas Aquinas and the later Scholastics; there must be a committal to the philosophy of law and government which gave heart to the Huguenots after the massacre of St. Bartholomew's Night; which inspired the Revolt of the Netherlands from the tyranny of Phillip II; which sustained Sir Edward Coke and other great Englishmen in the crisis of English liberty during the seventeenth century; and which flourished in the establishment of the American Republic.

As we shall see more fully presently, exponents of natural law during the seventeenth and eighteenth centuries attempted to cut the system off from its roots, with the result that, in a debased form, it fell upon evil days. The superficial generalizations of Rousseau and his school could not stand the scrutiny of nineteenth-century historical scholarship. In the result, during the nineteenth century, and the early decades of the present century, a strong reaction set in—and set in justifiably—against what had come to masquerade as natural law. But the old truths remained; and today, in the midst of travail, we are beginning to witness a revival of the real natural law, the world over.

It is no doubt still fashionable among many lawyers—both professional and academic, who like to think of themselves as 'realists', or 'clear-headed', or who simply shrink from discussing the ultimate problem of power—to scorn natural law, or to adopt an evasive attitude towards it. There is nothing very novel about this phenomenon—for some 2,500 years cynical and scornful statements about natural law have been made with quite as much self-assurance and plausibility, and often with more learning, than the best 'dynamic realists' (i.e. non-realists) of modern times can show.

Professor Kocourek, whose analytical acumen I admire, and whose familiarity with the work of the nineteenth-century German

[9] Above, p. 81.

Pandectists is becoming regrettably rare among modern lawyers, once described natural law as 'the world's greatest legal illusion'.[10] But a rhetorical flourish of this kind is not argument. And we will perhaps be in a better position to judge whether natural law is in fact an illusion after we have traced its history.

An attitude of evasion is just as bad. There are those who say that lawyers should not concern themselves with the historical and political factors that lie behind the establishment of a legal system; that they should content themselves with an initial hypothesis—a categorical imperative—of the kind 'let the law for the time being be observed'; that they should build a 'pure' science of law, and leave the rest to the politicians, the political scientists, the historians and the philosophers. This attitude—which was developed with intellectual vigour by Hans Kelsen—has its uses, which I need not here elaborate; but it is not good enough.

Basically Kelsen's attitude is itself a species of natural law thinking at a purely formal level. It is not really satisfactory, however, because a purely formal proposition such as 'the law for the time being must be observed', without reference to the content and quality of the law itself, would justify the binding force and validity of Hitler's laws. Hans Frank, one of the legal apologists of Hitler's regime, told us that law is that which is useful to the German nation, the scope of the national interest being determined exclusively by the head of the nation, Adolf Hitler.[11] Law, on this view, was the formulated will of the Fuehrer. Or to quote Alfred Rosenberg, 'Law is what Aryan men consider as law, non-law is what they reject';[12] and, of course, an Aryan view on this point depended on what Hitler said.

If we are to regard Hitler's system as a legal system, albeit a deplorable one, then we empty the word law of all ethical content. In common parlance, no doubt, we conjoin the words 'law and order', and there is significance in this usage; for without order there cannot be law, but order in itself should not be regarded as law. If, as Kelsen suggests, we are to have no regard to the content of the law in determining its validity or claim to obedience, then we legalize political absolutism, and identify law with sheer power and domination.

Nor will it do for lawyers to try to cut themselves off from the rest of reality, to divorce themselves from the very foundations in history and ethics and politics of the legal system—thereby abandoning,

---

[10] 30 *Illinois Law Review* 548; quoted by Richard O'Sullivan, *Christian Philosophy in the Common Law*, Blackfriars, 1942, p. 55.

[11] Quoted by Bodenheimer, *Jurisprudence*, 1940, p. 243.

[12] Bodenheimer, op. cit., p. 240.

as lawyers, all criteria for testing the validity of the decrees of men.
Lawyers may try to make this escape and avoid their responsibilities
—they may try to become competent craftsmen in their own carefully
insulated and technical legal compartments—but only at the cost of
consequences demoralizing to society, and, let me add, without
adding noticeably to the glory of their profession. This was not the
way, for example, of the lawyers who made great legal systems of
Anglo-American law and of Roman-Dutch law.

That the fields of law and morals are not identical is, of course, a
truism: there exist, for example, rules of law on points in respect of
which the precepts of morality are quite indifferent (e.g. whether
the rule of the road should prescribe driving on the right or on the
left); and on the other hand, there are rules of morality dealing, for
example, with the inward and unexpressed thoughts of men, of
which the law can take no account. Nevertheless, it remains true
that there cannot be a divorce between law and ethics: to a very
large extent these two fields overlap, leaving areas—far smaller
than it is commonly realized—which are exclusively the concern of
law or exclusively the concern of ethics.

THE NATURAL LAW

There are two approaches to an understanding of the nature and
significance of natural law; the first historical, the other more
directly philosophical. But if the concept is to be fully understood
both must be combined. Detailed discussion along these lines would
of course require not one chapter, but volumes, and the combined
scholarship of several disciplines. Moreover no man who has any
real knowledge of the subject would presume to undertake the task
without trepidation; for in this field some of the greatest minds have
been engaged. Nevertheless an attempt must here be made to sketch
the broad outlines of the subject, its architecture so to speak.
Fortunately, most of the basic research has already been done
and a short bibliography of the more readily accessible writing on
natural law will be found at the end of this chapter.

In the outline which follows my main object is to give prominence
to certain fundamental themes—to show how, in the course of
history:

(1) the idea of law as right reason, a discovery by man's intelligence
of principles rooted in his very nature, has been in perpetual
strife with the notion of law as arbitrary will;

(2) how the idea of law as right reason is very much less vague and
abstract, and far more practical, than is often thought;

(3) how, at decisive moments in history, the idea has been used to
tame the power of tyrants;

(4)   how men, in the exercise of their reason, have recognized the
      need for law to adapt itself to changing times and circumstances;
      and how in determining the content of natural law, therefore,
      it became necessary to distinguish between what admits of
      change and what is eternal and unchanging. For, let it be
      clearly understood, the natural law involves adaptability as
      well as stability, but it distinguishes between what is eternal
      and what is ephemeral;

(5)   how men have debated the need for an interpreter of the content
      of natural law—what conduct does right reason enjoin? And
      whose reason is to judge? And, finally,

(6)   how, even where lawyers have tried to divorce themselves in
      theory from the natural law, it has perpetually recurred in
      practice; how—in Etienne Gilson's words—natural law buries
      its undertakers.[13] It is still the vital force behind the successful
      American experiment in taming governmental power; and
      even in countries which make less overt use of the idea, it
      persists in the everyday work of the courts; for example, in
      the rules which prescribe the standards of conduct of 'the
      reasonable man', or the rule that statutes should be interpreted
      so as to avoid unfairness or injustice.

The Greeks

The Greeks were among the first to postulate clearly the existence
of certain fundamental principles of law and justice which can be
discovered by man's intelligence, but cannot be nullified by his will.[14]
Indeed among the poets, philosophers and statesmen of Greece
this was widely accepted as a truism. 'Every law', said Demosthenes,
'is a discovery, a gift of God—a precept of wise men.' Heraclitus
spoke of a divine law whence all human laws draw nourishment.
And similar passages occur in Plato, especially in *The Laws*.

At an early date, too, the Greeks gave expression to the dilemma
which faces a citizen when the laws enacted by public authority
run counter to the law revealed by reason—a dilemma which forms
the subject of Sophocles' tragedy *Antigone*. King Creon of Thebes
had issued an edict refusing decent burial to Antigone's brother,
contrary to what was accepted among the Greeks as a duty imposed
by divine law. To Creon it was enough that he was King of Thebes:
his declared will was the law; and as ruler of the city, he was not
prepared to recognize any other law. 'Whomsoever the city may

---

[13] *The Unity of Philosophical Experience*, p. 306; quoted by Rommen, *The
Natural Law*, p. 267.

[14] On the whole subject J. Walter Jones's *The Law and Legal Theory of the
Greeks*, Oxford, 1956, is invaluable.

appoint', he declared, 'that man must be obeyed in little things and in great, in just things and unjust.' To which Antigone, courting death, replied: 'It was not Zeus that published that edict; nor deemed I that thy decrees were of such force that a mortal could override the unwritten and unfailing statutes of heaven.'[15]

Socrates, by personal example, gave even greater poignancy and significance to this dilemma; for he preferred death in submission to an unjust law, rather than defiance, and refused to escape from the city whose institutions he loved and honoured.[16] As we shall see presently, the example of Socrates led St. Thomas Aquinas, in a later age, to give particular attention and very serious thought to the circumstances in which defiance of an unjust law is morally obligatory; for this indeed is a grave problem.

It is, however, in the works of Aristotle that we find the Greek conception of law and government most fully developed. Indeed constitutionalism, or the taming of power under law, may be said to be the legacy of Aristotle's treatises on Ethics and Politics.[17] Aristotle divided law into that which was 'in accordance with nature' and that which was conventional. The rules of natural law were eternal and universal, and discoverable by human reason, whereas the rules of conventional law were fashioned by human agencies in order to deal, in Sir Frederick Pollock's words, 'with matters which are indifferent or indeterminate until a definite rule is laid down by some specific authority. Such are rules fixing the amount of fines. The rule of the road may furnish as good a modern example as any.'[18]

In a famous passage Aristotle emphasized that law is reason without passion; and that the ultimate sovereign in any society of free men must be the command of reason itself and not exclusively the will of men.[19] He condemned the kind of democracy where the people, incited by demagogues, acknowledged no legal restraint.[20] Nor was it sufficient, he argued, merely to have law and order; there must be *good* law and order. And good institutions, says Aristotle, are those which enable individual human beings to achieve as far as possible, in the light of their reason, the fullness of their nature in society.[21] Here, then, in Aristotle's words, is as good a description of the idea of government and freedom under law as one may hope to find.

[15] Lines 450–60, 666–7, Jebb's translation.
[16] See, generally, J. W. Jones, op. cit., pp. 2, 112.
[17] The view of Sir Ernest Barker, Aristotle's *Politics*, Oxford, 1946, p. ix. Cf. A. E. Taylor's Introduction to his translation of Plato's *Laws*, 1934.
[18] *Essays in the Law*, 1922, p. 33.
[19] *Politics*, Bk. III, 15–16, Barker's ed., pp. 141 sqq., 367.
[20] Op. cit., Barker's ed., pp. 168, 233.
[21] Op. cit., pp. 142, 279, 284, 286, 289, 312.

It would be a mistake, moreover, to imagine that these were merely high-minded aspirations which had no practical bearing upon Greek life. To begin with, there existed an ingenious procedure for the guardianship of the laws. At any time within one year of the enactment of a measure, an action might be brought to secure its annulment on the ground that it was an ill-considered innovation, in conflict with the constitution. And what is more, an action lay for the punishment of the proposer of the offending law.[22] The parallel between the Athenian procedure for the annulment of laws and the modern American doctrine of judicial review has often been noted.[23]

In addition the Greek conception of the supremacy of law had effects on national life and character which far transcended the procedures of the courts. It was this conception which enabled the Greeks in their glory to say with justifiable pride that they enjoyed 'freedom under law'. Thucydides tells us how the Athenian general, Nicias, at a moment of supreme danger during the Sicilian campaign, gave heart to his captains by reminding them one by one that they were fighting for a country which was the 'freest of the free'.[24] Leaving aside, for the moment, the question of slavery, in what — we may ask — did this freedom consist? The answer is to be found in the Greek word *isonomia*, which means equal protection of the law for all.[25] It was to this that Herodotus referred when he spoke of 'the most beautiful of all words' in the political order.[26] And it was of this that Herodotus was thinking when he put into the mouth of the exiled Spartan King at the Persian Court, these words: 'Although the Greeks are free men, they are not free in every respect. Law is the master they own, and this master they fear more than any of thy subjects fear thee.'[27]

You will find the same ideas repeated in Pericles' great funeral oration:

> Our laws [he says] secure equal justice for all in their private disputes . . . [and] in our public acts we keep strictly within the control of the law. We acknowledge the restraint of reverence; we are obedient to whomsoever is set in authority and to the laws,

[22] See, generally, J. W. Jones, op. cit. ch. 6; Hignett, *A History of the Athenian Constitution*, Oxford, 1952, pp. 299; Vinogradoff, *Historical Jurisprudence* vol. ii, pp. 133 sqq.

[23] Haines, *The Revival of Natural Law Concepts*, 1930, p. 7; Vinogradoff, op. cit., p. 140; J. W. Jones, op. cit., p. 112.

[24] *History of the Peloponnesian War*, 7, 69.

[25] For an excellent general discussion, see Hayek, *The Political Ideal of the Rule of Law*, Cairo, 1955; and, with more detail, J. W. Jones, op. cit., pp. 84–7.

[26] *Histories*, III, 80.

[27] *Histories*, VII, 104.

more especially to those which offer protection to the oppressed, and those unwritten ordinances whose transgression brings admitted shame.[28]

One may, perhaps, sum this all up, in the words of Mr. J. W. Jones, by saying that for the Athenians true democracy was synonymous with the 'rule of law'; it meant, in short, good government and equality before the law.[29]

Of course, I am not suggesting that all Greek thought was of this kind. There was Thrasymachus who taught that laws were created by the group in power in order to promote their own advantage. Justice, he said, is nothing but the interest of the stronger.[30] And then you have Callicles who asserted that the laws were made by the weak and the many; and he contrasted the natural and more noble right of the strong man.[31] These are 'the realists' (modern style) among the Greeks. Then you had Protagoras stating exactly the views of modern positivists, and contending that the laws were binding simply because the men in power said so.[32] He flatly denied that there were any superior tests for determining the validity of law.

Nor do I suggest that Aristotle's attempt to justify slavery on the ground that some men were slaves by nature is convincing.[33] Indeed many centuries were to pass before reason on the subject of slavery prevailed over self-interest. But two things do appear very clearly from a study of the Greek sources. First, the conflict between the ideas of law as reason, and law as will, is plainly a very old one. And secondly, the political thought of Greece, at the time of her greatness, favoured right reason; it was hostile to tyranny and favourable to liberty.

The Romans

The influence of Greek ideas on the political thought of Republican Rome was enormous. Cicero and his contemporaries received the tradition of government under law to the full; and they added materially to it. Indeed Cicero's writings were to become one of the most influential channels for handing on the tradition.

[28] Thucydides, *History of the Peloponnesian War*, 2, 6.

[29] Op. cit., pp. 89–90.

[30] Plato, *Republic*, Book 1, Jowett's translation, *The Dialogues of Plato*, Oxford, 1892, vol. 3, pp. 15 sqq.

[31] Plato, *Gorgias*, Jowett's translation, *The Dialogues of Plato*, Oxford, 1892, vol. 2, pp. 370 sqq.

[32] Plato, *Protagoras*, Jowett's translation, *Dialogues of Plato*, vol. 1, pp. 129 sqq.

[33] For critical discussion of Aristotle on this point, see McIlwain, *The Growth of Political Thought in the West*, pp. 70 sqq.; R. W. Southern, *The Making of the Middle Ages*, 1952, pp. 98 sqq. Also, J. W. Jones, op. cit., pp. 58–9; Bryce, op. cit., vol. 2, p. 145 note 2.

In *De Republica* III, xxii (a passage preserved by Lactantius), he says:

> True law is right reason in agreement with nature; it is of universal application, unchanging and everlasting; it summons to duty by its commands, and averts from wrong-doing by its prohibitions. And it does not lay its commands or prohibitions upon good men in vain, though neither have any effect on the wicked. It is a sin to try to alter this law, nor is it allowable to attempt to repeal any part of it, and it is impossible to abolish it entirely. We cannot be freed from its obligations by senate or people, and we need not look outside ourselves for an expounder or interpreter of it. And there will not be different laws at Rome and at Athens, or different laws now and in the future, but one eternal and unchangeable law will be master and ruler, that is, God, over us all, for he is the author of this law, its promulgator, and its enforcing judge. Whoever is disobedient is fleeing from himself and denying his human nature, and by reason of this very fact he will suffer the worst penalties, even if he escapes what is commonly considered punishment . . .[34]

In the *De Legibus* Cicero identifies 'right reason' with the qualities of human nature whereby 'man is associated with the gods'; and the true source of law, he says, is to be found in the natural endowment and requirements of man's nature. This emphasis upon the nature of man as the true source of law was, as Dr. Carlyle pointed out, to become one of the most influential ideas in the whole range of political theory. For Cicero was proclaiming that all men equally, and all races of men, are by their very humanity to be considered capable of virtue, and equally entitled to the protection of the law.[35] It was appreciation of this principle which enabled the Emperor, Marcus Aurelius, to say: 'My city and country, so far as I am Antoninus, is Rome, but so far as I am a man, it is the world.'[36] All men too, said Cicero, are naturally free; 'if slavery is not actively opposed it is not—as Aristotle suggested—because slavery is according to nature, but only because man's outward status has become less important than his inward life'.[37]

Cicero's insistence upon man's capacity to discover basic principles of law in the light of his reason, was to bear fruit subsequently in the great discourse on the subject by St. Thomas Aquinas. Again, few writers have brought out more clearly than Cicero the proposi-

---

[34] On this passage, see Pollock, *Essays in the Law*, 1922, p. 39; Corwin, 'The Higher Law Background of American Constitutional Law', *Association of American Law Schools' Selected Essays*, 1938, vol. 1, pp. 7–11.

[35] *A History of Medieval Political Theory in the West*, vol 1, pp. 8–9; cf. Figgis, *From Gerson to Grotius*, p. 212.

[36] *Meditations*, VI, 44.

[37] McIlwain, op. cit., p. 98.

tion that justice is not the mere arbitrary construction of opinion.[38] 'Not all things are just', he says in the *De Legibus*, 'which are established by the civil laws and institutions of nations.'[39] And then comes a vital passage:

> If it were possible to establish justice simply by the commands of the people, by the decrees of princes, by the adjudications of magistrates, then all that would be necessary in order to make robbery, adultery, or the falsification of wills right and just would be a vote of the multitude.[40]

He goes on to say that many 'pernicious and harmful measures are enacted among peoples which do not deserve the name law'.[41] True law, he argues, is 'a rule of distinction between right and wrong according to nature'; and 'any other sort of law not only ought not to be regarded as law, it ought not to be called law'.[42]

At the same time Cicero was no anarchist. He recognized that conformity to established authority was in accordance with man's nature;[43] and that there was a duty to obey the promulgated laws of the land. Indeed it is probably with reference to the ordinary *ius civile* that he made his famous statement: 'We are slaves of the law that we may be free.'[44]

But there were limits to the authority of the enacted law. Professor Corwin has shown how Cicero frequently appealed to the Roman practice of inserting a saving clause or *adscriptio* in statutes to the effect that it was not the intention to abrogate what was sacred or just.[45] And on one occasion, in the Senate, he appealed directly to 'right reason' as against 'the written law'.[46]

It is sometimes objected that these quotations are all very well; but that they represent nothing more than philosophizing, whereas the actual practice of the Roman law was quite different. Indeed it has been claimed that in actual fact the Roman law was the embodiment of political absolutism; and in this respect it has been compared to its disadvantage with the common law of England.[47] But this is a very one-sided point of view, and hardly a fair judgment.

It is true that in that vast storehouse of legal principle, the *Corpus*

[38] *De Legibus*, 1.7.23; 1.15.16; 1.10.28; Corwin, op. cit., p. 8.
[39] Ibid., 1.15.42.
[40] Ibid., 1.16.43–4. Corwin's translation.
[41] Ibid., 2.5.13.
[42] Ibid., 2.6.13.
[43] Ibid., 3.1.2–3.
[44] *Pro Cluentio*, 53, 146. Corwin, op. cit. p. 9.
[45] Op. cit., p. 10.
[46] *Phil.*, XI, 12.
[47] O'Sullivan, *The King's Good Servant*, 1948, p. 19, quoting Mr. Justice O. W. Holmes.

Juris Civilis, which was compiled under Justinian's direction in the sixth century A.D., there are texts which were destined to play a role of paramount importance in giving support to the theory of political absolutism; chief among these being the statements by Ulpian that *princeps legibus solutus est* (the ruler is not bound by law),[48] and *quod principi placuit legis habet vigorem* (what the ruler wills is law).[49] Indeed, as the late Professor Esmein observed: 'few texts have had a more profound effect than these on the public law of certain European countries, notably France'.[50]

On the other hand, not only are the best authorities disposed to interpret Ulpian's statements in a less absolute sense than they might at first sight seem to warrant,[51] but there are other texts in the *Corpus Juris* which present a very different picture; as for example, the statement by Theodosius and Valentinian that *de auctoritate juris nostra pendet auctoritas* (our authority derives from the law).[52]

In fact, as Dr. N. P. Gilmore points out, the Roman law did not so much embody a theory of political absolutism as provide texts which could be used, and were used, in later ages, to support absolutism.[53]

But, in any event, there is more to it. The *ius naturale* of the Greeks was given actual practical application in Rome in the form of the *ius gentium*—a system of rules, based on reason and common sense, which was applied by the praetor peregrinus to transactions between Roman citizens and foreigners.[54] The influence of the *ius gentium* in giving an equitable character to the Roman law was enormous.

This is not the place to go into the technical differences in Roman law between the *ius gentium* and *ius naturale*. In practice, however, the two phrases were often equated, even though strictly speaking *ius naturale* should signify rules of conduct deducible by reason from the nature of human beings in society, and *ius gentium* so much of those rules as are actually acted upon by civilized people.[55] In the

[48] *Digest* 1.3.31.

[49] *Digest* 1.4.1.

[50] 'La maxime "princeps legibus solutus est" dans l'ancien droit public francais', in *Essays in Legal History*, Oxford, 1913, pp. 201, 299.

[51] Among the older authorities, Cujacius Gothrofredus, Noodt and Donellus all gave the maxim *princeps legibus solutus est*, a restricted meaning. Among modern authorities, see, especially Theodor Mommsen, *Römisches Staatsrecht*, 2nd ed., vol. 2, p. 728; H. F. Jolowicz, 'Political Implications of Roman Law', 22 *Tulane Law Review* 67.

[52] Code 1.14.4.

[53] *Argument from Roman Law in Political Thought*. Harvard, 1941, p. 131; also B. Z. Beinart, *Roman Law in South African Practice* (1952) *S.A.L.J.* 146.

[54] See, generally, H. F. Jolowicz, *Historical Introduction to Roman Law*, ch. 6.

[55] Pollock, *Essays in the Law*, p. 35.

Roman legal sources *ius naturale* is occasionally referred to as the principle on which all law rests; and though Buckland may be right when he says that this was more an ideal to which law should conform, than a test of the validity of rules of law,[56] enough, I think, has been said to show that the idea of law as reason was given much more than lip service in Roman times.

And, finally, it is relevant to note that in the writings of the medieval commentators on the Roman law, there is quite as much material in favour of government under law as there is in support of absolutism.[57] Indeed Professor Lawson of Oxford, who is hard-headed about the Roman law, sums up fairly when he says that through many centuries of political absolutism the system itself 'kept alive the notion that the lives of men could be ordered by a body of principle, rational, unarbitrary, and impersonal—the law'.[58]

The great Christian tradition

Graeco-Roman thought upon natural law—given even greater depths of meaning by Christianity—became the basis of the legal and political philosophy of the Middle Ages. And we would do well to consider deeply—with minds quite unprejudiced by attitudes to religion—the basic tenets of natural law as it was understood in those times, when the Church and Christianity had their strongest attraction for men.

Looking back upon this age, one is almost overwhelmed by the sweep and majesty of the available material on natural law, ranging from St. Augustine in the fifth century, to Suarez and Grotius more than 1,000 years later. For centuries the subject was developed and refined by the leading jurists, theologians and statesmen of their day. Here there is space only for a concise review.

St. Augustine, whose authority in later centuries was enormous, was clear that no human decree was entitled to the name of law unless it were just—*lex esse non videtur quae justa non fuerit*[59]; and it is to St. Augustine that we owe the famous tag: 'If justice be lacking what are kingdoms but robber bands'.[60] However, his

[56] Buckland, *A Manual of Roman Private Law*, 1925, 28.

[57] See, generally, Gierke, *Political Theories of the Middle Ages*, Maitland's translation; and *Johannes Althusius und die Entwicklung der natuurrechtlichen Staatstheorien*, 3rd ed., 1913 (Freyd's translation, under the title *The Development of Political Theory*, London, 1939). For a useful summary, see C. P. Joubert, 'Die gebondenheid van die sorvereine wetgewer aan die reg' (1952) *Tydskrif vir Hedendaagse Romeins-Hollandse Reg*, 7 sqq. And see Carlyle, op. cit. vol. 1.

[58] F. H. Lawson, *A Common Lawyer looks at the Civil Law*, Michigan, 1953, p. 211.

[59] *De Libero Arbitrio*, 1.5; quoted by St. Thomas Aquinas, *Prima Secundae*, Q–95, art. 2; Q–96, art. 4.

[60] *The City of God*, Book IV, ch. 4, Everyman Edition.

14

writings on the subject of the natural law, especially in regard
to its political aspects, are fragmentary and, in part, controversial.[61] We must therefore look to the later and more developed
treatises to appreciate the medieval Christian conception in its full
stature.

Probably the main function of natural law during the Middle
Ages was to provide a basis and test for all lawful power. It constrained the highest earthly powers; it held sway over Pope and
Emperor, over ruler and people, indeed over the whole community
of mortals.[62] Indeed, it is fair to say that the major contribution of
the Middle Ages to political theory was to develop the idea that all
political authority is intrinsically limited by law.

This was made very clear in the pages of John of Salisbury's
Policraticus or Statesman's Book. John of Salisbury, an Englishman,
who was the first systematic writer on politics in the Middle Ages,
based his work on the proposition that 'there are certain precepts
which have perpetual necessity, having the force of law among all
nations and which absolutely cannot be broken'.[63] Repudiating the
notion that law is exclusively an arbitrament of the ruler's will, he
distinguished between 'a tyrant' and 'a prince'. A tyrant is 'one
who oppresses the people by rule based on force', whereas a prince is
'one who rules in accordance with the laws'.

It remained, however, for John of Salisbury to deal with the two
troublesome texts of the Roman law; namely, that the prince is
not bound by law, and that what he wills has the force of law.
Neither of these propositions, he argued, justified absolutism under
the law of England. The prince was absolved from the obligations
of the law not 'in the sense that it is lawful for him to do unjust acts',
but only in the sense that his character should guarantee his doing
equity 'not through fear of the penalties of the law but through love
of justice'; and as to the 'will of the prince', he contended that in
respect of public matters, 'the prince may not lawfully have any will
of his own apart from that which the law of equity enjoins, or the
calculation of the common interest requires'.[64]

---

[61] Among the best available accounts in English of St. Augustine's political
thought, are those by C. H. McIlwain, *The Growth of Political Thought in the
West*, pp. 154–61; J. N. Figgis, *The Political Aspects of St. Augustine's City of
God*, London, 1921; and Norman H. Baynes, *The Political Ideas of St. Augustine's
De Civitate Dei*, London, 1936.

[62] Gierke, *Political Theories of the Middle Ages*. Maitland's translation, pp. 74
sqq.

[63] *The Statesman's Book of John of Salisbury*, 1927. Dickinson's translation,
p.33. For an admirable short survey see Corwin, *Liberty against Government*,
Baton Rouge, 1948, pp. 20–2.

[64] I have here followed Professor Corwin's summary, op. cit., p. 21.

Statements along the same lines recur throughout the Middle Ages and much learning and ingenuity was devoted to repudiating, distinguishing and qualifying the two Roman texts that the prince is not bound by law, and that what he wills has the force of law. But, for present purposes, there would be little point in multiplying authority here; moreover some of the discussion would take us too far afield.[65]

What does need elaboration, however, is the philosophical basis upon which medieval natural law rested; and we must also give attention to its actual content. Professor Dickinson has pointed out that John of Salisbury was not confronted with the difficulty which troubled later exponents of natural law of identifying any specific precepts as belonging to the natural law. Identifying the higher law very largely with scripture, and more particularly with the Ten Commandments, he found these precepts ready to hand in authoritative texts.[66] This is true; and the reason, in Sir Frederick Pollock's words, is that during the twelfth century the author or authors of the Decretum of Gratian identified the natural law with the law of God, 'with a thoroughgoing boldness which almost deserves the name of genius'.[67]

But more was needed. Thou shalt not kill; thou shalt not steal; thou shalt not bear false witness—these propositions and others in the Decalogue are no doubt first principles; but they are by no means full formulations. More specifically, 'thou shalt not kill' means 'thou shalt not kill an innocent person', just as 'thou shalt not steal' means 'do not take the goods of others against their will'.[68]

Here, then, was a great problem: how was a secure foundation to be laid for the natural law which would avoid a multiplicity of arbitrary constructions? How was satisfactory guidance to be obtained as to its content? The answer was given by St. Thomas Aquinas, in whose massive work the medieval tradition achieved its mature and comprehensive form.

For a proper understanding of St. Thomas it is necessary to begin with a few words of philosophical introduction.[69] Natural law, during its classical period of development in the hands of the Scholastic philosophers, presupposed an epistomology which is

[65] For full discussion, see Gierke, *Political Theories of the Middle Ages*; and Walter Ullman's very useful monograph on Lucas de Penna, *The Medieva Idea of Law*, 1946.

[66] Op. cit., introduction.

[67] *Essays in the Law*, p. 40.

[68] Cf. Rommen, *The Natural Law*, pp. 221–2.

[69] In this paragraph I am indebted to the brilliantly clear account given by Father John Murray, S.J., in 'The Natural Law' published in *Great Expressions of Human Rights*, ed. R. M. MacIver, 1950, pp. 95 sqq.

usually described as realist in the proper sense of that word, that is to say, it asserted that reality or the nature of being was not dependent for its creation or existence on man's perception; on the contrary, knowledge of reality as created by God, was discoverable by man's intelligence. More particularly, it asserted that the reality of man's nature is an ultimate and constant concept beneath all individual differences. Secondly, natural law, in its classical purity, presupposed a metaphysic of nature, especially the idea that nature is a teleological process, the 'nature' of a thing being its 'form' or 'final cause', its maximum perfection, or the goal of its becoming. More particularly, in the case of man, it asserted that there is a natural inclination for him to achieve the fullness of his nature as a social and God-loving being. Thirdly, natural law presupposed a natural theology, asserting that there is a God who is eternal Reason, *Nous*, at the summit of the order of being—the author of all nature—and whose will it is that all things in the order of being should fulfil their natures. And finally, it presupposed a natural morality, especially the principle that for man, a rational being, the order of nature was not a necessity to be fulfilled blindly, but an order of reason confronting his free will. In short, for the Scholastic philosophers the natural law was rooted in the nature of man, considered as part of a God-created order of being.

Let us now see how these ideas were developed in a practical way by St. Thomas. He distinguished between four different kinds of law:

(1) the eternal, (2) the natural, (3) the divine, (4) the human.

The eternal law is the divine wisdom itself directing all actions (of rational creatures) and all movements (of irrational creatures) to their due end.[70] In its entirety it is known only to God. No human being is capable of knowing this eternal law in its entirety except the blessed who are given grace to see God in his essence.

But although no human being can know the eternal law in its entirety, all men may partake of it by means of the faculty of reason with which God has endowed them. This participation in the eternal law by virtue of reason St. Thomas called the natural law.[71] And here, perhaps, we should allow St. Thomas to speak for himself. In a celebrated passage, he says:

> The precepts of the natural law are to the practical reason, what the first principles of demonstrations are to the speculative reason; because both are self-evident principles. Now a thing is said to be self-evident in two ways: first, in itself; secondly, in relation to

[70] *Summa Theologica, Prima Secundae*, Q.93, art. 1; Q.91, art. 2; Rommen, op. cit., p. 180. For a short and clear (though by no means superficial) exposition, see Cronin, *The Science of Ethics*, 1909, vol. 1, pp. 603 sqq.

[71] See, especially, Rommen, op. cit., pp. 180–2; Cronin, op. cit., pp. 607 sqq.

us. Any proposition is said to be self-evident in itself, if it predicate is contained in the notion of the subject; although, to one who knows not the definition of the subject, it happens that such a proposition is not self-evident. For instance, this proposition 'Man is a rational being', is, in its very nature, self-evident, since to say 'man', is to say 'a rational being'. And yet to one who knows not what a man is, this proposition is not self-evident. Hence it is that, as Boethius says (*De Hebdom.*), certain axioms or propositions are universally self-evident to all; and such are those propositions whose terms are known to all; as for example,

'Every whole is greater than its part', and 'Things equal to one and the same thing are equal to one another'. But some propositions are self-evident only to the wise.

Now a certain order is to be found in those things that are apprehended universally. For that which, before aught else, falls under apprehension is 'being', the notion of which is included in all things whatsoever a man apprehends. Wherefore the first undemonstrable self-evident principle is that 'the same thing cannot be affirmed and denied at the same time', which is based on the notion of being and not-being; and on this principle all others are based, as is stated in Metaph. iv., text 9. Now as 'being' is the first thing that falls under the apprehension simply, so 'good' is the first thing that falls under the apprehension of the practical reason, which is concerned with action; since every action seeks, or is directed towards, the good of the actor. Consequently, the first principle of the practical reason is one founded on the notion of good, viz., that 'good is that which all things seek after'. (*Bonum est quod omnia appetunt.*) Hence this is the first precept of law, that 'good is to be done and ensured and evil is to be avoided'. All other precepts of the natural law are based upon this: so that whatever the practical reason naturally apprehends as man's good (or evil) belongs to the precepts of the natural law as something to be done or avoided.[72]

It will not escape notice that St. Thomas in this passage moves from an Aristotelian proposition, stated in the indicative mood, namely that man in fact seeks his own good, to a proposition in the imperative mood, namely that the good ought to be sought. This follows, as Rommen points out, from the truth that ultimately, in God's created order, being and oughtness are identical.[73]

It will also be apparent that to say that 'good ought to be done and evil avoided' is on the face of it, and without more, a rather formal proposition without content. But Acquinas gave it content. Thus:

---

[72] *Prima Secundae*, Q.94, art 2. I have, on the whole, followed the Dominican translation, 1915–42, modifying it in the interest of clarity, by reference to the original.
[73] *The Natural Law*, p. 147.

Since, however, good has the nature of an end or purpose, and evil the nature of its contrary, hence it is that all those things to which man has a natural inclination, are naturally apprehended by reason as being good, and consequently as objects to be pursued; and hence it is that their contraries are apprehended as evil and as objects of avoidance. Accordingly the order of precepts of the natural law follows the order of man's natural inclinations. In the first place, there is an inclination to good which man shares with other substances, that is to say, inasmuch as every substance seeks the preservation of its own being, according to its nature, by reason of this inclination whatever is a means of preserving human life, and of warding off its obstacles, belongs to the natural law. Secondly, there is in man an inclination to ends or purposes that pertain to him more specially according to that nature which he has in common with other animals; and in virtue of this inclination, those things are said to belong to the natural law, which nature has taught to all animals, such as the procreation of species, education of offspring and so forth. Thirdly, there is in man an inclination to good according to the nature of his reason, which nature is distinctively proper to him. Thus man has a natural inclination to know the truth about God, and to live in society; and in this respect, whatever pertains to this inclination belongs to the natural law; for instance, to shun ignorance, to avoid offending those among whom one has to live, and other such things regarding the above inclinations.[74]

At this point two different kinds of objections to St. Thomas's reasoning have been raised. Montaigne remarked that no principle of conduct is self-evident, adding that among some people incest and thievery were considered virtuous acts. The answer, as it seems to me, has been given by Jacques Maritain: 'Men know the natural law with greater or less difficulty, and in different degrees, running the risk of error here as elsewhere.' The proposition that 'good must be done' is, he says, merely the first principle of the natural law, not its full content; the fact that error is possible merely proves that our sight is weak and that innumerable accidents may corrupt our judgment. Dealing specifically with Montaigne's objection, he says:

All this proves nothing against natural law, any more than a mistake in addition proves anything against arithmetic, or the mistakes of certain primitive peoples, for whom the stars were holes in the tent which covered the world, prove anything against astronomy. Man's knowledge of natural law has increased little by little as man's moral conscience has developed. The latter was at first in a twilight state.[75]

[74] *Prima Secundae*, Q.94, art. 2.
[75] *Man and the State*, Chicago, 1951, p. 90.

The second objection is that St. Thomas gives insufficient detailed guidance in the practical affairs of life, and insufficient certainty. Here, again, the scholastic tradition gives the answer. It will be remembered that St. Thomas recognized two other kinds of law in addition to the eternal law and the natural law, namely the divine law and the human law. Both of them, in St. Thomas's view, carry out the necessary supplementary function.

The divine law, as St. Thomas defined it, is the revelation of God's will as revealed through the sacred scriptures in the Old and New Testaments. By distinguishing between the divine and the natural law in this way, St. Thomas was able to give the concept of natural law more flexibility; in Lord Bryce's words, he went beyond Gratian and introduced 'a distinction which exercised an enduring significance'.[76] And even more comprehensive in supplementing the general provisions of the natural law, is the human law, which St. Thomas defines as 'an ordinance of right reason for the common good promulgated by him who has the care of the community'.[77]

St. Thomas is fully aware that as time moves on and conditions change, so too the basic principles of natural law require new methods of application. In short law in its practical application must be capable of growth;[78] and it is precisely the function of the human law-giver to deal specially with the problems presented by the changing circumstances and needs of the community. But as life is growth, it is not possible to map out, in advance, a blue-print of rules and instructions covering all human affairs.

It will be seen, therefore, that St. Thomas accorded a major role to human law in filling out the details left open by the national law. And, what is more, he recognized that human law was an act of volition; but—and it is a very big but—human law is not *merely* an act of volition on the part of the law-giver. For, to quote his words:

> in order that the volition of what is commanded may have the nature of law, it needs to be in accordance with some rule of reason. And it is in this sense that one must understand the saying that the will of the sovereign has the force of law; otherwise the sovereign's will would savour of lawlessness rather than of law.[79]

St. Thomas was also fully aware that laws require an interpreter. In his view, however, natural law both could and should be interpreted by the exercise of human reason; its basic principles (though

---

[76] Op. cit., p. 158.
[77] *Prima Secundae*, Q.90, art. 4.
[78] See Rommen, op. cit., pp. 50, 215 sqq.
[79] *Prima Secundae*, Q.90, art. 1 in *fin*.

not all their consequences) being within the comprehension of all who have reason. Interpretation of the Divine law was a matter ultimately for the Church; and—subject to the overriding force of the natural and the Divine law—human law was to be interpreted and applied in the ordinary courts.

And this brings us to a final question concerning St. Thomas's exposition of the natural law; namely the extent, if any, to which an unjust command of the law-giver is binding in conscience. The main passage on the point in the Summa Theologica reads as follows:

> Laws framed by man are either just or unjust. If they be just, they have the power of binding in conscience, from the eternal law whence they are derived, according to Prov. viii. 15: 'By Me Kings reign, and law-givers decree just things.' Now laws are said to be just, both by reference to their end or purpose, when, to wit, they are ordained to the common good; and by reference to their author, that is to say, when the law that is made does not exceed the power of the lawgiver; and also by reference to their content when, to wit, burdens are laid on subjects according to an equality of proportion and with a view to the common good.
>
> On the other hand laws may be unjust in two ways: first, by being contrary to human good, through being opposed to the requirements mentioned above:—either in respect of the end or purpose, as when an authority imposes on his subjects burdensome laws, conducive, not to the common good, but rather to his own cupidity or vainglory;—or in respect of the author, as when a man makes a law that goes beyond the power committed to him; —or in respect of the content, as when burdens are imposed unequally on the community, although with a view to the common good. The like are acts of violence rather than laws; because as Augustine says (De Lib. Arb. i.5), 'a law that is not just, seems to be no law at all'. Wherefore such laws do not bind in conscience, except perhaps in order to avoid scandal or disturbance, for which cause a man should even yield his right, according to Matth. v. 40, 41: 'If a man . . . take away thy coat, let go thy cloak also unto him; and whosoever will force thee one mile, go with him other two.'
>
> Secondly, laws may be unjust through being opposed to the Divine good: such are the laws of tyrants inducing to idolatry, or to anything else contrary to the Divine Law; and laws of this kind must nowise be observed, because, as stated in Acts v. 29, 'we ought to obey God rather than man'.[80]

St. Thomas, like Cicero, is therefore no anarchist. He recognizes that sedition is a social evil, and warns against rebellion in circumstances which would not justify the disturbance involved. Resistance,

[80] Prima Secundae, Q.96, art. 4.

he says, is a very grave step; nevertheless there are limits to the requirements of obedience. If the ruler persistently ignores the common good, then resistance is not rebellion against lawful authority; but, on the contrary, it becomes justifiable resistance to the abuse of authority.[81] The whole of this difficult subject is fully discussed by St. Thomas with admirable restraint in the treatise *De Regimine Principum*.[82]

Perhaps all this may now be summed up in a few sentences. Man was created by God to live in society; by his very nature, he is a political animal. But God, who created men to live in society, decreed also the means indispensable for its realization, namely government. Without government individuals—actuated by self-interest—would be in continual conflict. The authority of government is therefore necessary to ensure the harmonious and peaceful co-operation of individuals. But its *raison d'être* is the good of those whom it has the duty to control. The State, then, exists for a fixed purpose defined by God and discoverable by reason; and in that purpose we have the principle for the limitation of political authority.

Such, then, in broad outline, is the Christian concept of natural law as developed in the Middle Ages. We must now briefly trace its subsequent history and influence.

The natural law of the new learning

In the classical tradition of the natural law it was neither necessary nor usual to think or speak, as we do now, in terms of individual rights. The emphasis was more on conduct conforming to the natural law, more on man's condition, than on men's desires and their protection.[83] This does not mean that it was not possible to think in terms of substantive individual rights within the framework of medieval scholastic philosophy. Gierke is probably correct when he says that the germ of the modern idea is present in the writings of the Middle Ages, even though it was not often specifically formulated;[84] and indeed modern Thomists, like Maritain, have constructed systems on the basis of substantive natural rights.[85] But the point that needs to be stressed is that natural rights in the classical medieval

[81] See the essay on 'Law and Political Power' by J. F. Rogers S.J., in *Papers read to the More Society of London*, Second Series, ed. O'Sullivan, p. 149.

[82] Translated by Gerald Phelan, with notes by I. T. Eshmann, O.P., The Pontifical Institute of Medieval Studies, Toronto, 1849. See particularly chapter 6, pp. 23 sqq. Also Carlyle, op. cit., vol. 1, pp. 147 sqq.; vol. 3, pp. 115 sqq.

[83] Michel Villey, *Leçons D'Histoire de la Philosophie du Droit*, Paris, 1957, p. 283.

[84] *Johannes Althusius*, 2nd ed., p. 275, note 29. But see Villey, op. cit., p. 271 note 33.

[85] Maritain, *The Rights of Man and Natural Law*, New York, 1951, D'Entreves, op. cit., p. 45.

tradition are, and can only be, the product of natural law which comes first and is their source.[86]

An entirely different tradition and point of view was destined to develop slowly, and—after the Reformation controversies—to become manifest in full clarity in the seventeenth and eighteenth centuries. The new natural law, the natural law of the new learning, was based on radically different foundations from those which had sustained its predecessor. As in the Middle Ages, seventeenth- and eighteenth-century philosophers continued to speak in terms of the nature of man, and of his reason; but the old terms had been drained of much of their former content.

The new rationalistic universe, unlike the old, was anthropocentric and individualist. Each individual human being became an autonomous, discrete entity, willing and desiring his own satisfactions. The term *ius* or right began to be defined as an individual power (*potestas*) or faculty (*facultas*). Society was no longer regarded as natural to man; it became the artificial creation of wholly autonomous individuals who set it up, in various forms, for their own preservation and self-satisfaction. This they did either—as Hobbes would have it—by unreservedly attributing absolute law-making power to the state in order to preserve them from a life which would otherwise be 'nasty, poor, brutish and short', or—as Locke would have it—by conferring limited powers upon the state. Increasingly, however, all transcendental reference, all idea of a God-created order of things, came to be denied.'

No longer, as in the classical period, were natural rights the product of natural law; they had become its source—with consequences potentially disastrous to freedom. Weapons had been forged which were soon to be put to uses wholly alien to the thought of the Middle Ages. In the hands of Rousseau, and his fellow-systematizers, for example, the rights of man—stripped of all transcendental reference —both justify and necessitate the unqualified right of the people to do what they like, how they like; and the will of the people becomes the sole measure of right and wrong.

It is not possible within the limits of this book to trace the steps in the historical evolution from the classical conception of natural law to the natural law of the new learning in the seventeenth and eighteenth centuries.[87] But there are a few broad trends which it is relevant to mention here.

Villey has suggested that the beginnings of the individualistic approach to the subject of legal rights are to be found in the work of

[86] Murray, op. cit.
[87] This is a field, moreover, in which basic research remains to be done at several points.

philosopher-theologians like William of Occam, Duns Scotus and Gerson.[88] And he has put together sufficient evidence to make this a plausible proposition. For a time, however, there was sufficient dynamic in the old tradition to make the full implications of the new individualism barely perceptible. Locke, whose metaphysics were potentially dangerous to freedom, still believed sufficiently strongly in the idea of limited government, and gave it sufficiently cogent expression, to become the acceptable philosopher of the American Revolution and of the constitution-makers of the new world.[89]

Gradually, however, emphasis on the will rather than the reason of individuals became more marked; and by the time we reach Grotius and Suarez, one needs a firm grasp on the old faiths not to be swept away. But precisely because the new thinking was wholly individualist, wholly cut off from its roots in an order of nature; precisely because reason, as such, was being displaced by the will of individuals (under the name of reason), the new natural law could be used as an instrument to justify *any* system—from Locke's limited government to Hitler's tyranny of a master race.

Not, unnaturally, the natural law of the new learning could not stand up to critical scrutiny. Bentham and his followers—even without historical research—quite rightly contended that natural law had become individual fancy.[90] Finally, historical and legal scholarship, during the nineteenth century, destroyed the various 'social contract' theories which Hobbes, Locke and Rousseau—for example—had so laboriously constructed; and put in their place the idea that law was 'a product of the popular conscience', which supplies the data for the legislator to formulate. This, during the last century, was the view of writers like Savigny and Ihering; and more recently, it has been elaborated by Krabbe and Duguit. But the popular conscience, as Hitler's Germany proved, is an unstable foundation on which to build; and, in any event, in itself it provides no criterion for sorting out from the data the good and the bad. By the beginning of the twentieth century, it looked as if natural law was dead.

The modern revival

With growing realization that neither the rationalism of the eighteenth century, nor the historical scholarship of the nineteenth and early twentieth centuries, are adequate to satisfy human needs, men are today turning back to the real natural law—the natural law of the Christian tradition, whose truths were only temporarily

[88] Op. cit., pp. 272 sqq.
[89] For a good discussion, see Murray, *We Hold These Truths*, 1960, pp. 302 sqq.
[90] Pollock, *Essays in the Law*, p. 62.

obscured.[91] And I would suggest that if guaranteed human rights are to mean anything worth while—indeed if they are to survive— the real natural law must continue to be their inspiration. In Father John Murray's words:

> Today, as perverted social patterns are attempting to impose themselves on human life, to the destruction of human freedom, our problem in the West is ourselves to create a new social pattern, a pattern of freedom, that will be truly a pattern, but that will leave to freedom all its necessary energizing dynamism. Our problem is not simply to safeguard 'human rights', in the sense of fortifying each discrete individual in the possession of a heterogeneous collection of social empowerments; it is rather to erect, and secure against all assault, an *ordo juris*, an order of law that will be in consequence an order of rights and hence by definition an order of freedom. If this is so, as I think it is, the new 'age of order', of just law and true freedom must look to natural law as its basic inspiration.[92]

THE INFLUENCE OF NATURAL LAW IN MODERN HISTORY

History has given ample proof of the fact that whatever may be said and thought against the natural law, and whatever theories men may try to put in its place, it is in fact deeply rooted in human nature; for time and again men have asserted the idea of law as reason—as distinct from arbitrary will—and have used it to tame the power of tyrants.

The Huguenots

Most French political theorists during the sixteenth century, with the notable exception of Jean Bodin[93] and to a lesser extent Bossuet, 'elaborated liberal theories starting from natural law, and attempted to construct a secular state upon the idea of justice'.[94] On the other hand, among French civilian lawyers there was a strong body of opinion which supported political absolutism.[95]

The massacre of the Huguenots on St. Bartholomew's Night, 24 August 1572, gave dramatic relevance to this conflict—to the issue of the proper limits of governmental power; and gave rise to a series of declarations on the cause of freedom which still ring out whenever freedom is threatened. In 1572 François Hotman

[91] Rommen, *The Natural Law*, 1946.

[92] Op. cit., pp. 301–2. And see, generally, John Bowle's *Western Political Thought*, Jonathan Cape, 1947.

[93] See below, p. 231, note 41.

[94] Jean Brissaud, *A History of French Public Law*, Garner's translation, 1915, p. 536.

[95] One of the best short discussions is by Esmein, 'La Maxime "Princeps legibus solutus est" dans l'ancien droit public français', *Essays in Legal History*, 1913, pp. 201 sqq. See also Figgis, *From Gerson to Grotius*, 1907, p. 155.

proclaimed that the notion of an absolute monarch, free from the bonds of law, had no place in France.[96] Writing in 1573–4, the Calvinist, Theodore Beza, argued that the obedience due to princes was 'subject to the following condition, namely that they command nothing impious, nothing unjust'. And he defined unjust commands as those which prevented or prohibited the performance of 'that which every man is in charity bound to render to his neighbour'.[97] However, it is in du Plessis Mornay's *Vindiciae Contra Tyrannos*[98] that one finds the most cogent French Protestant refutation of unbounded political power.

Unlimited obedience, says du Plessis Mornay, is due to God alone; to the king, as his delegate, only a limited submission bound by God's law is due:

> Between the Almighty on the one hand and king and people on the other, there is an original contract, of which the covenant between Jehovah and the Israelites is the model; this contract is on God's side one of protection; on that of the nation, maintenance of the true religion. If the king violates this Covenant by persecuting the true religion, the people are absolved from allegiance to their *mesne* lord by their duties to God as the overlord. A prince who persecutes the faith is a rebel against God, and no more a lawful sovereign than a Pope deposed for heresy.[99]

No doubt the immediate occasion of the *Vindiciae* was the Huguenot revolt in defence of religious freedom; indeed the book was entirely a *livre de circonstance*. Nevertheless it has abiding value, for it breathes the spirit of constitutional liberty for all, and should find an echo wherever men honour true freedom. Law, for du Plessis Mornay, was something far higher than the positive edict of a transitory ruler. It was the embodiment of principles rather than of caprice. The king is a creature of law unchanged by time, unbiased by passion, unmoved by fear; law, which knows no partiality and expresses no personal idiosyncrasies but is the utterance of universal reason.[1]

The revolt of the Netherlands

The revolt of the Netherlands from the overlordship of Phillip II of Spain, during the latter half of the sixteenth century, is a classic illustration of the superiority of reason over force in human concerns.

[96] See, generally, A. H. Murray, The Franco-Gallia of François Hotman, in *Butterworth's South African Law Review*, 1956.

[97] *Concerning the rights of rulers*, Gonin's translation, H.A.U.M., Cape Town, 1956, p. 25.

[98] I follow Figgis and McIlwain in attributing the authorship of the *Vindiciae* to du Plessis Mornay.

[99] Dr. Figgis' summary in *From Gerson to Grotius*, 1907, p. 154.

[1] Figgis, op. cit., p. 156, commenting on du Plessis Mornay's conception of law.

Indeed the example of the Netherlands was to provide seventeenth-century Europe with 'a working model of free institutions—a centre of light'.[2]

In the Act of Abjuration of 1581, under which the states of the Netherlands deposed Phillip, it was boldly declared that if a prince, who is a shepherd, treats his subjects as though they were slaves, he is no longer to be regarded as their legitimate prince. A prince, it is said, must rule reasonably and with justice otherwise his subjects owe him no allegiance.[3]

When the principles underlying the Dutch revolt began to be crystallized into systematic treatises—notably by Johannes Althusius—emphasis was placed upon the pluralistic nature of a healthy society. Abjuring both the idea of State omnipotence, on the one hand, and an atomistic and artificial view of individual independence on the other, Althusius insisted that the State must not absorb the independent life of families, small associations and provinces.[4] He conceded the need for a central co-ordinating body, but its functions were to be limited. Once again St. Augustine's maxim, *remota justitia quid regna nisi latrocinia*, was invoked: 'If justice be lacking what are States but robber bands'; it was, in fact, Althusius' favourite tag.

There has been some dispute as to the extent to which the maxim *princeps legibus solutus est* was received in the Roman-Dutch law of Holland. But in an interesting article on the subject, Dr. Joubert has argued convincingly that the absolutist doctrine which that text may embody, had no place in the Netherlands.[5] Groenewegen (1613–52) is clear on the point;[6] and so too are the numerous other authorities to whom Dr. Joubert refers.

The crisis of English liberty

It has often been observed that the use to which natural law was put during the revolt of the Netherlands inspired Englishmen to put down the pretensions of the Stuarts during the seventeenth century.[7] While there is no doubt truth in this remark—Holland had become a refuge from Stuart wrath for English dissenters—it should not be forgotten that the English common law had its own powerful contribution to make.

[2] Figgis, *From Gerson to Grotius*, 1907, pp. 191, 198.
[3] Cau, *Groot Placaetboek*, vol. 2, p. 25; Z. W. Sneller, *Unie van Utrecht en Plakkaet van Verlatinge*, 1929. And see Figgis, op. cit., p. 199.
[4] Figgis, op. cit., p. 209.
[5] (1952) *Tydskrif vir Hedendaagse Romeins-Hollandse Reg* 47 sqq.
[6] *Ad Dig.* 1.3.31.
[7] See, for example, Figgis, *From Gerson to Grotius*, ch. VII; Corwin, *Liberty Against Government*, 1948, p. 44.

We have seen how during the thirteenth century the idea of natural law found great English expositors in men like Bracton and John of Salisbury. Yelverton, in the reign of Edward IV, said that, in the absence of authority, judges 'should resort to the law of nature which is the ground of all laws'.[8] In the fifteenth century, Sir John Fortesque, who had been Henry VI's Chief Justice, stated with pride that the laws of England knew nothing of that maxim of tyranny, 'admitted by the laws of France', *quod principi placuit legis habet vigorem.* On the contrary, he said, English law 'favours liberty, the gift of God to man in his creation'.[9]

Indeed, as Sir Frederick Pollock observes:

> It is not credible that a doctrine which pervaded all political speculation in Europe, and was assumed as a common ground of authority by the opposing champions of the Empire and the Papacy, should have been without influence among learned men in England.[10]

During the crisis of English liberty in the seventeenth century much of the inspiration of those who resisted Stuart absolutism, came precisely from the Greek, the Roman, and the medieval sources to which I have referred. Thomas Hobbes, who was anxious to defend the absolutism of kings, went so far as to suggest that the rebellious spirit of England—by which he meant the spirit of revolt against the tyranny of kings—was due mainly to the misguided zeal of Englishmen in 'reading the books of policy and histories of the ancient Greeks and Romans'.[11] And it was Hobbes who stated that it was just another error of Aristotle's politics that in a well-ordered commonwealth not men should govern but the law.[12]

However, Bracton's pronouncement that the king ought to be under God and the law was never really forgotten; and during the seventeenth century, in the hands of the Chief Justice, Sir Edward Coke, it was put to effective use. The story begins in Scotland. A case came before the Court of Session in 1599 in which Robert Bruce and Lord Hamilton were rival claimants to certain emoluments. James VI of Scotland disliked Bruce, and, appearing in person in the Court of Session, he demanded that the judges should dismiss

[8] Pollock, *Essays in the Law*, p. 56.

[9] *In Praise of the Laws of England.* See Corwin, op. cit., p. 29. A scholarly edition of the *De Laudibus Legum Angliae* has been published by S. B. Crimes, Cambridge, 1942.

[10] *The Expansion of the Common Law*, 1904, pp. 112–13; *Essays in the Law*, p. 57. See also Bryce, op. cit., p. 165; Holdsworth, *A History of English Law*, vol. II, pp. 133 sqq., 252, 256; vol. IV, 169.

[11] *Leviathan*, Oakeshott's edition (Blackwell), 2, 29.

[12] *Leviathan*, 4, 46.

Bruce's claim and grant Hamilton's. And this is how Lord Normand describes what happened:

> The President of the Court, Alexander Seton, thereupon stood up and said to the King that he was president and had first place to speak, and therefore, he said to the King, that he was their King and they his subjects, bound to obey him in all humility which they would do in all things for their lives, land and gear; but in the matter of law and conscience, being sworn to justice, they would do as their consciences led them, unless he commanded them to the contrary, in which case he said he would not vote at all nor no honest man there. The Lord of Newbattle, another judge, then also stood up and said to the King that it was said in the town, to his slander and theirs, that they durst not do justice but as the King commanded them; which he said should be seen to the contrary. He would vote against him in the right of his own presence. The Lords of the Session all but one voted for Mr. Robert Bruce 'whereat the King raged marvellously and is in great anger with the Lords of Session.' This account of the case we owe to the letter of an eye-witness, George Nicholson, addressed to Sir Robert Cecil, then a Minister of Queen Elizabeth in London. Nicholson added, 'the King swears he will have Mr. Robert Bruce's case reversed, which the President understanding, says he will pen in Latin, French and Greek to be sent to all the Judges in the world to be approved, and that by his vote it shall never be reversed, and so say the whole Session.' Surely never was the supremacy of the law over the state more fearlessly and resoundingly proclaimed.[13]

When James VI of Scotland became James I of England the scene was repeated. On a famous Sunday morning in November 1612, the King of England summoned the judges to appear before him, and declared, among other things, that he had the right to take away from the judges any cause he pleased, and decide it himself. The Archbishop of Canterbury, supporting the King, argued that the judges were merely royal delegates, and that therefore the King himself could decide causes which he usually left to his delegates. Sir Edward Coke answered on behalf of the judges that 'By the Law of England the King in person cannot judge any cause; all cases, civil and criminal are to be determined in a Court of Justice according to the law and the custom of the Realm.' The King then said he thought law was founded upon reason, adding 'I and others have reason as well as the Judges'.

To this, Coke replied:

> True it was that God had endowed His Majesty with excellent science as well as with great gifts of nature, but His Majesty was

[13] An address delivered in Edinburgh, 1951.

not learned in the laws of his Realm of England, and causes which concerned the life and inheritance of goods or fortunes of his subjects were not to be decided by natural reason, but by the artificial reason of the law, which law was an art which required long study and experience before that a man could attain to the cognizance of it.

The King was then much offended, saying that in such case he should be under the law, which it was treason to affirm. Coke answered, in the words of Bracton, that the King ought not to be under any man but that he should be under God and the Law.[14]

With the details of the struggle for constitutionalism in England in the seventeenth century, we need not here concern ourselves. They are part of the alphabet of history. But there are certain points which require emphasis; for the natural law tradition in England soon developed peculiarities of its own.

In the first place, as Professor Corwin has pointed out, by laying stress on the 'artificial' nature of the law's reason (acquired only by years of study), Sir Edward Coke in his dispute with King James was at the same time disclosing the fact that natural law in England was a matter for professional interpretation. Thus, to quote Corwin:

> The King is under the law, which only the judges know. English liberty as an effective restraint on authority has its source in a professional, a craft mystery.[15]

This emphasis upon the need for professional interpretation of the law, and the exclusive prerogative of the courts to supply that interpretation, had both strength and weakness. Its strength lay in the fact that whereas on the Continent natural law too often lacked institutional equipment to make good its claims, this deficiency was —for a time—supplied in England by a strong and influential Chief Justice, backed by Parliament. It was, however, the weakness of Coke's position which soon began to come to the fore in England. It was all very well to appeal to a judge-interpreted higher law against the pretentions of a king, especially when Parliament was disposed against the king, but could such an appeal prevail against the High Court of Parliament itself?

At first sight it would seem that an affirmative answer should be given to this question. Thus, for example, in the well-known case of Dr. Bonham, Coke asserted that it was 'a fundamental maxim' of the common law of England that no man can be a judge in his own cause. And quoting several authorities, he went on to say:

> It appears in our books that in many cases the common law will controul acts of Parliament and sometimes adjudge them to be

---

[14] See Campbell's *Lives of the Chief Justices*, 3rd ed., 1874, vol. 1, pp. 319–21.
[15] Op. cit., p. 31.

15

utterly void; for when an act of Parliament is against common
right or reason, or repugnant or impossible to be performed, the
common law will controul it and adjudge such act to be void.[16]

This is not the place to discuss at any length the question whether,
upon closer inspection, there are in fact specific cases on record in
which an English court has declared an Act of Parliament to be
void on the ground that it was against 'common right or reason'.
On this point it will suffice to make four observations. Firstly, there
has been much learned controversy as to what Coke meant in
Bonham's case by 'controuling' an Act of Parliament and adjudging
it to be void.[17] However, to the extent that Coke was asserting a
power on the part of the courts to ignore the clearly expressed will
of Parliament, the weight of scholarly opinion, including that of
Sir Frederick Pollock,[18] F. W. Maitland,[19] Sir William Holdsworth,[20]
Professor Plucknett,[21] and others, is adverse to Coke's claim;
and the better view is that the precedents which he cited do not
bear him out.

Secondly, whatever the position might have been in Coke's day,
after the Revolution Settlement in 1688, there can be no question
but that the duly declared will of the English Parliament was
absolutely binding on the courts.[22] It is true that as late as the
eighteenth century Blackstone wrote:

This law of Nature, being co-eval with mankind and dictated by
God himself, is of course superior in obligation to any other.
It is binding all over the globe, in all countries and at all times
no human laws are of any validity, if contrary to this; and such of
them as are valid derive all their force and all their authority,
mediately or intermediately from the original.[23]

But so far as the authority of the British Parliament was concerned,
this was at the time no more than a polite tribute to old and venerable
doctrines.

In the theory of English law Parliament was itself a court of Law;
it was the High Court of Parliament.[24] It was, therefore, never easy

---

[16] (1610) 8 Coke's Reports 114a.

[17] Among more recent surveys, see J. W. Gough, *Fundamental Law in English
Constitutional Theory*, Oxford, 1954, ch. III; S. E. Thorne, 'The Constitution
and the Courts', 54 *Law Quarterly Review* 543 sqq.; Haines, op. cit., pp. 33–5.

[18] *The Expansion of the Common Law*, pp. 121–2; *A First Book of Jurisprudence*,
6th ed., p. 267; *Essays in the Law*, p. 41.

[19] *The Constitutional History of England*, 1909, p. 301.

[20] *The History of English Law*, vol. 2, pp. 441–3; vol. 5, 428, 454, 491 sqq.

[21] *Statutes and their Interpretation in the first half of the 14th Century*, pp. 66–70;
'Dr. Bonham's Case and Judicial Review', 40 *Harvard Law Review* 35 sqq.

[22] For the meaning of 'duly declared', see below, p. 228, note 28; pp. 231–32.

[23] *Commentaries on the Laws of England*, 1, 41.

[24] See, generally, McIlwain, *The High Court of Parliament*, 1910.

for the judges to claim superior jurisdiction in the interpretation of law; and, as Holdsworth observes, after the Revolution Settlement, 'it was obviously difficult to assign any limits to the power of the Acts of a body which had effected changes so sweeping as those effected by the Revolution Parliament'.[25] Nor in fact did the judges attempt to place any obstacles in the way of parliamentary supremacy.[26] With Parliament's approval the judges in the seventeenth century had used the common law to curb the power of kings; but it was not to be used in England to curb the power of parliaments.

Indeed Holdsworth is probably correct when he says that as early as the sixteenth century, 'the supremacy of the law taught by Bracton had come to mean not the supremacy of an unchangeable law, but the supremacy of a law which Parliament can change'.[27] This is not to suggest that the doctrine of parliamentary sovereignty in England is a doctrine of lawlessness; but—as we shall see— there is in England very little law behind Parliament; only the law in accordance with which the constituent elements of Parliament must function in order to enact a law. In other words: as to what *is* Parliament, the law for the time being in force is supreme, but as to what may be done by Parliament, Parliament is supreme.[28] And this, as we have seen, is the position in South Africa today. The duly declared will of Parliament cannot be challenged in the courts on the score of unreasonableness.

But—in the third place—although Parliament emerged very largely *legibus solutus* in England, the old doctrines of natural law never wholly lost their vitality. In the everyday work of the English courts they have continued to play a subordinate but still very important role in such matters as the requirement of the standard of conduct of a reasonable man; the rule of statutory interpretation that, in the absence of clear words to the contrary, a statute should be interpreted so as to avoid injustice; and in numerous other rules which reveal the ethical content of English law.[29]

In the fourth place, however, when all this has been said, it remains true that the idea that the courts may adjudge an Act of Parliament to be void, did not flourish in England. The concept was destined to take root not in the original home of the English common law, but in its new home across the Atlantic.

---

[25] Holdsworth, op. cit., vol. IV, pp. 186–7.

[26] Holdsworth, op. cit., vol. IV, p. 189.

[27] Op. cit., vol. IV, pp. 186–7.

[28] Cf. (1935) *Law Quarterly Review* at 603. And see my article in (1953) 16 *Modern Law Review* at 290.

[29] See, especially, Roscoe Pound, *Law and Morals*, 1924; Sir Percy Winfield, 'Ethics in English Case Law' in *Select Legal Essays*, 1952 pp. 265 sqq.; Goodhart, *English Law and the Moral Law*, 1955.

The American tradition

It is one of the ironies of history that soon after the Stuart kings had been tamed by law, the English Parliament itself got out of hand. Parliament had supported the supremacy of law in the seventeenth century with great effect. In the eighteenth, it asserted its own omnipotence with an arrogance that cost Britain the American colonies. Indeed it was this arrogant assertion of legislative power which was largely responsible for the Americans' deep distrust of leaving absolute power to any legislature.[30]

The founders of the American Constitution were men of intellect and learning, very conscious of the difference between the ideas of law as reason and law as power. They were aware that in the writings of the English political philosophers were statements like Robert Filmer's proposition that a law binding kings was a contradiction in terms.[31] They were aware, too, of Harrington's answer: 'The art whereby a civil society is instituted and preserved upon the foundations of common right and interest, is to follow Aristotle, the Empire of Laws not of men.'[32] And they were even more familiar with Locke's propositions that:

> The legislative or supreme authority cannot assume in itself a power to rule by arbitrary decrees, but is bound to dispense justice. . . .
> These are the bounds which the trust that is put in them by the society and the law of God and nature have set to the legislative power of every commonwealth, in all forms of government; First: they are to govern by promulgated established laws, not to be varied in particular cases, but to have one rule for rich and poor, for the favourite at court and the countryman at plough. Secondly, these laws also ought to be designed for no other end ultimately but the good of the people. Thirdly, they must not raise taxes on the property of the people without the consent of the people.[33]

It remained for the Americans to find institutional machinery to give practical effect to the ideal of government and freedom under law. This they did by means of written constitutions, enacted by the people, and containing entrenched Bills of Human Rights enforceable by the courts. (As we saw in chapters 6 and 7.)

James Wilson, one of the principal authors of the federal constitution, and later a judge of the Supreme Court, disclosed the very core

[30] McIlwain, *The American Revolution*, New York, 1924, chapters 1 and 2.

[31] Quoted by Pollock, *Essays in the Law*, p. 83.

[32] *Oceana, The Political Writings of James Harrington*, Selections, ed. Blitzer, 1955, p. 41. The phrase 'government of laws' appears in so many words in the Constitution of Massachusetts, 1780.

[33] *Second Treatise of Civil Government*, Hafner Classics, 1947, pp. 188–94.

of the American philosophy of government when he said: 'Without law liberty loses its nature and name and becomes licentiousness. Without liberty law loses its nature and name and becomes oppression.'[34] By finding institutional means for realizing this ideal in practice, the Americans made their distinctive contribution to political science. Having sought inspiration for the taming of power in the best thought of the West—from Aristotle to Locke—they made of this thought a living force.

SOVEREIGNTY AND THE LAW

In an earlier chapter, when discussing the adoption of constitutions, the subject of the 'sovereign will of the people' was touched on; and the question was raised as to the scope of the people's authority.[35] It was pointed out, too, that the adoption in South Africa of a constitution along American lines, would involve the termination of the existing sovereignty of the Union Parliament.[36] And, in addition, mention should be made of a third aspect of sovereignty — state sovereignty.[37] Sovereignty, then, is a word which is used to designate several different ideas, each of which has a substantial history of its own. Though full discussion of this vast subject cannot here be undertaken, it is relevant to say a little more about the three aspects which have been mentioned.

State sovereignty

At the outset there is the topic of State sovereignty. In the well-known case of *Rex* v. *Christian*,[38] Sir James Rose-Innes pointed out that 'sovereignty is exercised in two directions; internally it relates to the power of making and enforcing laws, externally to freedom from outside control'. When we say that a *state* is sovereign, it is to the external aspect of sovereignty that we refer. In other words, the proposition that a state is sovereign means that no external authority, no other state, may lawfully control its affairs.[39]

And, in this connection, two points need to be emphasized. In the first place the fact that a particular state does not possess a sovereign legislature does not prevent the state itself from being sovereign. The text-book example is, of course, the United States of America —a sovereign state in which the search for a single organ of government possessing sovereign legislative power is generally regarded

[34] *Works*, ed. Andrews, 1896, vol. 1, quoted by Bodenheimer, *Jurisprudence*, pp. 147–8.
[35] Above, pp. 191–3.
[36] Above, pp. 146, 185.
[37] See, generally, Oppenheim, *International Law*, 7th ed. pp. 254 sqq.
[38] 1924 A.D. 106.
[39] The point is made crisply by Professor J. D. B. Mitchell in the *Juridical Review*, 1951, pp. 70–1.

by lawyers as being both pointless and futile.[40] If, for example, the Union of South Africa were to adopt American constitutional ideas and abolish the existing sovereignty of the Union Parliament, this would not in itself affect the sovereign status of the country.

But secondly, it should not be thought that state sovereignty, or complete independence, is in the modern world a really practical proposition; for increasingly, as Mr. Harold Macmillan observed in the speech quoted in chapter 1, states are realizing that they cannot live unto themselves alone.

The sovereignty of Parliament

Two aspects of Parliamentary sovereignty call for discussion here. In the first place, it is customary to emphasize the unlimited authority of the Parliament of the United Kingdom to enact any law. But—and this is not sufficiently recognized—even Parliament must observe the rules which make it Parliament.

In all cases where law-making authority is vested not in one person but in a number of persons, it is plain that those persons must combine for action in accordance with certain rules prescribing the manner in which their will is to be ascertained. This proposition has often been stated, but it needs emphasis.

Commenting on Bodin's advocacy of the principle that a sovereign lawgiver should be *legibus solutus*,[41] Sir Frederick Pollock observed that every composite sovereign must at least observe *some* rules in order that there may be any expression of its composite will. There may, for example, be a rule prescribing the majority principle or the principle of unanimity—but there must be *some* rule for ascertaining what is an authentic expression of the will of the composite sovereign. And Sir Frederick went on to indicate that in making new rules on the subject of its own definition, the composite sovereign 'must proceed according to the existing ones'.[42]

These principles apply also to a sovereign Parliament like the Parliament of the United Kingdom; for it should not be forgotten that the proposition that 'the Parliament of the United Kingdom is Sovereign' and can make and unmake any law—is itself a proposition of law.[43]

[40] See, generally, Orfield, *Amending the Federal Constitution*, 1942, chapter V.
[41] *Six Livres de la Republique* (Paris, 1576–7), Book I, ch. VIII, pp. 96, 104. According to the better view, Bodin did not equate sovereignty with lawlessness. See McIlwain, *Constitutionalism and the Changing World*, pp. 26 et seq., pp. 47 et seq., Shepard, 45 *Political Science Quarterly* 585 et seq., and Pollock, *History of the Science of Politics*, p. 54.
[42] *History of the Science of Politics*, p. 52, note 1.
[43] Jennings, *The Law of the Constitution*, 3rd ed., p. 114; Amos, *The English Constitution*, p. 24.

No doubt the law on the subject of how the Parliament of the United Kingdom is to be defined is not easy to state with any confidence; nor is it easy to state with any confidence the extent to which the courts in England would hold themselves free to go into the question whether the constituent elements of Parliament had duly functioned. But it is obvious that there must be some rules for ascertaining what is an authentic expression of the sovereign Parliament's will.[44]

It is, however, the second aspect of parliamentary sovereignty which is more relevant to this book. It is clear that when the courts are faced with an authentic expression of Parliament's duly declared will in countries where no limits are placed upon the power of Parliament, the courts must enforce that will; nor may they question its reasonableness or justice.[45] Now, this may be all very well in countries where conventional restraints are so strong and traditional that they have virtually the force of law.[46] But it is foolish to imagine that the system can be successfully exported to countries where the necessary traditions are lacking. And it is for this reason, among others, that I have advocated the introduction in Southern Africa of a court-enforced Bill of Rights entrenched in a rigid constitution.

Sovereignty of the people

We have seen that modern democratic theory regards the people as having authority to establish their own system of government — an idea which goes back to the Roman law. This raises two questions.

In the first place, where the people have established a constitution, and have laid down a specific procedure for its amendment, is that procedure binding on the people themselves? The answer to this question is clearly in the affirmative. Thus, in an American case on the subject it was said:

> No heresy has ever been taught in this country so fraught with evil as the doctrine that the people have a constitutional right to disregard the constitution, and that they can set themselves above the instrumentalities appointed by the constitution for the administration of law. It tends directly to the encouragement of revolution and anarchy.[47]

[44] See, generally, my article in 16 *Modern Law Review* 297 sqq.; and cf. Dr. H. W. R. Wade's valuable contribution on 'The Basis of Legal Sovereignty', in (1955) *Cambridge Law Review* 172 sqq.

[45] *Harris* v. *The Minister of the Interior* 1952 (2) S.A. 428 (A.D.) at 456.

[46] Goodhart, *English Law and the Moral Law*, p. 57.

[47] *Koehler* v. *Hill* (1883) 60 Iowa 543 at 616, quoted by L. B. Orfield, *Amending the Federal Constitution*, 1942, p. 38.

And there is abundant authority to the same effect.[48] As Kelsen would put it, the law in force for the time being must be observed.

But, as pointed out earlier, the proposition that the law in force for the time being must be observed, may result merely in the perpetuation of injustice. And this raises the second and basic question. Is the validity of a constitution to be measured solely by the fact that the people have ordained it. This, according to Mr. Justice Learned Hand, is in fact the case. Thus, he says:

> I shall, however, ask you *arguendo* to assume with me that the Constitution and the 'Bill of Rights' neither proceed from, nor have any warrant in, the Divine Will, either as St. Thomas or Jefferson believed; but on the contrary that they are the altogether human expression of the will of the state conventions that ratified them; that their authority depends upon the sanctions available to enforce them; and their meaning is to be gathered from the words they contain, read in the historical setting in which they were uttered.[49]

If this view is sound, if the validity of a constitution depends solely on the fact that the people have ordained it, quite apart from its content, then on what basis, I would ask, would one distinguish between the American and the Russian constitutions? If they are both to be considered as equally valid, legally speaking, and equally moral, there is no point in proclaiming the virtues of 'a free society'. If, however, it is claimed that both constitutions are equally valid in their respective legal systems, because they rest on the will of the people, but that only the American one is 'moral', then where do the criteria of 'morality' come from? And why should not the people's will determine these criteria as well?

I know of only one satisfactory answer to these questions. The people's will can never make wrong right. There are rules of law binding even on the people themselves; and these rules are contained in the natural law. This was universally recognized in the Christian Middle Ages,[50] and there is no escape from it today.

If what I have said is felt to infringe the 'sovereignty' of the people, if the people's will is to be entirely unrestrained by law, then I would, in humility, say with Jacques Maritain: 'The two concepts of Sovereignty and Absolutism have been forged together on the same anvil. They must be scrapped together.'[51]

---

[48] Orfield, *Amending the Federal Constitution*, 1942, pp. 38–9; Jameson, *Constitutional Conventions*, 1887, 4th ed., p. 599; Rottschaeffer, *Constitutional Law*, 1939, p. 8; Wheare, *Modern Constitutions*, 1951, pp. 89–90.

[49] *The Bill of Rights*, Harvard, 1958, pp. 2–3.

[50] Gierke, *Political Theories of the Middle Ages*, Maitland's translation, pp. 37 sqq.

[51] *Man and the State*, p. 53.

CONCLUSION

I have maintained in this book that, in the ultimate analysis, no constitution can be stronger than the character of the people who work it and for whom it is made. And it has been shown that the natural law itself derives from the nature of man as a being endowed with reason to discover the good and the just, and a free will and responsibility to seek after them.

This throws responsibility back on to each individual. The price of liberty, it has been said, is eternal vigilance; this is true; but it is only part of the truth, part of the price. The price of freedom is to serve God under the law.

A SHORT BIBLIOGRAPHY ON NATURAL LAW

This bibliography is confined to a few of the more important books and essays, written in English in modern times, which were used in writing chapter 10. It has been put together in the hope that it may help to encourage general interest in the subject and, for this reason, in selecting titles I have kept in mind the needs of the non-professional reader; books marked with an asterisk may be particularly helpful to them.

1. WORKS OF A GENERAL INTRODUCTORY CHARACTER

Barker, E., Introduction to Gierke, *Natural Law and the Theory of Society*, Cambridge, 1950, pp. xxiv–1

*D'Entreves, A. P., *Natural Law*, Hutchinson, 1951.

Haines, C. G., *The Revival of Natural Law Concepts*, Harvard University Press, 1930.

Jones, J. Walter, *Historical Introduction to the Theory of Law*, Oxford, 1940, pp. 98–138.

*Murray, John Courtney, *We Hold These Truths*, Sheed and Ward, New York, 1960. An exciting discussion of the contemporary relevance of natural law.

*Rommen, H. A., *The Natural Law*, translated by T. R. Hanley, Herder Book Company, 1949.

2. HISTORICAL BACKGROUND AND DEVELOPMENT

Barker, E., *Natural Law and the Theory of Society*, a translation of part of Gierke's work, Cambridge, 1950.

Becker, Carl, *The Heavenly City of the 18th Century Philosophers*, New Haven, 1932.

Bodenheimer, E., *Jurisprudence*, McGraw-Hill, New York, 1940.

Bowle, John, *Western Political Thought*, Jonathan Cape, 1947.

Brown, B. F., *The Natural Law Reader*, Oceana Publications, 1960.

Bryce, Lord, The Law of Nature in *Studies in History and Jurisprudence*, 1901, vol. 2, pp. 112–71.

Carlyle, R. W. & A. J., *A History of Medieval Political Theory in the West*, 6 vols. 1903–36, William Blackwood & Sons. An invaluable source book.

Corwin, Edward S., *Liberty Against Government*, Baton Rouge, 1948. Several of Professor Corwin's scholarly and stimulating articles were published in the Association of American Law Schools' *Selected Essays on Constitutional Law*, Foundation Press, 1938.

D'Entreves, A. P., *Medieval Contributions to Political Thought*, The Humanities Press, New York, 1959.

Figgis, J. N., *From Gerson to Grotius*, Cambridge, 1907; *The Political Aspects of St. Augustine's 'City of God'*, Longmans, 1921; *The Divine Right of Kings*, Cambridge, 2nd ed., 1934.

Freyd, B., *The Development of Political Theory*, a translation of Gierke's *Johannes Althusius*, Allen & Unwin, 1939.

Friedrich, Carl, *The Philosophy of Law in Historical Perspective*, Chicago, 1958.

Gierke, Otto von, *Das deutsche Genossenschaftsrecht*, 1868–1881; *Johannes Althusius*, 3rd ed., 1913. Gierke's work is basic. As Figgis once said, next to Gierke most writing on the subject is prattle. English translations include those by Maitland, Barker, and Freyd. See, therefore, under translators' names.

Gilby, Thomas, *Between Community and Society*, 1953; *Principality and Polity*, London, 1958.

Gilmore, M. P., *Argument from Roman Law in Political Thought, 1200–1600,* Harvard University Press, 1941.

Gilson, Etienne, *The Christian Philosophy of St. Thomas Aquinas,* Shook's translation, New York, 1956; *History of Christian Philosophy in the Middle Ages,* New York, 1955.

Greenidge, A. H. J., *A Handbook of Greek Constitutional History,* Macmillan, 1902.

*Hayek, F. A., *The Constitution of Liberty,* London, 1960; *The Political Ideal of the Rule of Law,* Cairo, 1955.

Hearnshaw, F. J. C., *Social and Political Ideas of the Middle Ages,* A series of lectures edited by Hearnshaw, London, 1923.

Hignett, C., *A History of the Athenian Constitution,* Oxford, 1952.

Jolowicz, H. F., *Historical Introduction to the Study of Roman Law,* 2nd ed., Cambridge, 1952.

*Jones, J. Walter, *The Law and Legal Theory of the Greeks,* Oxford, 1956. A most useful book.

Kern, Fritz, *Kingship and Law in the Middle Ages,* translated by S. B. Chrimes, Basil Blackwell, 1948.

Maitland, F. W., *Political Theories of the Middle Ages,* Cambridge, 1900. A translation of Gierke with a famous introduction.

*McIlwain, C. H., *The Growth of Political Thought in the West,* Macmillan, 1932; *Constitutionalism and the Changing World,* Cambridge, 1939; *Constitutionalism: Ancient and Modern,* Cornell, 1947.

*Pollock, Sir Frederick, The History of the Law of Nature in *Essays in the Law,* Macmillan, 1922, pp. 31–79; *An Introduction to the History of the Science of Politics,* Macmillan, 1923.

Pound, Roscoe, *Law and Morals,* London, 1926; *Interpretations of Legal History,* Cambridge, 1923.

Ritchie, D. G., *Natural Rights,* Swan Sonnenschein & Company, London, 1903.

*Southern, R. W., *The Making of the Middle Ages,* Hutchinson, 1953.

Strauss, Leo, *Natural Right and History,* Chicago, 1953.

Ullmann, Walter, *The Medieval Idea of Law,* Methuen, 1946.

Wild, J., *Plato's Modern Enemies and the Theory of Natural Law,* Chicago, 1953.

Windolph, F. Lyman, *Leviathan and Natural Law,* Princeton, 1951.

3. WORKS ON THE NATURE AND CONTENT OF NATURAL LAW

Bourke, Vernon J., *Ethics,* Macmillan, New York, 1951. An introduction to St. Thomas.

Cronin, M., *The Science of Ethics,* Gill & Sons, Dublin, 1909, 2 vols. A standard introduction to St. Thomas.

Davitt, T. E., *The Nature of Law,* Herder Book Company, 1953.

Del Vecchio, G., *The Formal Bases of Law,* Husik's translation, Boston, 1914; *Justice,* ed. A. H. Campbell, Edinburgh. 1952; *General Principles of Law,* Forte's translation, Boston, 1956.

*Goodhart, Arthur, *English Law and the Moral Law,* London, 1955; *Interpretations of Modern Legal Philosophy,* in Essays in Honour of Roscoe Pound, ed. P. Sayre, New York, 1947.

Kelsen, Hans, *General Theory of Law and State,* Harvard, 1949; *What is Justice,* Berkeley, 1957.

*Maritain, Jacques, *Man and the State*, Chicago, 1951; *The Rights of Man and the Natural Law*, New York, 1951; *The Social and Political Philosophy of Jacques Maritain*, selected readings, eds. Evans and Ward, London, 1946.

*Murray, John Courtney, The Natural Law in *Great Expressions of Human Rights*, ed. R. M. MacIver, Harper, New York, 1950.

The Natural Law Forum: This journal, published by the Notre Dame Law School, is full of interest.

O'Sullivan, Richard, *Christian Philosophy in the Common Law*, Blackfriars, 1947; and (O'Sullivan ed.) *Papers Read to the Thomas More Society*, 1st series, 1948; 2nd series, 1949.

*Pieper, Josef, *Justice*, translated by L. E. Lynch, Pantheon Books, New York, 1955.

Raphael, D. Daiches, *Moral Judgment*, Allen & Unwin, 1955.

Rommen, H. A., *The Natural Law*, translated by T. R. Hanley, Herder Book Company, 1949.

Symposium on Human Rights, edited by UNESCO, New York, 1949.

St. Thomas Aquinas, *Summa Theologica* and *De Regimine Principum*. The sections in the *Summa Theologica* on Law, *Prima Secundae*, Quaestiones 90 to 108, and on Justice, *Secunda Secundae*, Quaestiones 57 to 80, are basic. The Dominican Fathers in England have published an English translation (Burns Oates) vols. 8 and 10; but while useful, it is not entirely satisfactory. A short but good selection of texts, very well translated by Thomas Gilby, was published by Oxford University Press in 1951: *St. Thomas Aquinas, Philosophical Texts*. More extensive texts, edited and annotated by Anton Pegis, were published by Random House, *The Basic Writings of St. Thomas Aquinas*, New York, 1944, 2 vols. See especially vol. 2, pp. 742–978. The *De Regimine Principum* (On Kingship) translated by Gerald Phelan and revised, with notes, by I. T. Eschmann, was published by the Pontifical Institute of Medieval Studies, Toronto, 1949.

Winfield, P. H., Ethics in English Case Law, in *Select Legal Essays*, 1952 pp. 266–87.

N.B.—I have not included references to the plethora of books on the semantic approach to ethical and legal problems. Though not very sustaining, they do help—often considerably—to define issues, which after all is a necessary step in advancing knowledge. R. M. Hare's *The Language of Morals*, Oxford, 1952, is a useful introduction to this literature.

THE UNIVERSAL DECLARATION OF HUMAN RIGHTS

Adopted by the General Assembly of the
United Nations on 10 *December* 1948

PREAMBLE

WHEREAS recognition of the inherent dignity and of the equal and inalienable rights of all members of the human family is the foundation of freedom, justice and peace in the world,

WHEREAS disregard and contempt for human rights have resulted in barbarous acts which have outraged the conscience of mankind, and the advent of a world in which human beings shall enjoy freedom of speech and belief and freedom for fear and want has been proclaimed as the highest aspiration of the common people,

WHEREAS it is essential, if man is not to be compelled to have recourse, as a last resort, to rebellion against tyranny and oppression, that human rights should be protected by the rule of law,

WHEREAS it is essential to promote the development of friendly relations between nations,

WHEREAS the peoples of the United Nations have in the Charter reaffirmed their faith in fundamental human rights, in the dignity and worth of the human person and in the equal rights of men and women and have determined to promote social progress and better standards of life in larger freedom,

WHEREAS Member States have pledged themselves to achieve, in co-operation with the United Nations, the promotion of universal respect for and observance of human rights and fundamental freedoms,

WHEREAS a common understanding of these rights and freedoms is of the greatest importance for the full realization of this pledge, Now, therefore,

THE GENERAL ASSEMBLY PROCLAIMS

THIS UNIVERSAL DECLARATION OF HUMAN RIGHTS as a common standard of achievement for all peoples and all nations, to the end that every individual and every organ of society, keeping this Declaration constantly in mind, shall strive by teaching and education to promote respect for these rights and freedoms and by progressive measures, national and international, to secure their universal and effective recognition and observance, both among the peoples of Member States themselves and among the peoples of territories under their jurisdiction.

ARTICLE 1

All human beings are born free and equal in dignity and rights. They are endowed with reason and conscience and should act towards one another in a spirit of brotherhood.

ARTICLE 2

Everyone is entitled to all the rights and freedoms set forth in this Declaration, without distinction of any kind, such as race, colour, sex, language, religion, political or other opinion, national or social origin, property, birth or other status.

Furthermore, no distinction shall be made on the basis of the political, jurisdictional or international status of the country or territory to which a person belongs, whether it be independent, trust, non-self-governing or under any other limitation of sovereignty.

ARTICLE 3

Everyone has the right to life, liberty and security of person.

ARTICLE 4

No one shall be held in slavery or servitude; slavery and the slave trade shall be prohibited in all their forms.

ARTICLE 5

No one shall be subjected to torture or to cruel, inhuman or degrading treatment or punishment.

ARTICLE 6

Everyone has the right to recognition everywhere as a person before the law.

ARTICLE 7

All are equal before the law and are entitled without any discrimination to equal protection of the law. All are entitled to equal protection against any discrimination in violation of this Declaration and against any incitement to such discrimination.

ARTICLE 8

Everyone has the right to an effective remedy by the competent national tribunals for acts violating the fundamental rights granted him by the constitution or by law.

ARTICLE 9

No one shall be subjected to arbitrary arrest, detention or exile.

ARTICLE 10

Everyone is entitled in full equality to a fair and public hearing by an independent and impartial tribunal, in the determination of his rights and obligations and of any criminal charge against him.

ARTICLE 11

(1) Everyone charged with a penal offence has the right to be presumed innocent until proved guilty according to law in a public trial at which he has had all the guarantees necessary for his defence.

(2) No one shall be held guilty of any penal offence on account of any act or omission which did not constitute a penal offence, under national or international law, at the time when it was committed. Nor shall a heavier penalty be imposed than the one that was applicable at the time the penal offence was committed.

ARTICLE 12

No one shall be subjected to arbitrary interference with his privacy, family, home or correspondence, nor to attacks upon his honour and reputation. Everyone has the right to the protection of the law against such interference or attacks.

ARTICLE 13

(1) Everyone has the right to freedom of movement and residence within the borders of each state.

(2) Everyone has the right to leave any country, including his own, and to return to his country.

ARTICLE 14

(1) Everyone has the right to seek and to enjoy in other countries asylum from persecution.

(2) This right may not be invoked in the case of prosecutions genuinely arising from non-political crimes or from acts contrary to the purposes and principles of the United Nations.

ARTICLE 15

(1) Everyone has the right to a nationality.

(2) No one shall be arbitrarily deprived of his nationality nor denied the right to change his nationality.

ARTICLE 16

(1) Men and women of full age, without any limitation due to race, nationality or religion, have the right to marry and to found a family. They are entitled to equal rights as to marriage, during marriage and at its dissolution.

(2) Marriage shall be entered into only with the free and full consent of the intending spouses.

(3) The family is the natural and fundamental group unit of society and is entitled to protection by society and the State.

ARTICLE 17

(1) Everyone has the right to own property alone as well as in association with others.

(2) No one shall be arbitrarily deprived of his property.

ARTICLE 18

Everyone has the right to freedom of thought, conscience and religion; this right includes freedom to change his religion or belief, and freedom, either alone or in community with others and in public or private, to manifest his religion or belief in teaching, practice, worship and observance.

ARTICLE 19

Everyone has the right to freedom of opinion and expression; this right includes freedom to hold opinions without interference and to seek, receive and impart information and ideas through any media and regardless of frontiers.

ARTICLE 20

(1) Everyone has the right to freedom of peaceful assembly and association.

(2) No one may be compelled to belong to an association.

ARTICLE 21

(1) Everyone has the right to take part in the government of his country, directly or through freely chosen representatives.

(2) Everyone has the right of equal access to public service in his country.

(3) The will of the people shall be the basis of the authority of government; this will shall be expressed in periodic and genuine elections which shall be by universal and equal suffrage and shall be held by secret vote or by equivalent free voting procedures.

ARTICLE 22

Everyone, as a member of society, has the right to social security and is entitled to realization, through national effort and international co-operation and in accordance with the organization and resources of each State, of the economic, social and cultural rights indispensable for his dignity and the free development of his personality.

ARTICLE 23

(1) Everyone has the right to work, to free choice of employment, to just and favourable conditions of work and to protection against unemployment.

(2) Everyone, without any discrimination, has the right to equal pay for equal work.

(3) Everyone who works has the right to just and favourable remuneration ensuring for himself and his family an existence worthy of human dignity, and supplemented, if necessary, by other means of social protection.

(4) Everyone has the right to form and to join trade unions for the protection of his interests.

ARTICLE 24

Everyone has the right to rest and leisure, including reasonable limitation of working hours and periodic holidays with pay.

ARTICLE 25

(1) Everyone has the right to a standard of living adequate for the health and well-being of himself and of his family, including food, clothing, housing and medical care and necessary social services, and the right to security in the event of unemployment,

sickness, disability, widowhood, old age or other lack of livelihood in circumstances beyond his control.

(2) Motherhood and childhood are entitled to special care and assistance. All children, whether born in or out of wedlock, shall enjoy the same social protection.

ARTICLE 26

(1) Everyone has the right to education. Education shall be free, at least in the elementary and fundamental stages. Elementary education shall be compulsory. Technical and professional education shall be made generally available and higher education shall be equally accessible to all on the basis of merit.

(2) Education shall be directed to the full development of the human personality and to the strengthening of respect for human rights and fundamental freedoms. It shall promote understanding, tolerance and friendship among all nations, racial or religious groups, and shall further the activities of the United Nations for the maintenance of peace.

(3) Parents have a prior right to choose the kind of education that shall be given to their children.

ARTICLE 27

(1) Everyone has the right freely to participate in the cultural life of the community, to enjoy the arts and to share in scientific advancement and its benefits.

(2) Everyone has the right to the protection of the moral and material interests resulting from any scientific, literary or artistic production of which he is the author.

ARTICLE 28

Everyone is entitled to a social and international order in which the rights and freedoms set forth in this Declaration can be fully realized.

ARTICLE 29

(1) Everyone has duties to the community in which alone the free and full development of his personality is possible.

(2) In the exercise of his rights and freedoms, everyone shall be subject only to such limitations as are determined by law solely for the purposes of securing due recognition and respect for the rights and freedoms of others and of meeting the just requirements of morality, public order and the general welfare in a democratic society.

(3) These rights and freedoms may in no case be exercised contrary to the purposes and principles of the United Nations.

ARTICLE 30

Nothing in this Declaration may be interpreted as implying for any State, group or person any right to engage in any activity or to perform any act aimed at the destruction of any of the rights and freedoms set forth herein.

CONVENTION FOR THE PROTECTION OF HUMAN RIGHTS AND FUNDAMENTAL FREEDOMS

Rome, 4 *November* 1950

PREAMBLE

The Governments signatory hereto, being Members of the Council of Europe,

Considering the Universal Declaration of Human Rights proclaimed by the General Assembly of the United Nations on 10th December, 1948;

Considering that this Declaration aims at securing the universal and effective recognition and observance of the Rights therein declared;

Considering that the aim of the Council of Europe is the achievement of greater unity between its Members and that one of the methods by which that aim is to be pursued is the maintenance and further realization of Human Rights and Fundamental Freedoms;

Reaffirming their profound belief in those Fundamental Freedoms which are the foundation of justice and peace in the world and are best maintained on the one hand by an effective political democracy and on the other by a common understanding and observance of the Human Rights upon which they depend;

Being resolved, as the Governments of European countries which are like-minded and have a common heritage of political traditions, ideals, freedom and the rule of law, to take the first steps for the collective enforcement of certain of the Rights stated in the Universal Declaration:

Have agreed as follows: —

ARTICLE 1

The High Contracting Parties shall secure to everyone within their jurisdiction the rights and freedoms defined in Section I of this Convention.

SECTION I

ARTICLE 2

(1) Everyone's right to life shall be protected by law. No one shall be deprived of his life intentionally save in the execution of a sentence of a court following his conviction of a crime for which this penalty is provided by law.

(2) Deprivation of life shall not be regarded as inflicted in contravention of this Article when it results from the use of force which is no more than absolutely necessary —

243

(*a*) in defence of any person from unlawful violence;
(*b*) in order to effect a lawful arrest or to prevent the escape of a person lawfully detained;
(*c*) in action lawfully taken for the purpose of quelling a riot or insurrection.

ARTICLE 3

No one shall be subjected to torture or to inhuman or degrading treatment or punishment.

ARTICLE 4

(1) No one shall be held in slavery or servitude.
(2) No one shall be required to perform forced or compulsory labour.
(3) For the purpose of this Article the term 'forced or compulsory labour' shall not include—

(*a*) any work required to be done in the ordinary course of detention imposed according to the provisions of Article 5 of this Convention or during conditional release from such detention;
(*b*) any service of a military character or, in case of conscientious objectors in countries where they are recognized, service exacted instead of compulsory military service;
(*c*) any service exacted in case of an emergency or calamity threatening the life or well-being of the community;
(*d*) any work or service which forms part of normal civic obligations.

ARTICLE 5

(1) Everyone has the right to liberty and security of person.
No one shall be deprived of his liberty save in the following cases and in accordance with a procedure prescribed by law:—

(*a*) the lawful detention of a person after conviction by a competent court;
(*b*) the lawful arrest or detention of a person for non-compliance with the lawful order of a court or in order to secure the fulfilment of any obligation prescribed by law;
(*c*) the lawful arrest or detention of a person effected for the purpose of bringing him before the competent legal authority on reasonable suspicion of having committed an offence or when it is reasonably considered necessary to prevent his committing an offence or fleeing after having done so;
(*d*) the detention of a minor by lawful order for the purpose of educational supervision or his lawful detention for the purpose of bringing him before the competent legal authority;
(*e*) the lawful detention of persons for the prevention of the spreading of infectious diseases, of persons of unsound mind, alcoholics or drug addicts or vagrants;
(*f*) the lawful arrest or detention of a person to prevent his effecting an unauthorized entry into the country or of a

person against whom action is being taken with a view to deportation or extradition.

(2) Everyone who is arrested shall be informed promptly, in a language which he understands, of the reasons for his arrest and of any charge against him.

(3) Everyone arrested or detained in accordance with the provisions of paragraph 1(c) of this Article shall be brought promptly before a judge or other officer authorized by law to exercise judicial power and shall be entitled to trial within a reasonable time or to release pending trial. Release may be conditioned by guarantees to appear for trial.

(4) Everyone who is deprived of his liberty by arrest or detention shall be entitled to take proceedings by which the lawfulness of his detention shall be decided speedily by a court and his release ordered if the detention is not lawful.

(5) Everyone who has been the victim of arrest or detention in contravention of the provisions of this Article shall have an enforceable right to compensation.

ARTICLE 6

(1) In the determination of his civil rights and obligations or of any criminal charge against him, everyone is entitled to a fair and public hearing within a reasonable time by an independent and impartial tribunal established by law. Judgment shall be pronounced publicly but the press and public may be excluded from all or part of the trial in the interests of morals, public order or national security in a democratic society, where the interests of juveniles or the protection of the private life of the parties so require, or to the extent strictly necessary in the opinion of the court in special circumstances where publicity would prejudice the interests of justice.

(2) Everyone charged with a criminal offence shall be presumed innocent until proved guilty according to law.

(3) Everyone charged with a criminal offence has the following minimum rights:—

- (a) to be informed promptly, in a language which he understands and in detail, of the nature and cause of the accusation against him;
- (b) to have adequate time and facilities for the preparation of his defence;
- (c) to defend himself in person or through legal assistance of his own choosing or, if he has not sufficient means to pay for legal assistance, to be given it free when the interests of justice so require;
- (d) to examine or have examined witnesses against him and to obtain the attendance and examination of witnesses on his behalf under the same conditions as witnesses against him;
- (e) to have the free assistance of an interpreter if he cannot understand or speak the language used in court.

ARTICLE 7

(1) No one shall be held guilty of any criminal offence on account of any act or omission which did not constitute a criminal offence under national or international law at the time when it was committed. Nor shall a heavier penalty be imposed than the one that was applicable at the time the criminal offence was committed.

(2) This Article shall not prejudice the trial and punishment of any person for any act or omission which, at the time when it was committed, was criminal according to the general principles of law recognized by civilized nations.

ARTICLE 8

(1) Everyone has the right to respect for his private and family life, his home and his correspondence.

(2) There shall be no interference by a public authority with the exercise of this right except such as is in accordance with the law and is necessary in a democratic society in the interests of national security, public safety or the economic well-being of the country, for the prevention of disorder or crime, for the protection of healthier morals, or for the protection of the rights and freedoms of others.

ARTICLE 9

(1) Everyone has the right to freedom of thought, conscience and religion; this right includes freedom to change his religion or belief and freedom, either alone or in community with others and in public or private to manifest his religion or belief, in worship teaching, practice and observance.

(2) Freedom to manifest one's religion or beliefs shall be subject only to such limitations as are prescribed by law and are necessary in a democratic society in the interests of public safety, for the protection of public order, health or morals, or for the protection of the rights and freedoms of others.

ARTICLE 10

(1) Everyone has the right to freedom of expression. This right shall include freedom to hold opinions and to receive and impart information and ideas without interference by public authority and regardless of frontiers. This Article shall not prevent States from requiring the licensing of broadcasting, television or cinema enterprises.

(2) The exercise of these freedoms, since it carries with it duties and responsibilities, may be subject to such formalities, conditions, restrictions or penalties as are prescribed by law and are necessary in a democratic society, in the interests of national security, territorial integrity or public safety, for the prevention of disorder or crime, for the protection of health or morals, for the protection of the reputation or rights of others, for preventing the disclosure of

information received in confidence, or for maintaining the authority
and impartiality of the judiciary.

ARTICLE 11

(1) Everyone has the right to freedom of peaceful assembly and
to freedom of association with others, including the right to form
and to join trade unions for the protection of his interests.

(2) No restrictions shall be placed on the exercise of these rights
other than such as are prescribed by law and are necessary in a
democratic society in the interests of national security or public
safety, for the prevention of disorder or crime, for the protection
of health or morals or for the protection of the rights and freedoms
of others. This Article shall not prevent the imposition of lawful
restrictions on the exercise of these rights by members of the armed
forces, of the police or of the administration of the State.

ARTICLE 12

Men and women of marriageable age have the right to marry
and to found a family, according to the national laws governing
the exercise of this right.

ARTICLE 13

Everyone whose rights and freedoms as set forth in this Convention
are violated shall have an effective remedy before a national authority
notwithstanding that the violation has been committed by persons
acting in an official capacity.

ARTICLE 14

The enjoyment of the rights and freedoms set forth in this Convention shall be secured without discrimination on any ground
such as sex, race, colour, language, religion, political or other
opinion, national or social origin, association with a national
minority, property, birth or other status.

ARTICLE 15

(1) In time of war or other public emergency threatening the life
of the nation any High Contracting Party may take measures
derogating from its obligations under this Convention, to the extent
strictly required by the exigencies of the situation, provided that
such measures are not inconsistent with its other obligations under
international law.

(2) No derogation from Article 2, except in respect of deaths
resulting from lawful acts of war, or from Articles 3, 4 (paragraph 1)
and 7 shall be made under this provision.

(3) Any High Contracting Party availing itself of this right of
derogation shall keep the Secretary-General of the Council of
Europe fully informed of the measures which it has taken and the
reasons therefor. It shall also inform the Secretary-General of the
Council of Europe when such measures have ceased to operate and
the provisions of the Convention are again being fully executed.

ARTICLE 16

Nothing in Articles 10, 11 and 14 shall be regarded as preventing the High Contracting Parties from imposing restrictions on the political activity of aliens.

ARTICLE 17

Nothing in this Convention may be interpreted as implying for any State, group or person any right to engage in any activity or perform any act aimed at the destruction of any of the rights and freedoms set forth herein or at their limitation to a greater extent than is provided for in the Convention.

ARTICLE 18

The restrictions permitted under this Convention to the said rights and freedoms shall not be applied for any purpose other than those for which they have been prescribed.

Signatories: BELGIUM   ITALY
                  DENMARK   LUXEMBOURG
                  FRANCE   THE NETHERLANDS
                  GERMAN FEDERAL REPUBLIC NORWAY
                  GREECE   THE SAAR
                  ICELAND   SWEDEN
                  THE IRISH REPUBLIC   TURKEY
                                                    THE UNITED KINGDOM

Index